CRITICAL ISSUES IN ASIAN DEVELOPMENT
Theories, Experiences and Policies

CRITICAL ISSUES IN ASIAN DEVELOPMENT

Theories, Experiences and Policies

EDITED BY

M.G. Quibria

Published for the Asian Development Bank
by Oxford University Press

HONG KONG
OXFORD UNIVERSITY PRESS
OXFORD   NEW YORK
1995

Oxford University Press

Oxford New York
Athens Auckland Bangkok Bombay
Calcutta Cape Town Dar es Salaam Delhi
Florence Hong Kong Istanbul Karachi
Kuala Lumpur Madras Madrid Melbourne
Mexico City Nairobi Paris Singapore
Taipei Tokyo Toronto

and associated companies in
Berlin Ibadan

Oxford is a trade mark of Oxford University Press

First published 1995

Published for the Asian Development Bank by Oxford University Press

Library of Congress Cataloging-in-Publication Data
Critical issues in Asian development : theories, experiences, and
policies / edited by M.G. Quibria.
        p. cm.
        "The proceedings of the Second Asian Development Bank Conference
on Development Economics"--Foreword.
        Includes bibliographical references and indexes.
        ISBN 0-19-586606-1
        1. Asia--Economic conditions--1945- 2. Households--Asia.
3. Income distibution--Asia. 4. Rural credit--Asia.
5. Agriculture--Economic aspects--Asia. 6. Economic development-
-Environmental aspects. 7. Sustainable development--Asia.
I. Quibria, M.G. (Muhammad Ghulam) II. Asian Development Bank
Conference on Development Economics (2nd : 1993)
HC412.C75 1995   94-23393
338.95--dc20   CIP

Printed in Hong Kong
Published by Oxford University Press (Hong Kong) Ltd.
18/F Warwick House, Taikoo Place, 979 King's Road, Quarry Bay, Hong Kong

Contents

Chapter One
Introduction
M.G. QUIBRIA

Chapter Two
Inequality Within and Between Households in Growing and Aging Economies
ANGUS DEATON

Chapter Three
Gender and Household Dynamics: Recent Theories and Their Implications
GILLIAN HART

Chapter Four
Income Distribution in Developing Economies: Conceptual, Data, and Policy Issues in Broad-Based Growth
GARY S. FIELDS

Chapter Five
Rural Credit and Interlinkage: Implications for Rural Poverty, Agrarian Efficiency, and Public Policy
KAUSHIK BASU

Chapter Six
Is Land Reform Passé? With Special Reference to Asian Agriculture
SALIM RASHID and M.G. QUIBRIA

Chapter Seven
Economic Development and the Environment: Issues, Policies, and the Political Economy
PARTHA DASGUPTA

Chapter Eight
Trade and Sustainable Development
ROBERT REPETTO

Chapter Nine
The Implications of New Growth Theory
for Trade and Development: An Overview
PRANAB BARDHAN

Chapter Ten
Recent Advances in Trade and Growth Theory
RONALD FINDLAY

List of Tables

List of Figures

Foreword

Development economics is an active area of economic research. In recent years, the discipline has made significant intellectual advances that have deep ramifications for economic policies.

In 1992, the Asian Development Bank initiated a series of annual conferences on development economics to discuss recent advances in the field and their empirical significance and policy implications for developing Asia.

This volume represents the proceedings of the Second Asian Development Bank Conference on Development Economics. The authors discuss a wide range of important development issues facing Asian developing economies. It is hoped that these papers will contribute to a deeper understanding of the issues involved and the means to their resolution.

The views and opinions expressed in this volume are those of the authors and do not necessarily reflect the views and policies of the Asian Development Bank.

A.I. Aminul Islam
Officer-in-Charge
Economics and Development Resource Center
Asian Development Bank

Preface

This collection of essays is the outcome of the Second Asian Development Bank Conference on Development Economics held in Manila on 24-26 November 1993.

The conference, attended by a diverse group of participants, including academic economists, policymakers, staff of the Asian Development Bank, and representatives of other international organizations, was inaugurated by Vice President G. Schulz. The newly appointed President M. Sato, who arrived at the Bank during the Conference, was kind enough to make the closing remarks despite heavy demands on his time. A number of senior officials of the Bank, namely, Vice President B. S. Lee, Vice President W. Thomson, N. Morita, E. Watanabe, S. C. Jha, and K. F. Jalal, presided over the various sessions. In addition to the papers published in this volume, there was a roundtable discussion, 'Financing a Better Environment', with K. F. Jalal, K. Kato, P. Rogers, and J. Warford as panelists.

The conference was a considerable success. It could not have been so smoothly organized without the tireless efforts of S. C. Jha, the then dynamic Chief Economist of the Economics and Development Resource Center, and the help and cooperation of a number of other ADB officials, including J. M. Dowling, A. I. Aminul Islam, and K. F. Jalal. The economists of the Economics and Development Resource Center and the supporting staff there, in particular, Lutgarda T. Labios, Ma. Lourdes Antonio, Anita P. Angeles, Zenaida M. Acacio, Elizabeth Leuterio, and Ellen Reyes, must be thanked for their organizational contributions.

The papers, featured at the conference and presented in this volume, address a number of basic themes relating to gender and family, poverty and inequality, rural credit and land tenure, the environment and economic policies, and recent advances in trade and growth theories. They highlight important analytical and policy issues germane to the development process of Asian developing countries as well as lacunas in the present state of economic knowledge.

Given the heterogenous nature of the participants, the essays presented at the conference were nontechnical. The level of technicality was equivalent to that of a typical paper in the *Journal of Economic*

Perspective, a journal addressing nonspecialized economists. Given this, it is hoped that the present volume will be accessible to a wide readership interested in the issues of economic development.

The papers in this book benefited from the comments of a large number of individuals, many of whom also acted as designated discussants at the conference. They include A. T. M. Nurul Amin, Tariq Banuri, Sutanu Behuria, Yeong-Yuh Chiang, Marian de los Angeles, Anil Deolalikar, J. M. Dowling, Raul Fabella, Rodney Falvey, Junichi Goto, Godfrey Guantilleke, Francis Harrigan, Mahabub Hossain, K. F. Jalal, Chung-Young Jung, Basant Kapur, Hun Kim, Jeffrey Liang, Pak-Wai Liu, Bindu Lohani, S. M. Naseem, Gene Owens, Ernesto M. Pernia, M. S. Rao, Narhari Rao, Chalongphob Sussangkarn, Mokhtar Tamin, Min Tang, M. A. Taslim, and Mao Yushi. Also acknowledged, gratefully, is the cooperation of the authors in meeting the deadlines, addresssing the comments of the reveiwers, and responding to frequent queries from the editor.

The following individuals deserve special thanks for their cooperation and conscientiousness. Judith A. Banning, the editorial consultant, put in extraordinary efforts to convert the manuscripts to a publishable typescript. Further editorial assistance was provided by Stephen J. Banta and Alex V. Gordevich. A team of expert word processors, including Anita P. Angeles, Zenaida M. Acacio, Wilhelmina M. Jacinto, and Lorna Protacio, worked on various drafts of the book. Cherry Lynn Zafaralla prepared the index, and Lutgarda T. Labios provided valuable research assistance.

M. G. Quibria
Asian Development Bank

List of Contributors

M. G. Quibria
Asian Development Bank

Pranab Bardhan
Professor
Department of Economics
University of California at Berkeley

Kaushik Basu
Professor
Delhi School of Economics
London School of Economics

Partha Dasgupta
Professor
Faculty of Economics and Politics
University of Cambridge

Angus Deaton
William Church Osborn Professor of Public Affairs
Professor of Economics and International Affairs
Center for International Studies
Princeton University

Gary S. Fields
Professor
Department of Labor Economics
School of Industrial and Labor Relations
Cornell University

Ronald Findlay
Ragnar Nurkse Professor of Economics
Department of Economics
Columbia University

Gillian Hart
Professor
Department of City and Regional Planning
University of California at Berkeley

Salim Rashid
Professor
Department of Economics
University of Illinois at Urban-Champaign

Robert Repetto
Vice-President and Senior Economist
World Resources Institute

Terms and Abbreviations

ADB   -   Asian Development Bank
CFC   -   chlorofluorocarbon
FAO   -   Food and Agriculture Organization
FDI   -   foreign direct investment
GATT   -   General Agreement on Tariffs and Trade
GDP   -   gross domestic product
GNP   -   gross national product
HYV   -   high-yielding variety
ICP   -   International Comparison Programme
IPP   -   international purchasing power
IPR   -   intellectual property rights
LDC   -   less developed country
NAFTA   -   North American Free Trade Agreement
NIE   -   newly industrializing economy
NNP   -   net national product
OECD   -   Organisation for Economic Co-operation and Development
R&D   -   research and development
PRC   -   People's Republic of China
US   -   United States of America

Note: References to Taipei,China are to the island of Taiwan.

Chapter One

Introduction

M.G. Quibria

The developing economies of Asia experienced a tremendous wave of dynamism over the past 30 years or so. Some economies afflicted by widespread poverty graduated into vibrant newly industrializing economies (NIEs), while a few others came on the verge of becoming so. However, not all the economies in Asia could join this journey of prosperity: many lagged behind. And this is amply reflected in the vast majority of the global poor who live in developing Asia. Contrary to popular perception, the economic challenge facing developing Asia, as measured by the metric of poverty, is far from over, and may have only begun. In addition to poverty, there are other problems that have accompanied the process of development. Some of these issues are highlighted in the collection of essays featured in this volume. An important criterion for selection of these essays is their general analytical and policy significance, especially in relation to Asian developing countries.

Achieving an equitable distribution of income and welfare remains a primordial objective for many societies. Indeed, the global experimentation with socialism was inspired by this ideal. However, in many societies, inequalities remain a nagging problem despite economic improvements. These inequalities manifest themselves in many different forms and dimensions. They are found not only across households, but also within the household: between sexes, and between different age groups. It is widely believed that gender disparity, within and across the household, is pervasive in traditional Asian societies. Similarly, inequality in income distribution between households, as well as factors of production, remains a problem, even among the most dynamic economies. As a matter of fact, inequality has become more pronounced in some of the Asian NIEs. Some critical analytical, and empirical issues regarding inequalities of income and welfare are discussed in the papers by Angus Deaton, Gillian Hart, and Gary Fields.

1

As is widely recognized, the problem of poverty in developing Asia is predominantly one of rural poverty (see Quibria 1993). Two measures that are often put forward to mitigate this problem are rural credit and land reform. It is argued that rural credit enables poor farmers without past savings to acquire purchased inputs, to buy food and subsist until the harvest, and to smooth out harvest fluctuations. Credit also helps the rural poor to climb out of their poverty through productive investment. The contribution of land reform, if it can be effectively implemented, is to provide the farmer access to a productive asset and therefore to a stream of otherwise unavailable incomes. These two topics, which are obviously of great empirical and policy significance in the context of developing Asia, are discussed by Basu, and Rashid and Quibria.

A new awareness has developed of the importance of environmental preservation and sustainable development. This awareness has paradoxically been accompanied by many misconceptions about the relationship between economic development and environmental degradation. An important policy issue that arises in this context involves finding the growth strategy that ensures economic development in the shortest possible time but does not inflict undue damage to the environment. Those countries in Asia that achieved spectacular economic development within a short span of 20 to 30 years have followed an outward-oriented strategy of development that relied on trade as the engine of growth. A pertinent question then is, What ramifications does such a strategy have for the environment? Some of these issues of so-called sustainable development and the environment-trade nexus are addressed by Dasgupta, and Repetto.

Finally, as noted earlier, some Asian economies, such as the NIEs, as well as Thailand, Malaysia, and Indonesia, have in recent years shown a dynamism, which is in some sense unparalleled in recent world economic history. A good deal of research, both analytical and empirical, has been devoted to the issue of, How does one explain the 'mechanics' of development? Much of the recent analytical literature has placed great import on the role of trade and come up with well articulated formal models to aid our understanding. A review of this literature as well as a discussion of their relevance in the light of the Asian experience is provided by Bardhan, and Findlay.

The following brief summaries of the papers are meant to provide a helpful overview.

Inequality: Gender and Household

Angus Deaton (chapter 2) provides a selective survey of the empirical work on two aspects of inequality that prevail in Asian developing countries. The first aspect relates to inequality within the household between males and females, and the second relates to inequality among households and how this inequality is affected by the rate of population growth. The latter issue is becoming increasingly important in the context of the Asian newly industrializing economies where fertility has undergone a significant decline in recent decades, leading to a concomitant increase in income inequality.

Deaton notes that data on infant mortality, anthropometrics, and education tend to indicate a disparity in intrahousehold allocation of resources between boys and girls. The question Deaton then poses is, How far is this inequality borne out by supplementary evidence from household surveys? Recent studies that sought to address the question drew on the recent methodological work of numerous authors such as Chiappori, Bourguignon, and Deaton himself. This recent methodological work, which builds on the earlier literature on equivalence scales by such authors as Rothbarth, is based on a simple idea: If parents accept greater reduction in their consumption with the birth of a boy than with that of a girl, then there is discrimination.

Earlier empirical work on this issue by Deaton in Cote d'Ivoire and Thailand, found no evidence that girls were discriminated vis-a-vis boys in the intrahousehold allocation of resources. Recent studies by Subramanian and Deaton in Maharashtra (India), Rudd (Taipei,China), Ahmad and Morduch (Bangladesh), and Deaton (Pakistan), all tend to suggest that there was no discrimination between gender with respect to household expenditure. This seems to be at odds with other existing evidence on gender discrimination. It provides an empirical puzzle and needs to be resolved through further analytical and empirical investigations.

The second issue addressed by Deaton relates to inequality between households and the impact of population growth and aging. He argues that standard theories of intertemporal choice under uncertainty imply an increase in inequalities in income and consumption within a fixed cohort of people as the cohort ages. In the simplest version of the theory, the consumption of each member of the cohort follows an independent random walk, implying that even if everyone starts at the same level of consumption, over time as the cohort ages, their individual consumption levels will 'fan out'. Deaton notes that this theory can be generalized to allow for different initial positions for different individuals.

An important implication of the above theory is that in stable demographic equilibrium, with lower fertility and consequently a relative high proportion of older people, income and consumption inequality will be higher. The latter will follow from a *composition effect*—that is, as the proportion of the old increases, and as consumption and income among the old are more unequally distributed, aggregate inequality increases. However, aggregate inequality is made up of within-cohort and between-cohort inequalities. Under fairly standard assumptions, Deaton notes, it can be shown that the between-cohort effect tends to reinforce the within-cohort effect. Therefore, lower fertility unambiguously results in increases in consumption and increases in income inequality across stable demographic equilibria.

The empirical evidence from Taipei,China, the United States, and Great Britain cited by Deaton indicates that the intracohort dispersions of consumption and income increase with cohort age. The increased inequality in Taipei,China that has emerged in the last decade, Deaton argues, can be attributed at least in part to the changing demographic composition of the population. While the paper raises interesting analytical and policy issues pertaining to aging, it is somewhat reticent about discussing public policies to address the economic problems arising from it. Nevertheless, the work undertaken by Deaton and his collaborators creates an edifice on which useful future policy work can be anchored.

The paper by Gillian Hart (chapter 3) addresses the debates in the literature on gender inequality, household models, and economic development. Until recently, economists have treated the household as a black box and the economic decision-making process, especially with respect to resource allocation within the household, has been something akin to an enigma. However, things have changed in recent years and a large economic literature has emerged on this subject.

There are two principal approaches to explain intrahousehold allocation of resources—namely, the unitary model and the bargaining model. In the unitary model, the household is assumed to possess a consistent preference function (however derived) and intrahousehold allocation is determined by this preference. On the other hand, in the bargaining model, it is assumed that the household is comprised of spouses who have concern for each other but whose preferences are not necessarily the same, and that intrahousehold allocation of resources is determined by mutual bargaining of the spouses. It may be noted that the unitary model and the bargaining model (which comes in numerous variants) are subsets of a general class of models, termed the collective models. The thrust of the collective approach is that the household should be viewed as a group of self-interested individuals among whom collective decisions take place. Depending on the particular mathematical game-theoretic approach adopted to resolve the problem of collective decision making, collective models can be either *cooperative* or *noncooperative*.

While the unitary model is simpler to handle mathematically, its principal shortcoming as an analytical construct stems from its disregard of the fact that household decisions involve a collective process, involving more than one individual. On the other hand, the bargaining models that have been brought to bear on the issue of intrahousehold allocation of resources have been developed in the context of two-member (husband and wife) families. To the extent that real world families are multimember families and that children's preferences are often independent of parents, the utility of the framework for explaining the sex bias in the intra-household allocation of resources remains at least limited, unless the framework can be extended to multimember families. However, the shortcoming that is common to both approaches is the static nature of the framework itself. This shortcoming is especially telling on the bargaining model, as it is well-known from game theory that the results of static bargaining models are not necessarily isomorphic to those of a repeated game.

It is difficult to test unitary and bargaining models empirically as both these models have the same reduced form (Behrman 1990). However, recently, Chiappori and Bourguignon, in a series of papers, developed a methodology that allows empirical testing between the models and, under appropriate assumptions, allows recovery of the rules by which resources are allocated within the household. However, Hart argues that this methodology is far from free of problems. She argues that sharing rules cannot be unproblematically recovered from aggregate survey data because the way data are collected will determine the conclusions. Since household survey data collection exercises require predefined categories, the rules that are recovered from the data will reflect these assumptions and definitions. In addition, even the most basic issue of what and where is the 'household' is far from self-evident. The usual definition used in many surveys and censuses is the *kitchen* definition—that is, those who eat from the same kitchen are considered a household. This definition can be misleading because of the dynamic processes of household formation and partition and of spatially extended resource flows and sharing arrangements (see Greenhalgh 1985, for discussion on Taipei,China).

After the review of the major economic approaches, Hart provides an outline of a 'relational and processual approach', the critical element of which is gender. Hart argues 'there is a need to focus on relationships within and between households, as well as in nonhousehold institutions, and on the way these relationships are defined in terms of gender . . . . A gendered approach focuses on how multiple understandings of "male" and "female" are socially constructed and are embodied in everyday practices both within and beyond the household.'

The relational approach seems to be more elaborate, as it seeks to incorporate many more dimensions of reality than those included in the usual economic models. This is both a strength and a weakness. Given that it is a more encompassing framework, it is difficult to express the framework formally and thereby test the model through rigorous data and quantitative analyses. However, it appears that the framework may be amenable to some form of mathematical codification, as some aspects of the framework seem to allude to a form of a repeated bargaining game between husband and wife. If viewed in this way, the framework seems to open up a rich panopoly of possibilities, which need to be explored further.

Despite the considerable literature that has emerged on the topic, the policy content of much of it remains limited. Different economic models have different implications for policies as well as different degrees of capabilities to handle policies. The models that incorporate interdisciplinary elements, such as the relational approach as espoused by Hart, appear to be too malleable to provide a framework for rigorous exploration of policies. Our understanding of household behavior is still rudimentary. The gender disparity that exists within the household feeds upon and, in turn, is fed by the gender disparity that exists outside of the family. For the development of appropriate kinds of public policy, it is important to understand the behavior of the household, as well as that of other nonhousehold mediating institutions, which together form an interlocking resource allocation mechanism through which public policy would generally operate.

Gary Fields (chapter 4) looks into the problem of income distribution, which bedevils many developing countries at various stages of development. As Deaton has noted, the problem has become more acute in the NIEs as their population ages. Fields starts his paper by advocating the desirability of broad-based growth, a concept that implies rising standards of living for all socioeconomic levels. As the upper and middle income groups do not require much special assistance, he argues that broad-based growth should translate into development efforts directed toward raising the standards of living of the poor, an approach that is in accord with the Rawlsian 'maximin principle'.

Fields notes that measures to determine the extent of broad-based growth fall into two categories, namely, measures of absolute poverty and those of relative inequality. Depending on the issue being investigated, one needs to look into the available distributional statistics. Fields argues that depending on the approach being adopted, the evidence indicates conflicting results regarding the distributional effects of growth. Despite Kuznets' well-known hypothesis and the corroborating cross-sectional data, Fields argues that currently available data do not support any stable relationship between economic growth and changing income inequality. On the other hand, steady growth seems to be always accompanied by reductions in poverty. This provides a strong case for the trickle down hypothesis and for the promotion of growth through conducive policies.

As regards evidence from Asia, Fields notes that rapid growth in the NIEs has also been accompanied by reductions in relative inequality as well as in absolute poverty. Fields highlights a number of policies that have led to the success of NIEs in achieving this broad-based growth. First, the labor market has been relatively free of distortions, thus allowing full employment. Distortion can be introduced by raising the returns to labor beyond its marginal product or by repressing the returns to labor below its marginal product. Both policies help to impede economic development. Fields rightly argues that Asian developing countries should promote labor intensive growth as these countries have an abundant supply of labor relative to capital. Second, the NIEs have made relatively high investments in education. Fields finds an overwhelming case for investment in primary education as it does not involve any trade-off between equity and efficiency. A marginal investment in primary education adds to the productive capacity of the economy as well as spreads the benefit of growth to a wider segment of society. Third, growth has been facilitated by an egalitarian distribution of land and other assets. An egalitarian distribution, besides being equitable and efficient, creates a congenial political environment in which social policies can succeed. Fourth, government policies in the NIEs have been market friendly. In the NIEs the government has played an important role in ensuring fair competition to private enterprise and thereby eliciting socially acceptable outcomes. Finally, these economies have adopted outward-oriented policies in trade and industries. An important guiding principle in this context is that of comparative advantage, which for the East Asian NIEs has meant adopting trade and industrialization strategies that correspond to comparative advantage in the dynamic sense.

The policies discussed by Fields, while extremely important, are by no means exhaustive. Governments can, and should, take measures to curb excessive population growth, to improve the health and nutritional status of the poor, and to ensure the stability of macroeconomic environments. Finally, while Fields provides a useful discussion of the issue of inequality in the course of economic development, his paper features much in common with the existing literature, the static aspect of income distribution. In particular, it does not shed light on how a particular individual or a group figures over time. In other words, the discussion does not provide an assessment of income dynamics and the related policy issues.

Rural Credit, Land Tenure, and Land Reform

Basu (chapter 5) provides a selective survey of the literature on rural credit and interlinkage, limiting himself to issues and areas where he has something new or interesting to report. Interlinkage has been an important feature of agriculture of many Asian developing countries, especially those in South Asia. Some important questions that have been raised are, Is this interlinkage equitable and efficient? What is its implication for rural poverty? If it is inefficient or inequitable, how does one remedy the deficiency through public policy?

Markets are defined as interlinked if the prices of two products are determined simultaneously and the agreement to buy or sell is contingent on buying or selling the other. In the agriculture context, transactions in the land market may be interlinked with transactions in the credit market. Basu provides a simple model to illustrate the idea that interlinkage may often be imposed on an agent by the principal in the context of a principal -agent problem to circumvent the moral hazard problem. He argues that in the face of moral hazard, it is often preferable for both the worker and the employer to come to an agreement where the level of effort is imposed by the landlord. This sacrifice of worker sovereignty may lead to an increase of welfare for the contending parties in the transaction.

Basu goes on to explain agricultural tenancy, an important feature of many economies, in terms of limited liability. As the landlord cannot collect what is contractually due to him if the tenant's financial position drops to a precarious position, Basu argues, this leads to the wide prevalence of share tenancy in many parts of India. And this conjecture has been vindicated by his casual empiricism of India as well as the historical research from Nellore. He argues that tenancy, based on limited liability, has important implications for poverty. In particular, he notes that the less wealthy individual, because of the limited liability clause, would be at a disadvantage in contracting tenancy; therefore tenancy, rather than mitigating poverty, may magnify the inequities that persist in the system.

With respect to the credit market, Basu notes that the formal market often excludes the poor, who usually borrow from the private money lender at exorbitant interest rates. This feature tends to exacerbate the problems of equity as the poor are excluded from the cheaper sources of credit. This situation becomes further complicated and rendered more inequitable as triadic relations come into existence. These triadic interactions make possible further extortion by the rich and the powerful. The government can play a role to curb inequity and inefficiency; but Basu argues, as the opposite can also happen, there therefore is a need to design policies carefully.

In a provocative and controversial paper, Rashid and Quibria (chapter 6) examine the question of whether land reform is passé in the context of Asian developing countries. The paper reviews the basic arguments in favor of land reform—in terms of equity and efficiency—and arrives at conclusions that are at odds with the existing orthodoxy. The authors argue that there are no sound reasons, either theoretical or empirical, to support tenancy regulations. If the tenancy market is allowed to function in an unfettered way, this would encourage the relatively large landowners to lease out part of their holding to the landless, perhaps interlinked with a credit, if the credit market is inefficient.

In contrast with their position regarding tenancy reform, Rashid and Quibria are much more enthusiastic about redistributive land reform. The authors note that the fact that there are no significant economies of scale in agriculture—especially in the rice economies of Asia where skill-intensive and scale-neutral cultivation is the norm—makes the case for land distribution an appealing one. However, despite the many arguments in favor of redistributive land reform, both in terms of distributional equity and in terms of production efficiency, land reform seems to have become passé.

The reason, according to Rashid and Quibria, lies partly in the domain of the political economy and partly in the domain of the history of economic development. No land reform was endogenous—in Taipei,China, it was forced by an alien military power; in the Republic of Korea, it was instigated by a military government. Efforts at endogenous land reform—reform introduced by a democratic regime—are few and far between. On the other hand, there is no agreement on the contribution of land reform to economic development. In Korea, land reform succeeded in bankrupting the existent landlord class, and little agriculture surplus was generated to support industrialization. Rashid and Quibria argue that Korea's industrial success, which came over a decade later, arose out of seemingly unrelated circumstances. Similarly, in Thailand, land reform has affected essentially the marginal farmers, yet the performance of the economy remains impressive. In Indonesia, the economy has shown an unprecedented degree of vitality, despite no land reform.

Advocates of land reform often seek to achieve diverse objectives through land reform. Rashid and Quibria argue that there are more efficient ways of achieving those objectives than land reform: if poverty alleviation is the goal, this can be tackled through land-contingent poverty alleviation schemes; if commercial and export farming is the goal, systems of contract farming can be encouraged; if achieving economies of scale is the desired goal, then administrative agencies or associative farming may be used. They further argue that if a noneconomic but development goal such as education is to be encouraged, then compulsory education may be fostered. However, they note that the one goal that cannot be achieved is a change of political power.

Even if one can overcome the issue of political power in implementing land reform, Rashid and Quibria caution, land reform is no magic solution for poverty alleviation. While effective land reform may help, it cannot substitute for a program of comprehensive economic reform and sustained economic growth that is required to create employment and reduce poverty.

Economic Development, Trade, and the Environment

Dasgupta (chapter 7) provides a selective survey of issues that arise in relation to the environment as the country strives to achieve economic development. The paper notes that poor countries, including those in developing Asia, are biomass-based subsistence economies and rural people in these countries derive their subsistence from products obtained from plants and animals. These plants and animals are examples of a genre of resources that are regenerative but are often threatened with the possibility of excessive use. Dasgupta rightly notes that the earlier literature identifies the failure of market institutions as the cause of environmental problems, followed by another strand of the literature that identifies the failure of government policies as the cause of environmental problems. The author argues that institution failure, which is defined as market and government failures, as well as poverty is the root cause of environmental problems. Consequently, there are many who would view environmental problems as the reflection of the wrong type of economic growth and there are many who would view environmental problems as the reflection of poverty. There are elements of truth in both. The existence of an apparent relationship between economic growth and environmental quality (or degradation) has led some economists to search for an environmental Kuznets' curve. A critical discussion of the concept as well as the empirical basis of the relationship leads the author to conclude—and correctly so—that like all broad generalizations in the social sciences, 'the environmental Kuznets' Curve is almost certainly something of a mirage'.

The environmental Kuznets' curve is drawn against national income as conventionally measured. The author argues that as the conventionally measured national income is misleading, it should be replaced by an index of real national income, a concept that takes into account changes in the natural resource base. If this correction is incorporated, then obviously a different Kuznets' curve would be implied.

Dasgupta argues that if real national income is to reflect aggregate well-being, appropriate accounting prices should be used. Current estimates of net national product are biased because depreciation of environmental resources are not taken into account. Alternatively, net national product estimates are based on a set of biased prices—in particular, those imputed to environmental resources. This bias, the extent of which varies from country to country and project to project, leads to the adoption of wrong technologies.

The environmental degradation that takes place in poor countries also leads to higher fertility, according to Dasgupta. The basic mechanism through which this takes place is delineated as follows: 'Poverty, the thinness of markets, and an absence of basic amenities make it essential for households to engage in a number of complementary production activities . . . Each is time consuming. . . . Children are then continually needed as workers by their parents, even when parents are in their prime . . . A small household simply will not do. Each household needs many hands and it can be that the overall usefulness of each additional hand increases with declining resource availability.' While the above description is plausible, there is yet to emerge any rigorous empirical tests of the precise mechanism noted above. The important and positive conclusion that follows from the paper is that in poor countries there is no tradeoff between growth, on the one hand, and the environment and fertility, on the other.

Much of the economic success of the Asian developing countries can be traced to their success in exploiting opportunities afforded by international trade. The question posed by Repetto (chapter 8) is, Does trade liberalization also support the goal of environmentally sustainable development? Repetto notes that outward-looking trade policies have had a significant environmental impact and illustrates this proposition by drawing on the experiences of Thailand, the People's Republic of China (PRC), and Indonesia. He argues that the growing environmental problems these countries are encountering do not imply that trade liberalization and outward-looking policies are inconsistent with sustainable development. On the other hand, these policies have enabled the countries to achieve a high rate of growth, to reduce poverty, and to raise their standard of living—a factor that engendered social, economic, and political conditions for enhanced environmental quality. According to Repetto, the important challenge for these fast growing economies is to ensure that their newly acquired resources and capabilities are directed to containing environmental problems.

The main reason countries suffer from environmental problems, according to Repetto, is that they have underinvested in institutional capacity and infrastructure for environmental management. While trade restrictions are not the first-best measure to address market failures arising out of environment problems, in the absence of domestic environmental policies, trade restrictions may emerge as a second-best option. Repetto argues that an important implication of his analysis is that international development agencies should undertake policies that ensure rapid export-led growth and, at the same time, promote investment to strengthen institutional capacity and provide necessary infrastructure. Repetto argues that these investments should be made prior to export liberalization as the prevention of environmental damage is much less expensive than remediation.

As outward-oriented policies have adverse ramifications for the environment, so have inward-looking, trade-restricting development policies. The experience of pre-reform PRC indicates that state-owned heavy industries generated a large quantity of pollution. Similarly, in India, environmental degradation stemmed from poverty, obsolete technology, and an overemphasis on highly polluting industries.

It is widely feared in developing countries that if they are obliged to adhere to the standards of developed countries in environmental matters, they would be unable to compete internationally. But Repetto argues that empirical studies do not bear out this fear: differences in regulatory stringency in environmental control do not explain patterns of international trade and investment, nor do changes in the location of production. Indeed, India and the Eastern block countries, despite their lax environmental standards, have not been particularly competitive in world markets. Repetto argues that while it is irrational for developing countries to forego reasonable environmental control, it would be irrational for Northern environmentalists to demand that developing countries adopt the same standards as member countries of the Organisation for Economic Co-operation and Development (OECD). It is now well recognized that countries differ in environmental objectives and standards, reflecting differing absorptive capacities and social preferences.

Repetto concludes his paper with a number of policy recommendations, with the most controversial one being the principle, 'the polluter pays'. While it seems eminently sensible in terms of natural justice, internalization of costs, and correction of distorted price signals, there are circumstances when it leads to difficulties—particularly at transnational levels, where the interests of nations diverge, and the polluter is comparatively poor. It can be argued that a preferable solution to the 'game' would be side payments by the rich victims to the poor polluter, which may take the form of opening up markets to the poor country if it stops the 'mining' of tropical timber. The polluter pays principle, when applied to the national level, leads to a set of problems similar to those at the international level, which are also amenable to similar solutions.

Advances in Trade and Growth Theories

Bardhan (chapter 9), and Findlay (chapter 10) discuss a set of complementary issues. The former discusses the implications of the so-called new growth theory for trade and development while the latter reviews the new advances in trade and growth theory and their implications for the development of Asian countries. Bardhan points out that there are two misconceptions about the so-called new growth theory. First, the hallmark of the new growth theory is that it endogenizes technological progress, whereas the old growth theory did not. As a matter of fact, there is a body of literature in old growth theory—as contributed by Arrow, Kaldor-Mirrless, Uzawa, and Shell, among others—that did endogenize technical progress. It has been claimed that the distinction between capital accumulation and technical progress vanishes in the new growth theory. However, this feature is not a novel one. The major contribution of the new growth theory, according to Bardhan, is to posit an analytical framework that combines the above features with that of a 'tractable imperfect competition framework' in which private motivation exists for investment in research and development. Second, the new growth theory provides a theoretical demonstration of the salutary effects of trade expansion on the pace of economic development. It is now widely acknowledged that the new growth theory has yielded new insights into the effect of trade on growth and sharpened analytical tools to explore this question. However, as Bardhan forcefully argues, this new literature has by no means provided an unambiguous theoretical demonstration of the relationship between outward orientation and economic development, as is widely believed.

The open economy literature within this strand of growth models (as exemplified by Grossman and Helpman 1992) provides some new insights as to the impact of trade on growth, through such mechanisms as research and development, learning by doing, and technological diffusion. An important result of this literature, as Bardhan reports, relates how economic integration with the world market, as compared to a situation of autarky, helps long-run economic growth in similar developed economies by eschewing duplication of research and thus increasing the productivity of resources in the research and development (R&D) sector, which is subject to economies of scale. However, this result gets modified, or overturned, when it comes to trade between rich and poor countries. Discussing the recent formal models in the area of R&D, the author focuses on the controversial issue of intellectual property rights, and concludes that the recent literature does not provide any unambiguous guidance as to whether stricter intellectual property rights are beneficial to innovation, or to the economic development of poor countries.

The new growth theory has helped to formalize some aspects of the relationship between trade and development, yet there are others that have received little attention. It is argued that economic development does not happen in a vacuum, but takes place in the context of political and social institutions. These institutions have been virtually ignored in the new literature. In particular, it is argued that the government has a role to play, a role that may encompass providing a stable macroeconomic environment, protecting property rights, and investing in public goods. In a similar vein, labor market institutions have important bearings on the process of economic development. While the experience of the NIEs indicates that institutions matter, it is not well articulated in the existing theoretical literature.

Foreign direct investment (FDI) can be a source of capital and technology, management know-how, as well as a means for obtaining access to foreign markets. FDI has made an important contribution toward the economic dynamism of the Asian NIEs. While the role of FDI in economic development is widely recognized, this has not been captured in a meaningful manner in the theoretical models.

Finally, the new literature has attempted to formalize the relationship between trade and growth, yet it has paid inadequate attention to the issue of empirical verification of the theoretical propositions derived therefrom. While some preliminary work has been undertaken to confirm the hypotheses derived from the new growth models, the evidence of the link between trade and productivity growth remains both sparse and mixed. The author rightly notes that for all their recent advances, the theoretical models have a 'long way to go' before they can catch up with the complexity of the real world.

Findlay (chapter 10) notes that the fact that growth is endogenous is hardly new, as it is indeed a salient feature of the growth models as varied as those of Marx, Von Neumann, Lewis, and Domar. Findlay considers two particular models that generate endogenous growth. In the first, endogenous growth is generated by learning by doing on the part of the workers. In the second, endogenous growth is generated by an R&D activity that generates technical progress. In the first model, the key hypothesis is that the more capital intensive the production process is, the greater the degree of learning by doing for the workers involved. The average rate of labor augmenting technical progress, which applies to all workers, depends on the average capital intensity. There are a number of important issues involved here: Is this specification empirically verifiable? Is there no distinction between the production of different products and alternative input mixes being used to produce the same product? How reasonable is it to assume a constant rate of learning by doing for the production of the same goods over the years? Does the same criticism apply to the production of the same set of goods at different capital intensities? What is the implication of sustained endogenous growth for the production of new products?[1]

In the second model, endogenous growth is generated by an R&D activity that produces Hicks-neutral technical progress for other production activities. The R&D industry, in fact, produces public goods. Two policy options present themselves. First, private producers can form a 'club' and undertake this R&D collectively. One wonders whether this outcome would lead to the optimal provision of R&D, given the free rider problem. Presumably, the more likely outcome is the one adopted by Findlay, where the government provides the R&D activity, financed by taxes. A closer look at this activity seems to suggest that there is an externality that is economy wide in scope, but does not affect the R&D activity. This activity resembles the characteristics of infrastructure, but the question remains whether it is plausible to build a model of sustainable growth on the provision of infrastructure.

Leaving aside the mechanics of these models, many important and significant weaknesses remain with regard to their ability to explain the real world phenomenon of growth. In the Asian NIEs, it is widely believed that trade played an important role in accelerating their growth. While the traditional theory does not provide any guidance with regard to this link, the new growth theory identifies some factors that might shed important light on this. First, one strand of this theory claims that R&D —either private or public—is the basic impetus for growth, a claim, which has, however, been refuted by empirical evidence that suggests such R&D effort was rather modest in these countries. Second, the other strand of the theory claims that growth was propelled by learning by doing. However, this learning by doing occurs more in the export rather than import sectors. Empirical studies suggest that this may indeed be the case, as many export industries have emerged rather quickly in response to opportunities afforded by outward-oriented policies.

Findlay, however, argues that the success of East Asian NIEs is largely due to 'catching up' rather than the development of new technology. This 'catching up' was made possible because of increasing contact opened by trade and foreign investment. There is increasing empirical support for the proposition that technology transfer is achieved principally through foreign investment. As in many areas of economics, the theory seems to have fallen behind the complex reality, with the issue of growth and development being no exception. Empirical evidence suggests that there is a critical role for a conducive policy environment that encourages liberal trade and investment, an insight that is worth taking to heart.

Concluding Remarks

The essays in this volume address a number of critical issues facing Asian developing economies. Summarizing, in a nontechnical way, the state of empirical and theoretical knowledge, the essays highlight the policy options facing these economies. While most of the issues do not yield any simple solutions, it is hoped that the analytical and policy insights offered will be useful to policymakers and development economists alike.

Acknowledgments

The author is grateful to Pranab Bardhan, Kaushik Basu, Angus Deaton, Gary Fields, Gillian Hart, and S. Rashid for comments.

Note

1. These remarks are owed to Rod Falvey.

References

Behrman, J. R., 1990. "Intrahousehold Allocation of Nutrients and Gender Effects: A Survey of Structural and Reduced Form Estimates." In S. R. Osmani, ed., *Nutrition and Poverty*. Oxford: Oxford University Press.

Greenhalgh, S., 1985. "Sexual Stratification: The Other Side of 'Growth with Equity' in East Asia." *Population and Development Review* 11:265-314.

Grossman, G. M., and E. Helpman, 1992. *Innovation and Growth in the Global Economy*. Cambridge, M.A.: MIT Press.

Quibria, M. G., 1993. *Rural Poverty in Asia: Priority Issues and Policy Options*. Hong Kong: Oxford University Press.

Chapter Two

Inequality Within and Between Households in Growing and Aging Economies

Angus Deaton

Introduction

This paper provides an overview and synthesis of some recent work by the author and others on various aspects of inequality. Two topics will be discussed. The first is inequality in the allocation of resources within the household, with a focus on how to use data on household consumption to disentangle who gets what, and, in particular, whether males and females are equally treated. There exists a large and growing literature on gender issues in household behavior, much of it reviewed by Gillian Hart in chapter 3. Most of the evidence on gender differences comes from direct measurements of outcomes such as nutrition, anthropometrics, infant mortality, and education. Of concern here is whether the analysis of household consumption patterns can tell us anything about allocations by gender. A methodology for extracting information on individual consumption from household data will be presented, and the results of the analyses that have been carried out so far will be discussed. These present something of a puzzle; even in areas of Asia where there is strong evidence that girls are treated worse than boys, there seems to be no evidence of bias in household expenditure patterns.

The second topic is the allocation of resources between households. A mechanism whereby declines in the rate of population growth can be expected to widen aggregate inequality in both income and consumption will be discussed. The author and Christina Paxson (1993a) show that many of the standard theories of intertemporal choice have the implication that consumption inequality within any given cohort of individuals

---

Note: References to Taipei,China are to the island of Taiwan. Data for Taipei,China reported in this paper were collected from the whole island, not from a specific locality.

18

will widen as the cohort ages. They provide evidence that the inequality of consumption of earnings, and of income, do indeed widen in the United States, Great Britain, and Taipei,China. As a result, in the absence of secular changes in inequality, older cohorts will typically be more unequal than younger cohorts, so that decreases in mortality or in fertility that increase the fractions of old, relative to young, will also increase aggregate measures of consumption and income inequality. These changes are particularly relevant for those countries in Asia where fertility has declined in the last two decades; the theory and empirical evidence predicts that they will experience an increase in inequality, but it is an increase that is an automatic and harmless consequence of declines in fertility that are typically welcome on other grounds.

This paper is divided into two parts; the first, on intrahousehold inequality, the second, on interhousehold inequality.

Inequality Within Households

Allocation within households has been much researched in recent years, with a particular focus on gender issues. The topic is of interest in its own right; we want to know whether males and females are treated equally, and, if not, under what circumstances. But intrahousehold allocation is also important for standard measures of welfare and poverty. Because our data are nearly all household, and not individual, data, and because we measure living standards using per capita measures of consumption or income, we measure welfare, inequality, and poverty under the implicit assumption that everyone in the household receives the same. We count the number of children in poverty by counting the number of children in poor households, defined as those whose per capita consumption or income is below some threshold, without any real idea of how much children get, and we make estimates of the living standards of the elderly by measuring the consumption levels of the households in which they live. If we are to move from household to individual welfare, which is our ultimate concern, we have to be able to look within the household and to discover who gets what.

There is much direct evidence from statistics on infant mortality, on anthropometric measures, and on education, for example, that girls are treated less favorably than boys, at least in some countries. The research reviewed in this paper looks at whether household surveys can be used to provide supplementary evidence on this question. In general, it is not possible to infer anything about individual welfare from grouped data, but we can certainly examine how household consumption patterns are affected by the demographic composition of households. Recent work by Chiappori (1988, 1992), and by Bourguignon and Chiappori (1992) has shown how data on exclusive goods—goods that are consumed only by individual persons or groups—or on assignable goods—goods where the consumption of each individual can be measured—can be used to (at least partially) identify the *sharing rules* that are used to allocate resources within the household. This new approach develops older ideas in the equivalence scale literature, in particular Rothbarth's (1943) approach of using expenditures on adult goods to measure the costs of children.

Rothbarth's method was extended by the author (Deaton 1989) as a tool to investigate the allocation to boys and girls within the household. Rothbarth's idea is to look at expenditures on adult goods, and to assess the cost of a child by seeing how much such expenditures are cut to make room for the child. In my work, the idea is to calculate these reductions separately for boys and girls, and to see whether a preference for boys causes households to 'make more room' for boys than for girls. Figure 2.1 illustrates how the method works. The horizontal axis shows total outlay (expenditure or income) and the vertical axis household expenditure on adult goods, defined as goods that are not consumed by children— tobacco, alcohol, or adult clothing being the most obvious examples. The solid line AB shows the relationship between expenditures on adult goods and total outlay for a two-adult household without children; the positive slope indicates that adult goods are normal goods, whose expenditures respond positively to increases in outlay. Suppose now that a child is added to the household. The child brings no additional resources to the household, but does bring needs, such as food and clothing. To meet these, the parents must sacrifice some of their own consumption, not only on adult goods, but also on food, clothing, and on, presumably, the whole range of expenditures. But since the children consume none of the adult goods, household expenditure on these goods must fall, as illustrated in Figure 2.1 by the two lines A_gB_g and A_bB_b, which show the new adult good Engel curves for the cases where the child is a girl or boy respectively. As illustrated, the curve for the two adults and a boy—the dotted curve—is lower than the solid curve for two adults and a girl. This is the case where the girl is being allocated less than the boy, so that the parents need to make less room in their budget for the girl than for the boy.

Using this analysis, there are a number of ways of measuring the extent of the discrimination. Perhaps the obvious method is to measure the distances CD and CE, the reductions in expenditures on adult goods

Figure 2.1
The Effect of Boys and Girls on Adult Expenditures

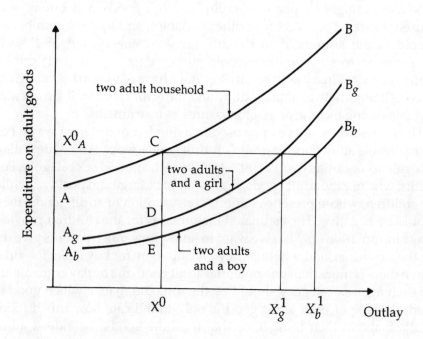

associated with a girl and a boy, and to see whether they are different. Alternatively, the impact of the child can be converted into an 'outlay equivalent' by measuring the additional outlay that would be necessary to restore expenditure on adult goods to its level prior to the addition of the child. These are shown in the figure by the distances $x_g^1-x^0$ and $x_b^1-x^0$ respectively. It is often convenient to express these outlay equivalents as ratios of initial total outlay x^0, in which case they are referred to as 'outlay equivalent ratios'. In this form, we might find that a boy is equivalent in his effect on adult good expenditure to a 30 per cent reduction in total outlay, while a girl is equivalent to 25 per cent.

In practice, these magnitudes are calculated from a regression analysis of expenditures on adult goods. A convenient functional form relates the *share of the budget* on adult goods to the logarithm of total outlay, the logarithm of household size variable representing the age and sex structure of the household, and other relevant sociodemographic characteristics. This is written as

$$w_i = \alpha_i + \beta_i \ln(x/n) + \eta_i \ln n + \sum_{k=1}^{K-1} \theta_{ik}(n_k/n) + \psi_i.z + u_i \qquad (1)$$

where i indexes the commodity number, so that i might be all adult goods, or it might be one of a group of adult goods, x is outlay, n is household size, z is a vector of other variables, and n_k is the number of people in the household in the kth age-sex category, out of K such categories in total. Given household survey data, equation (1) can be estimated by ordinary least squares, or if we have reason to be concerned by correlations between total outlay and the error term, by instrumental variables using income or asset measures as instruments.

The regression results can be used in a number of different ways. For each possible adult good or group of adult goods, we can calculate outlay equivalents or outlay equivalent ratios for each age and sex category. For adults, who use the adult goods, these should be large and positive, while for children, whose presence inhibits consumption of adult goods, they should be negative. The estimated magnitudes for the children provide direct information on what we want to know, how much parents give up for their children, and whether they give up more for boys than for girls. When there is more than one potential adult good, the outlay equivalents for each age-sex category should be the same no matter which good is used; the role of each adult good is only to indicate how much room adults make in their budget, so that if all the goods are indeed adult goods, all should give the same answer. Whether or not this is the case provides a test of the model given a predefined set of at least two adult goods. Alternatively the result can be used to start from a single adult good and to test whether others can legitimately be added. The significance of gender differences in the outlay equivalents is most simply tested by comparing the θ-coefficients in (1). In the absence of discrimination, they should be the same for boys and girls, a hypothesis that can be tested using standard F-tests on the regression coefficients.

In Deaton (1989), the data used were from World Bank's 1985 Living Standard Survey of Côte d'Ivoire and from the 1981 Socio-Economic Survey of Thailand. For Côte d'Ivoire, there were seven adult goods: adult clothing, fabric for adult clothing, adult shoes, alcohol, tobacco, meals eaten away from home, and entertainment. For none of these individually, nor for them all taken together, was there any significant difference between boys and girls; indeed, if anything the adults seemed to make slightly more room in their budgets for girls than for boys. Using the Thai data, it was rather more difficult to find a satisfactory set of adult goods. There are fewer plausible candidates in the survey, and a grouping of alcohol, tobacco, and meals away from home produced different outlay equivalents depending on which goods were used, a result that casts doubt particularly on the use of meals away from home as an adult good. Indeed, although such meals are unlikely to be eaten by small children, the presence of children is likely to affect work patterns, which is what seems to determine the consumption of such meals, so that the effect of children on such expenditures is not determined by their pure income effect. This is a recurrent problem with the methodology to which we will return below. However, and even given these difficulties with the Thai data, there was no evidence that boys were favored over girls.

That there should be evidence of gender bias in neither Côte d'Ivoire nor Thailand is not surprising. Neither of these countries has figured in the direct evidence of differential treatment of boys and girls, and in both countries, women participate productively and profitably in the labor force—the absence of women is often associated with unequal treatment of girls. The Thai and Ivorien data therefore provide a useful illustration of the technique, but they cannot be expected to demonstrate its ability to discover gender bias.

A more likely venue was provided by the Indian data from the state of Maharashtra analyzed by Shankar Subramanian and the author (1991). Since Maharashtra is largely a southern state, and since most of the direct evidence of gender bias comes from the north of the subcontinent, once again we might not expect to find very much. Even so, some of the northern districts of the state appear to have excess infant mortality among girls, so that there was some hope that the expenditure data might also reveal gender differences. The data are the microlevel household expenditure records from the Maharashtran state sample of the 38th round (1983) of the National Sample Survey, and attention is focused on the behavior of 5,600 rural households. A number of adult goods was considered, although only two, alcohol, and tobacco and *pan*, were clearly uncontaminated by consumption by children. Of these, alcohol is less than satisfactory because its consumption is reported by only a very small fraction of rural Maharashtran households. Tobacco and *pan* is a more useful adult good. With total outlay held constant, additional children cause expenditure to fall; for boys aged from 0 to 4 years, this effect is estimated to be equivalent to a 42 per cent drop in total outlay, while for those aged 5 to 9, and 10 to 14, the respective estimates are 12 and 13 per cent. When the same figures are calculated for girls, an additional infant is equivalent to only a 4 per cent cut in outlay, and the two older groups have estimated ratios of 1 and 17 per cent respectively. For the infants, aged 0 to 4, although not for the other two groups, these differences are statistically significant, and they are in the expected direction, indicating that these rural households make more room in their budgets for boys than they do for girls.

Although these results are suggestive, they are hardly conclusive. Maharashtra is not the ideal site for the investigation, and the estimated gender differences appear only for one commodity group—tobacco and *pan*—and for one age group, albeit the group that seems most relevant given the direct evidence on infant mortality. With only a single adult good, there must also be a concern that special factors are at work that might explain the results in some other way. In particular, the estimated Engel curves for tobacco and *pan* show large positive effects on consumption when adult males are added to the household. There are no corresponding effects associated with adult females. This suggests that consumption is mostly by men, and that it is men who spend less on the commodity after the birth of a son but do not change their behavior on the birth of a daughter. There is still no reason to interpret this in terms of anything other than unequal treatment of boys and girls, but it would be premature to claim a full understanding of the mechanisms at work.

In the last two years, there has been a series of other studies using the same methodology, including work on Pakistan and Bangladesh, areas where we would have a high expectation of finding gender effects in the household expenditure data. Asif Ahmad and Jonathan Morduch (1993) have examined the 1988 Household Expenditure Survey from Bangladesh and find no evidence of gender differences in expenditure patterns on adult goods, even though the survey itself shows an excess of boys over girls of more than 10 per cent, and although they find evidence from a contemporaneous child nutrition survey that the nutritional status of boys rises more rapidly with household income than does the nutritional status of girls. These results provide what appears to be an example of the methodology failing to find gender bias in intrahousehold allocation even when it is demonstrably present.

The absence of gender effects in Pakistan is replicated in my own work using the 1984 Household Income and Expenditure Survey of Pakistan and reported in Deaton (forthcoming). The most promising adult goods in this survey are men's footwear, women's footwear, and tobacco and *pan*. As in the Indian data, the consumption of the last is strongly associated with the number of men in the household, but unlike the Indian case, the effects of small children are not uniformly negative. Although most of the estimated θ-coefficients for children are insignificantly different from zero, there is a *positive* and marginally significant effect of boys aged 0 to 2 on expenditures on tobacco and *pan*. Such a result, with children apparently driving their fathers to the use of stimulants, might be thought of as a substitution effect between children and adult goods, and if genuinely present means that tobacco and *pan* cannot be used as an adult good, and also casts doubt on the results from Maharashtra. (Although it remains unclear why it is only boys and not girls that cause their fathers to behave in such a way.) The results for the two footwear categories are more consistent with the conventional interpretation of adult goods. Holding total outlay constant, the expenditure on both men's and women's footwear is diminished by the addition of young children of either sex, and as in Ahmad and Morduch's results for Bangladesh, the effects are the same for boys and girls. Older boys exert a positive influence on the demand for men's shoes, an effect that is not replicated for girls on women's shoes, but for the two youngest age categories, in this case, ages 0 to 2, and 2 to 4, respectively, the reductions in expenditures on both men's shoes and women's shoes are the same whether the additional child is a boy or a girl.

Two other similar studies should also be noted. Jeremy Rudd (1993) examined Taipei,China data from the 1990 Survey of Personal Income Distribution. There is less direct evidence of discrimination against girls in Taipei,China than in either Pakistan or Bangladesh, but traditional Chinese attitudes tend to favor boys over girls in a number of ways, and evidence of differential treatment has been uncovered in studies by Susan Greenhalgh (1985), and William Parrish and Robert Willis (1992). But using the same methodology as the other studies reviewed here, Rudd finds no evidence of discrimination in the expenditure data.

Gregory Fischer (1993), whose Princeton senior thesis investigates the situation in the United States, provides an interesting comparison between developing and developed countries. There are serious methodological problems with using the two most obvious adult goods, alcohol and tobacco. Such expenditures tend to be grossly underestimated in survey data, and the combined group has a close to zero response to income, so that it is impossible to compute the income reductions that would have the same effect on adult expenditures as an additional child. This difficulty has arisen before in the literature, which attempts to use Rothbarth's method to measure the cost of children in developed countries (see in particular the discussion in Jan Cramer 1969). Partly because of these problems, Fischer finds no evidence of discrimination in expenditure patterns in the United States. However, he finds that the labor force participation decisions of women after the birth of a child are affected by the gender of the child, although the effects of these decisions are startlingly different by race. The relationship between child gender and adult leisure is a topic that would benefit from more research, both in developed and developing countries. Indeed, this whole literature can be faulted for its neglect of the labor/leisure choice.

With the exception of the results from Maharashtra in India, the evidence from all these studies suggests the same thing, that at least as far as household expenditures are concerned, there is no evidence of discriminatory treatment by gender. This is somewhat of a puzzle, given the direct evidence on gender discrimination. While it is always possible that it is the *direct* evidence that is flawed, that explanation is less likely than a number of other possibilities.

First, there may be pervasive problems with the adult good methodology. Indeed, some of these have already become apparent in the discussion: the difficulty of finding adult goods, possible substitution effects of children on various adult goods, and problems of measurement error. However, while it is easy to think of reasons why any of these might bias coefficients and thus confound attempts to measure the cost of children, it is much more difficult to explain why any of them would act differentially by gender, so as to obscure any genuine differences between boys and girls in the data. For example, children demand parental leisure, so that adding children to the household will enforce a reallocation of time, which will affect the pattern of demand for apparently unrelated goods— including adult goods—as the parents substitute away from goods that are relatively time intensive.

If parents allocate less time to girls than to boys, we would expect substitution effects to make it easier to observe gender differences in consumption patterns—not more difficult. If the consumption of adult goods requires relatively little time compared with other goods—which seems implausible in any case—and if boys are favored over girls and so raise the shadow price of time by more, then there might be a time-price substitution effect toward adult goods in the presence of boys that could offset the larger negative income effect. This argument is not at all plausible, and it is surely *very* implausible that the substitution effects would exactly offset the income effects.

Second, the specification of these models may be too simple to capture the reality. This argument has been made by Ahmad and Morduch (1993), and reinforced by arguments by Monica Das Gupta (1987) that discrimination against girls in India is related to birth order. Even so, and in the absence of an argument to the contrary, the presence of a more complicated mechanism would usually show up in the simpler specification, even if the latter failed to give an adequate account of the phenomenon.

Third, we might accept the findings and try to reconcile the direct evidence of discrimination with the absence of such effects in the expenditure data. Most obviously, the unequal allocation may be confined to such things as hospital care or calling in the doctor when the child is sick, while food itself is equally allocated. It is not easy to imagine why parents would behave in such a manner, treating girls identically to boys in the everyday business of food allocation, but withholding vital medical care when their lives are at risk. One possibility is based on a distinction between capital account and current account transactions. If the cost of medical care is large, or even possibly so, poor families risk going into debt to pay for medical care, a debt that may be worth incurring for a boy, whose future earnings make him a valuable asset, but not for a girl, for whom absence of labor market opportunities and the need for a dowry make her a financial liability. Parents may therefore be able to afford medical care for boys but not for girls, a story that is essentially that told by Rosenzweig and Schultz (1982), who also find empirical evidence in India relating excess infant mortality of girls to differentials in wage rates between boys and girls.

The final explanation also comes from consideration of intertemporal allocation. In regions where girls require dowries at marriage, the birth of a girl should promote a decrease in consumption as the household begins the saving necessary to meet her later marriage expenses. When this happens, it may or may not explain what we see, depending on how the household allocates resources. If adult expenditures are differentially cut to make room for the additional saving, an additional girl could cut adult expenditures by *more* than would an additional boy, an affect that would offset the tendency to make more room for the current expenses of boys. However, if preferences are intertemporally separable, so that saving for dowries comes from a reduction of current total expenditure, the procedure here, which is conditional on current total expenditure, should still give the right answer. Some of these issues have been investigated using the panel data, from the International Crop Research Institute for the Semi Arid Tropics (India), presented in a recent paper by Ramesh Subramaniam (1992). Subramaniam finds that boys have an advantage in food equations that control for total expenditure, but that when household fixed effects are included, fixed effects that can be interpreted as capturing the lifetime marginal utility of money in a life-cycle model, gender differences disappear. While such evidence can be interpreted in a number of different ways, it certainly suggests that too little attention has been given to the investigation of gender differences in a dynamic context.

Inequality Between Households
in Growing and Aging Economies

This part of the paper reviews recent joint research by the author and Christina Paxson—research that is the first step in a five-year research project to examine the relationships between aging, saving, and inequality, with a particular, but not exclusive, focus on Asia. Many of the more rapidly growing economies of the region have already experienced substantial declines in fertility, and those furthest along in this process are already seeing an aging of their populations, a phenomenon that will become even more pronounced in the future. There are a host of policy questions associated with this aging process, many of which have been little researched in the Asian context. Living arrangements of the elderly are likely to change, as will saving patterns if people come to expect to be independent in old age, as opposed to the traditional pattern of living with children. There will also be demands for social security to prevent poverty among the increasing proportion of the elderly who will have no children upon whom to rely. However, the topic of concern here is that discussed in Deaton and Paxson (1993a, b), where a link is drawn between population aging and inequality, with increased aging associated with a greater dispersion of income and consumption in the population as a whole.

The basic idea can be elucidated by analogy with the standard life-cycle model of Modigliani and Brumberg (Modigliani 1986). As Modigliani has frequently emphasized, a simple life-cycle theory of intertemporal choice under certainty implies that there should be a relationship between the rate of population growth and the rate of national saving. In an economy where saving is a life-cycle phenomenon, and its main motive is to build up wealth for retirement, the average age of savers is considerably less than the average age of dissavers. In consequence, an increase in the rate of population growth, which in demographic equilibrium increases the numbers of young relative to the numbers of the old, will also increase the number of savers and decrease the numbers of dissavers, so that the aggregate rate of saving will increase. Our work is also based on the life-cycle story of saving, but adds the crucial ingredient of uncertainty. We argue that this version of life-cycle theory implies that inequality of both consumption and income should increase with age, so that if we were to track a single cohort of people through their working lives, retirement, and death, we would find gradually increasing inequality among them in both income and consumption. As a result, and in the absence of secular changes in inequality, inequality among the old will generally be greater than is inequality among the young. Hence, just as increases in the rate of population growth in the simple life-cycle model generate more saving by redistributing population from old to young, so will the same phenomenon in the life-cycle model under uncertainty imply that there will be a decrease in inequality, as high inequality older people are replaced by low inequality younger people. In the context of current developments in Asia, a *decline* in the rate of population growth is the relevant phenomenon. Hence, if our story is correct, we can expect the 'greying' of Asia to generate increases in national measures of inequality.

In the remainder of this paper, we will look at why the life-cycle theory predicts such an effect, and examine the empirical evidence to see whether there is any evidence that inequality does indeed increase with age. An assessment of what this implies for the consequences of aging for saving and inequality in Asia will be made based on the argument that, in spite of the life-cycle theory, there is little evidence that reductions in population growth rates will decrease national saving rates, but that we can expect aging to be a force for greater inequality, though its effects might well be swamped by the many other forces that are at work.

The theoretical basis of the work comes from the life-cycle model. In the simplest version of the life-cycle hypothesis under certainty, Modigliani's (1986) 'stripped-down' model, consumption is constant throughout life, while earnings follow some lifetime trajectory, typically zero after retirement. The age profile of life-cycle earnings has no effect on the age profile of life-cycle consumption, although the level of the consumption profile is set by lifetime resources and the requirement that the discounted present value of lifetime consumption and earnings be the same. If uncertainty about earnings is added to this simple model, instead of consumption being constant, it will be constant in the absence of new information, so that in expectation, future consumption is always the same as current consumption. This is the famous martingale or random-walk property of consumption (Hall 1978), which can be written in the following form

$$c_{it} = c_{it-1} + u_{it} \tag{2}$$

where c is consumption and the indices i and t refer to an individual and a time period respectively. The innovation u_{it} has the property that its expectation at time $t-1$ (or earlier) is zero, so that it is orthogonal to any information dated t or earlier, and in particular, must be uncorrelated with lagged consumption c_{it-1}.

Equation (2) has implications for the behavior of the variance of consumption over time for any given cohort of individuals. Indeed, given any group of individuals whose members are present at both time t and $t-1$ the equation predicts that the variance of consumption at t should be larger than the variance at $t-1$ or any earlier date, provided that the covariance between u_{it} and c_{it-1} is zero. This proviso is guaranteed by the theory only for a single individual over time, and need not hold in the cross section, although it can be shown that it will hold over an average of cross sections under reasonable assumptions. As a result, the variance of consumption for any given cohort of people must be increasing over time, if not in every year, at least over a run of years. Indeed, equation (2) has the much stronger prediction that the cross-sectional distribution of consumption at any time is second-order stochastically dominated by the distribution of consumption in all earlier periods, so that inequality will increase according to *any* measure of inequality that respects the principle of transfers, that a transfer from a richer to a poorer person decreases inequality. Whatever measure of inequality we use, the cross-sectional distribution of consumption within a cohort of individuals should be 'fanning out' as the cohort grows older.

The intuition behind this result can perhaps be developed by thinking about consumption as a function of lifetime resources, as the life-cycle theory requires, and thinking about the impact of luck on lifetime resources. On any given date, each individual's earnings may differ from what they previously expected. If consumption was simply equal to current earnings, and if the earnings of the cohort showed no tendency to disperse over time, there would be no fanning out of consumption either. But lifetime earnings include, not only the current earning shock, but the sum of all previous earning shocks, so that making consumption depend on lifetime resources also makes consumption depend on the sum of all shocks, or in the language of time-series analysis, makes consumption an integrated process. While the *average* of shocks will converge to zero over a long enough time period, their *sum* is a process that can become infinitely large or infinitely small, some people will go in one direction and some in the other, so that the spread between them will expand over time.

There are a number of extensions and caveats that are explored in the earlier work. First, it is important to note that the fanning-out result holds only for a given cohort of people, all of whose members are present over time. It does not hold for the economy as a whole, where the population as a whole is constantly being renewed by the process of births and deaths. Indeed, it is quite possible for inequality to be increasing for every cohort in the population, but to be constant for the population as a whole, since the unequal older generations are constantly being replaced by more equal young generations. Second, equation (2) also implies that the dispersion of *income* is increasing over time. This is far from obvious, but is nevertheless true, and depends crucially on maintaining the distinction between earnings and income, where the latter includes income from assets. For a cohort whose inequality of earnings is constant over time, the growing dispersion of consumption is supported by a growing dispersion of assets, and thus of asset income and income in total. Third, the simple life-cycle model of (2) can be extended to include more realistic preferences than the simple certainty equivalent forms that underlie the martingale result. Perhaps the most important reason for doing so is that precautionary motives for consumption are thereby permitted. The analysis shows that, although the result can continue to hold with precautionary motives, a sufficiently large amount of caution is capable of inhibiting the spread of consumption within the cohort. The spread of inequality is generated by individuals responding to the opportunities that fortune presents to them; some do well, some not so well, and dispersion increases. But if consumers are too cautious to respond to such opportunities, inequality may remain constant over time.

Precautionary motives also suggest a further result that is particularly relevant in the current Asian context. The introduction of social insurance systems, whether in the form of old age, poverty, or unemployment insurance, can be expected to reduce the degree of precaution in consumption and saving behavior. As a result, the introduction of such measures can be expected to increase the rate at which inequality spreads with age, at least in the distribution of consumption and income prior to the operation of the social security system. This is no more than the familiar concept that insurance can induce risk taking, but expressed here through the consequences of the spread of inequality.

What does the empirical evidence say about the relationship between age and inequality? In Deaton and Paxson (1993a) we examine the relationship between inequality and age using household survey data from Taipei,China (1976–90), Great Britain (1969–1990), and the United States (1980–90). None of the sources provide panel data, so we do not have the ability to track a given set of households over time. Instead, each of these countries has a succession of annual household surveys, with new selections of households each year. We use these to track cohorts— defined by their year of birth—by means of their members who are randomly selected into each survey. Consider, for example, the cohort born in Taipei,China in 1945. In 1976, the first year of the Taipei,China data, the members of this cohort are 31 years old, and we estimate cohort inequality in that year by calculating the variance of the logarithm of consumption for 31-year-olds in the 1976 survey. In 1977, the same cohort is 32 years old, so that the variance of the logarithm of consumption of 32-year-olds in the 1977 survey provides as an estimate of consumption inequality among the cohort of 1945 in the second year. This process is continued for the 15 years of survey data until we lose the cohort after 1990 in which year they were 45 years old. Exactly the same procedure is followed for each cohort whose members make an appearance in at least one of the surveys.

Provided the sample design throws up a random sample of each cohort in each year, the fact that we are not following the same households is of no importance; indeed, repeated random sampling avoids the attrition that is often a difficulty in genuine panel data. The main difficulty is not the sampling issue, but the fact that we do not observe consumption (nor all of income) for individuals, but for households. This presents us with a choice between two alternatives, neither of which is entirely satisfactory. In the first, we deal cleanly with the cohorts by working with individual data, and make some attempt to impute consumption and income for each individual based on the household data. In the second, we preserve the household data and deal with cohorts by tracking, not the age of the individuals, but the age of the household head. We have investigated both possibilities, and the results are not very sensitive to the choice. The first alternative requires quite arbitrary assumptions about intrahousehold allocation, and the age profiles that result appear to have as much to do with the assumptions as with the data. The second, which is what we prefer, requires fewer arbitrary assumptions, but will raise difficult selectivity issues when the membership of households is changing over time. While this can happen at any time, we think that it is likely to be a serious problem (at least in Taipei,China) only among the older heads, where households are rapidly dissolving as the elderly either move in with their children or die.

Figure 2.2 shows some results from the Taipei,China data. The horizontal axis plots the age of the household head, and the vertical axis, the variance of the logarithm of household consumption. The figure shows four cohorts of household heads, those born in 1955, 1945, 1935, and 1925; others could be added, but this would not change the shape of the picture, making it only more difficult to read. As it is, the experience of the four cohorts, each observed for 15 years, can be pieced together to make a picture of life-cycle consumption inequality in which there is little change until around age 40, at which point there is a steady increase, at

Figure 2.2
Within Cohort Inequality for Four Taipei, China Cohorts

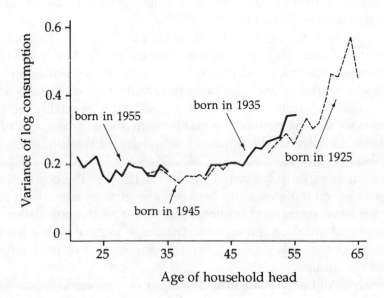

least until somewhere around age 60. What is particularly notable about the Taipei,China case is the absence of cohort effects in inequality. At age 40, those born in 1945 had essentially the same level of consumption inequality as did the cohort born in 1935 when they were 40; even though aggregate inequality in Taipei,China is slowly increasing over the period of these surveys, it is not the case that the later born cohorts are experiencing higher lifetime inequality.

The relationship between inequality and age in Figure 2.2 also appears in similar analyses for the British and American data. Indeed, the increase in the variance over the life cycle is very similar in all three countries, although in Britain and the United States, the increase starts earlier than in Taipei,China. In all three countries, the spread of consumption inequality appears to stop at around the normal age of retirement, something that the theory predicts if the primary source of uncertainty is shocks to earnings. Again in line with the theory, the distribution of *income* also fans out with age, as does the distribution of earnings. Of course, these results are consistent not only with the theory discussed above, but also with a number of other models of behavior, for example those in which consumption is fairly closely tied to earnings. But whatever the cause, there appears to be very good evidence that inequality increases with age, so that, everything else being the same, inequality of earnings, income, and consumption is larger among households with older heads.

Given this fact, we can turn to the impact on aggregate inequality of changes in the demographic composition of the population, particularly those brought about by reductions in the rate of population growth. Increases in mortality and decreases in fertility will each increase the fraction of older people in the population, so that if inequality increases with age, so will aggregate inequality with the average age of the population. In spite of the apparent simplicity of the argument, it is incomplete. Aggregate inequality depends not only on the inequality within each age group weighted by the fractions of the population in each, but also on the inequality between age groups, something about which we have so far said nothing. The aging of the population will increase the 'within' age group contribution to inequality, but the final outcome also depends on what are the effects, if any, on inequality between age groups.

An analysis of the ultimate effects of aging on aggregate consumption inequality is undertaken in Deaton and Paxson (1993b). They work with the variance of the logarithms of consumption, which is convenient because it can be decomposed into within and within age-group components, and consider what happens in demographic equilibrium when the rate of population growth is constant and has been so for some time. Because inequality increases with age for individual cohorts, decreases in the rate of population growth unambiguously increase the within age-group component of aggregate inequality, the result that we have already seen. To make progress in discussing the effects on the between age-group component, we need a theory of the cross-sectional age profile of consumption. The obvious candidate is, once again, the life-cycle model. According to this, the age profile of consumption for a single cohort is determined by tastes, independently of the life-cycle profile of earnings, so that we can derive various possible profiles from different standard intertemporal utility functions. In particular, the usual isoelastic specification yields a profile of steady growth with age, where the growth rate can be positive, negative, or zero. For this case, it is possible to show that the within age-group effect of lower rates of population growth on inequality is reinforced by a further negative effect on the between age-group component, so that lower rates of population growth inevitably lead to higher aggregate inequality of consumption.

While this result is useful, its assumptions are unrealistic in one important respect. The assumption that consumption grows, or declines, steadily with age makes some sense for single individuals, or for indissoluble but childless marriages, but it makes very little sense for households with children. In particular, small children have relatively low consumption needs, so that young households that have a relatively large number of children will typically have relatively low per capita consumption. As a result, the cross-sectional profile of consumption by head's age may well be lowest among the youngest households, although such an effect will be less pronounced and possibly even reversed at high enough rates of economic growth. Under the life-cycle hypothesis, where consumption is set in relation to lifetime resources, economic growth makes the young wealthier than their elders, and must therefore tip the cross-sectional consumption to age profile in favor of the young.

Suppose first that per capita economic growth is low, and that the lowest consumption levels in the age-profile are among the youngest households, which are therefore the major source of between age-group consumption inequality. A decrease in the equilibrium rate of population growth will decrease the numbers of such people relative to the older groups, and will therefore *decrease* between age-group inequality, an effect that can be large enough to swamp the unambiguously positive effect on inequality through the within age-group effect. However, as the rate of growth increases, the younger households' consumption should increase relatively, and the depressing effect on inequality will be eliminated or become positive as in the simple version of the life-cycle model where children are ignored.

To summarize these results, if the life-cycle model of consumption is correct, and if the rate of economic growth is not too low—and recent rates of growth in Taipei,China and elsewhere in Asia are well above the threshold—declines in the rate of economic growth will increase consumption inequality in the population as a whole. What then should we expect to see? Are the assumptions underlying these results sufficiently credible that we can confidently expect to see inequality rising in Asia? Is the mechanism sufficiently robust so that we should revise our expectations about Kuznets' curve, with income growth leading to lower rates of population growth and to higher inequality? As usual, the answers are mixed, with some elements of the story more credible than others.

The first point to make is a methodological one. The results discussed in this section should be seen as an addition to the general toolbox of applied economists. The life-cycle model has for many years provided the framework in which economists have thought about saving rates, economic growth, and population growth, and our argument is that this framework also has implications for inequality, implications that are worth bearing in mind, and that will occasionally be important. More substantively, there is a good deal of evidence that at least some of the implications of the life-cycle hypothesis are incorrect, an issue reviewed elsewhere (Deaton 1992). In particular, the life-cycle profile of consumption is not as firmly detached from the life-cycle profile of earnings as the theory would suggest, and there is strong evidence against the proposition that higher rates of economic growth tip the consumption to age profile in favor of younger households (see, in particular, Carroll and Summers 1991). As a result, the part of the argument that uses the life-cycle hypothesis to pin down the effects of population growth on the between age-group contribution to inequality is likely to be of greater theoretical than practical interest. As a result, and although the inequality to age relationship is robust so that population aging will exert a force toward greater inequality, there is no general reason to suppose that this effect might not be offset by other effects. Indeed, this is about as much as could reasonably be expected in any case. There are many links between demographic change and inequality, and the mechanism identified in this paper is only one.

It should also be noted that there is an increasing amount of evidence (Deaton and Paxson 1994) from Taipei,China, and from other countries around the world, that fails to support the prediction of the life-cycle hypothesis that the average age of saving is lower than the average age of dissaving. It should always be remembered that saving behavior among older households is extremely difficult to measure, partly because of the general difficulties in measuring saving, but also because of increasingly severe sample selection with age. Even so, the supposed dissaving of the elderly is becoming more and more an article of faith in a world in which the evidence seems to point to substantial bequest motives and an unwillingness by the elderly to run down their capital. In such circumstances, there is no reason to believe the prediction of the life-cycle theory that slower rates of population growth will cause saving rates to decline. Indeed, we would attach more credibility to the prediction that inequality will rise with aging than to the prediction that saving rates will fall.

Acknowledgments

The author is grateful to Yeong-Yuh Chiang, J. Malcolm Dowling, Jr., and Chung-Young Jung for helpful comments. He also wishes to acknowledge the collaboration of Christina Paxson, who is the joint author of the work reported in the second part of the paper.

References

Ahmad, A., and J. Morduch, 1993. "Identifying Sex Bias in the Allocation of Household Resources: Evidence from Limited Household Surveys from Bangladesh." Harvard University. Processed.

Bourguignon, F., and P. A. Chiappori, 1992. "Collective Models of Household Behavior: An Introduction." *European Economic Review* 36:355–64.

Carroll, C. D., and L. H. Summers, 1991. "Consumption Growth Parallels Income Growth: Some New Evidence." In B. D. Bernheim and J. B. Shoven, eds. *National Saving and Economic Performance*. Chicago: Chicago University Press for National Bureau of Economic Research.

Chiappori, P. A., 1988. "Rational Household Labor Supply." *Econometrica* 56(1):63–89.

———, 1992. "Collective Labor Supply and Welfare." *Journal of Political Economy* 100(3):437–67.

Cramer, J. S., 1969. *Empirical Econometrics*. Amsterdam: North-Holland Publishers.

Das Gupta, M., 1987. "Selective Discrimination against Female Children in Rural Punjab, India." *Population and Development Review* 13:77–100.

Deaton, A. S., 1989. "Looking for Boy-Girl Discrimination in Household Expenditure Data." *World Bank Economic Review* 3:1–15.

———, 1992. *Understanding Consumption*. Oxford: Clarendon Press.

———, forthcoming. *The Analysis of Household Surveys: Microeconomic Analysis for Development Policy*. Research Program in Development Studies, Princeton University.

Deaton, A. S., and C. H. Paxson, 1993a. "Inequality and Aging: An East Asian Perspective." Research Program in Development Studies. Princeton University. Processed.

———, 1993b. "Intertemporal Choice and Inequality." Research Program in Development Studies. Princeton University. Processed.

———, 1994. "Saving, Growth, and Aging in Taiwan." In David Wise, ed., *Issues in the Economics of Aging*. Chicago: Chicago University Press for National Bureau of Economic Research.

Fischer, G., 1993. "I Love You Just the Same." Senior Thesis. Princeton University.

Greenhalgh, S., 1985. "Sexual Stratification: The Other Side of 'Growth with Equity' in East Asia." *Population and Development Review* 11:265–314.

Hall, R. E., 1978. "Stochastic Implications of the Life-Cycle Permanent Income

Hypothesis: Theory and Evidence." *Journal of Political Economy* 86(6):971–87.

———, 1988. "Intertemporal Substitution in Consumption." *Journal of Political Economy* 96(2):339–57.

Modigliani, F., 1986. "Life Cycle, Individual Thrift, and the Wealth of Nations." *American Economic Review* 76(3):297–313.

Parrish, W. L., and R. J. Willis, 1992. "Daughters, Education, and Family Budgets: Taiwan Experiences." Chicago: National Opinion Research Center. Processed.

Rosenzweig, M. R., and T. P. Schultz, 1982. "Market Opportunities, Genetic Endowments, and Intrafamily Resource Endowments." *American Economic Review* 72(4):803–15.

Rothbarth, E., 1943. "Note on A Method of Determining Equivalent Income for Families of Different Composition." In C. Madge, ed., *War Time Pattern of Saving and Spending*. Occasional Paper Number 4, Appendix 4. London: National Institute of Economic and Social Research.

Rudd, J. B., 1993. "Boy-Girl Discrimination in Taiwan: Evidence from Expenditure Data." Princeton University. Processed.

Subramaniam, R., 1992. "Gender-Bias in Intrahousehold Allocation: The Importance of Household Fixed Effects." Working Paper No. 92-25. McMaster University Department of Economics, Hamilton, Ontario.

Subramanian, S., and A. Deaton, 1991. "Gender Effects in Indian Consumption Patterns." *Sarvekshana* 14:1–12.

Chapter Three

Gender and Household Dynamics: Recent Theories and Their Implications

Gillian Hart

Introduction

Economic analyses have by and large treated the household as a black box in which the preferences of all household members can be aggregated in a single joint utility function. Until recently the strongest critiques of this unitary view of the household have come from noneconomists and nonneoclassical economists who insist on the importance of recognizing both conflict and cooperation in intrahousehold relations. In response to these criticisms an alternative bargaining model of the household emerged during the 1980s and, until very recently, the debate has been cast in terms of unitary versus bargaining models of the household.

Over the past year or so, the terrain of debate has shifted quite dramatically with the emergence of an explicitly neoclassical critique of the unitary model. The main thrust of this critique is that individuals should be characterized by their *own* preferences, rather than aggregated within the ad hoc fiction of the unitary model: 'individualism should be referred to even when one is modeling household behavior; that is, the latter should be explicitly recognized as a *collective* process involving (except for singles) more than one decision unit' (Chiappori 1992, 440). Since the rules governing intrahousehold allocation can assume multiple forms, collective modelers maintain that the unitary model is no more than a special subset of the collective approach, which also encompasses bargaining models (Chiappori et al. 1993).

Collective modelers' challenge to the unitary model carries far-reaching policy implications (Alderman et al. 1993; Chiappori et al. 1993; Haddad et al. 1993). The neglect of intrahousehold resource allocation, they maintain, is likely to result in a number of serious policy failures—these include the wrong choice of policy instrument, the inappropriate implementation of a particular policy instrument, and failure to recognize the variety and reach of potential policy handles. The policy failures that they associate with the unitary model, discussed more fully below, are closely analogous to longstanding arguments in the literature on women and development—namely that resources should be channeled to women on grounds not only of equity but also of efficiency.

Having recognized the diversity of intrahousehold resource allocation processes, collective modelers now confront the question of how to identify which of the myriad possible collective models applies in a particular setting. The prevailing view is that this is an open question to be resolved empirically through generating testable restrictions rather than imposing them on the data a priori, and recovering the household's sharing rule from the data with the help of some additional assumptions.

The most obvious problem with this approach is that the collection of quantitative survey data is itself contingent on assumptions about intrahousehold and interhousehold relations. Precisely what is meant by the household is far from self-evident, and the predefined categories used in any quantitative data collection exercise will determine what is recovered from the data. The problem is rendered even more formidable when one takes into account dynamic processes of household formation and reconstitution, particularly in rapidly industrializing economies such as those in much of contemporary Asia. For example, rather than a straightforward process of rural-urban migration, what seems to be emerging in many parts of Asia are complex systems of labor circulation and spatially extended sharing arrangements. Far from a natural unit, the household is a complex, culturally varied, and dynamic set of institutional arrangements.

One of the strengths of the collective approach is its recognition of the multiplicity and complexity of household forms, and the need for interdisciplinary collaboration. Calls for such collaboration are hardly new; since the inception of household studies in the 1970s they have been raised with some regularity, but the rift between unitary modelers and those who argue for the need to look inside the black box has remained insurmountable. By focusing directly on intrahousehold allocation, the collective approach appears to have narrowed the rift: 'Generally, the very nature of intrahousehold research—being so rooted in cultural concepts of division of labor, attitudes toward status within households, and perceived versus actual contributions—would seem to benefit from a multidisciplinary approach' (Alderman et al. 1993, 28). The authors identify two particularly promising areas of work: (i) the use of information collected in a qualitative manner and yet accessible to 'quantifiers', such as the creation of variables for 'respect', 'status', or 'apparent prosperity', and (ii) an investigation of cultural norms that often override the intent of social legislation.

These suggestions for a more culturally informed set of data are all very well, but they do not get at the basic problem—the need for a conceptual understanding of intrahousehold and interhousehold *relations* as a guide to empirical research. Rather than simply shifting from the household to the individual, there is a need to focus on *relationships* within and between households, as well as in nonhousehold institutions, and on the way these relationships are defined in terms of gender. Taking account of gender is not simply a matter of adding women. Nor is it just a question of discrimination. A gendered approach focuses on how multiple understandings of 'male' and 'female' are socially constructed and embodied in everyday practices both within and beyond the household.

Gender in this sense is crucial to understanding not only *what* the culturally variable rules are that govern access to and control over resources and labor, but also *how* definitions of rules, rights, and obligations are reinforced, renegotiated, and, on occasion, openly challenged. A key insight of this gendered, politicized understanding of the household is that policies and macroeconomic changes not only have different effects on different household members, but may also provoke renegotiations of gendered relations within as well as beyond the household. Gender thus provides the key to understanding the processes of household formation and dissolution, as well as dynamic processes more generally.

The first part of this paper outlines the shift from unitary to collective models of the household, showing how the latter represent a step forward but also encounter insuperable problems that represent the limits of economism. The second half of the paper presents the outlines of a gendered approach and the insights that flow from it.

From Unitary to Collective Models of the Household

Unitary Models of the Household

The problem of preference aggregation forms the core of neoclassical household models. Posed most forcefully by Samuelson (1956), the problem is, How can we expect family demand functions to obey any consistency conditions? Samuelson's solution is revealing of his own preferences. He rejected the notion of a household dictator with sovereign power such that family demand reflected this individual's consistent indifference curves, and opted instead for a 'social welfare function' in which household members internalize one another's preferences such that 'the family acts *as if* it were maximizing their joint welfare'.

The need to conjure up a justification for equating the household to an individual with a consistent preference ordering has remained a central theme, and is a defining feature of the unitary model. With growing substantive interest in the household, the justifications have become more sophisticated. They have nevertheless remained inherently problematic and the disintegration of these justifications has contributed to the recent return to the individual as the unit of analysis.

It was the discovery of housework that was primarily responsible for transforming the household from an analytical nuisance into an object of interest. Becker's (1965) celebrated notion that the household is a unit, not only of consumption but also production even in advanced industrial economies, depicts household members combining time with market goods and household capital to produce consummables (or Z-goods) that yield direct utility. Becker's 'Theory of the Allocation of Time' (1965) coincided with the publication in English of Chayanov's *Theory of Peasant Economy* (1966). They form the starting points of two closely parallel streams of empirical literature on unitary models—the former focusing on human capital, the latter on models of the farm household.[1]

Chayanov's theory of the peasant household, constructed from his reading of Russian rural survey data at the turn of the century, is a model of utility maximization, subject to a land and a labor constraint defined by household size and composition. The key assumption is the absence of a labor market. In these circumstances, the allocation of time between leisure and work on the family farm will be determined by preferences —the 'subjective equilibrium'. The farm-household model, which has come to play quite an important role in the development literature, incorporates a perfectly competitive labor market into Chayanov's model. This simple manoeuvre, performed by Nakajima (1969), is crucial for econometric estimation because it allows for the separability of production and consumption decisions. The production side of the farm household can be estimated independently of the consumption side, and farm profits are then used to explain consumption and labor supply behavior.

In one of the first econometric estimations of the farm-household model, Barnum and Squire (1979a) used data from the Muda region of Malaysia to show that the elasticities of own consumption of padi, consumption of nonfarm good, and labor supply estimated from the integration of production with consumption differed significantly from elasticities estimated in isolation. More generally, farm household modelers underscore the importance of the integration of production and consumption in estimating the effects of changes in prices and technology (Singh et al. 1986).

Farm-household models exemplify the unitary approach, with the preferences of all household members aggregated in a joint utility function so that the household can be treated in effect like an individual. The second key assumption is that of a perfectly competitive labor market. Any departure from the perfectly competitive labor market assumption poses major estimation problems because it means that household preferences and endowments will affect production decisions, that is, it violates the separability conditions. Lopez (1986) rejects separability, and Deolalikar and Vijverberg (1983) argue that family and hired labor are not perfect substitutes in India and Malaysia. Benjamin (1992), in contrast, reasserts the separability assumption on the grounds that farm employment is independent of family composition in Java.

The farm-household literature has remained entirely separate from work on sharecropping, agrarian institutions, and market interlinkages (for example, see P. Bardhan 1989b; Stiglitz 1989). The Muda region of Malaysia provides an example of the problems inherent in abstracting from the organization of work. In providing descriptive 'background' information from this region, Barnum and Squire (1979a, 24) note that rice transplanting and harvesting activities are organized in groups, and that agricultural wage data reveal considerable variations in earnings per unit of time within the same area. However, this point drops out of sight in the estimation of the farm-household model, which requires a uniform wage rate to measure the opportunity cost of labor (Barnum and Squire 1979b). In fact, it is women's labor that is organized in groups, and for many small landholders the work group rather than the household is the salient unit of production (Hart 1992). As will be more fully argued later, a direct understanding of the organization of work is extremely important from the viewpoint of policy.

Household models, which trace their descent to Becker, have focused primarily on human capital decisions, including fertility, education, and health, as well as labor supply and consumption. Becker's original formulation proved difficult to operationalize because of its reliance on unobserved variables such as household technology and genetic endowments (Pollak and Wachter 1975). Modifications by Gronau (1973, 1977) produced an operational model that closely resembles the farm-household model, with household members allocating their time between market work, home production, and leisure. Like the farm-household models, human capital models entail the estimation of a production function for home produced 'goods' such as health and children. In general, however, these models drop the separability assumption, so the reduced form equations used to estimate the determinants of goods, such as health, include not only variables from the production side such as input prices, but also consumption side variables such as the education of household members. The theoretical predictions that can be generated from these models are quite limited because income and substitution effects often operate in opposite directions. Accordingly, empirical work has come to play a particularly important role in this literature.

Since their initiation in the 1970s, empirical studies have grown rapidly in number and sophistication (for useful reviews, see Behrman 1990, 1992; Behrman and Deolalikar 1988; and Strauss and Thomas 1993). Summarizing these studies, Behrman (1992, 80) notes that:

> ... even the best studies in this tradition are characterized by some strong maintained hypotheses, though with some variance regarding the exact assumptions (implicit and explicit) in different studies: unified household, or at least parental, preferences, perhaps with strong additional assumptions regarding separability; no problems with dynamics or with imperfect information; all of the relevant choice variables are observed in the estimation of household production functions; [and] the determinants of household structure are not addressed and are assumed not to be critical.

As data sets have become more sophisticated and refined, the literature has increasingly come to focus on questions of intrahousehold resource allocation. One of the earliest efforts to deal with intrahousehold allocation on the basis of household-level data was Rosenzweig and Schultz's (1982) estimation of differential male-female child survival rates in rural India. Invoking the logic of the unitary model, they posit that male-female survival differentials depend on expected relative returns to male and female labor because these will determine parental investments in sons and daughters. Assuming that expectations are static, they use predicted current employment rates for men and women as proxies for investment in boys and girls. Their main finding is an inverse relationship between predicted female employment rates and male-female survival differentials, which they interpret as evidence that household resources are allocated differentially to children who are more likely to become economically productive adults. In other words, intrahousehold inequality is economically rational and optimal from the viewpoint of the household as a whole. Data and estimation techniques have become increasingly sophisticated, but the logic invoked to explain intrahousehold inequality has remained essentially the same (see Pitt et al. 1990).

Well before the collective approach made its appearance, critiques of the unitary model focused on the problem of preference aggregation in the joint utility function. One set of critiques, embodied in the bargaining approach discussed below, challenges the unitary interpretation of intra-household inequality. In one of the earliest applications of the bargaining approach, Folbre (1984) pointed out that an entirely different interpretation can be placed on the relationship between male-female survival differentials in India and relative returns to labor—namely that women with higher incomes wield greater influence in intrahousehold allocation, and are more inclined to divert resources to daughters. Rosenzweig and Schultz (1984) contest this interpretation on grounds discussed below. The problem of distinguishing between unitary and bargaining interpretations has, until recently, been a central theme in the economic literature on the household.

While bargaining models focus on gender inequality, a second set of critiques of the unitary model address the problem of intergenerational resources transfers and conflicts. Much of this criticism has been directed at the Rotten Kid theorem, Becker's (1974, 1981) rather ingenious device for legitimating the unitary model in terms other than domestic dictatorship or utopian communism. So long as the household is headed by an altruist 'who cares sufficiently about other household members to transfer general resources to them', then no matter how selfish the kids (or the wives) may be, it will be in their individual interests to maximize the welfare of the household as a whole. Efficiency is thus accomplished through paternalistic manipulation, rather than through brute force or perfect consensus. The beauty of the Rotten Kid theorem is that it resolves not only the awkwardness of preference aggregation, but also the problem of enforcement.

Closer inspection of the Rotten Kid theorem reveals, however, some rather serious warts. Not only must the paternalistic altruist control sufficient resources to prevent coalitions of Rotten Kids from forming but, as Hirschleifer (1977, 500) shows, household welfare is maximized 'only if Big Daddy has the last word, i.e. controls the last action taken in an intertemporal sequence'. In addition, as Bernheim and Stark (1988) show in 'Do Nice Guys Finish Last?', there are circumstances under which altruism may be inversely related to social efficiency. The basic problem —also termed the Samaritan's dilemma—is that altruists are subject to exploitation by other household members (see also Lindbeck and Weibull 1988; N. Bruce and Waldman 1990). To preempt exploitation, the altruist has to take averting action that is inefficient: 'in cases where altruism is stronger, these actions must be more extreme, and so the resulting inefficiency is greater' (Bernheim and Stark 1988, 1035). For example, a Rotten Kid will consume too much in period one if it is possible to freeload in period two. To reduce the attractiveness of freeloading, the altruist will have to increase consumption in period one even though this is inefficient.

More generally, high levels of altruism in Becker's sense provide no guarantee of efficient outcomes. The authors conclude that, unless altruism arises endogenously through marriage choices and child-rearing practices, 'family decisions are more properly modeled as negotiations by self-interested individuals' (Bernheim and Stark 1988, 1044). This is precisely the conclusion other analysts have arrived at by different routes.

Bargaining Models and Other Critiques of the Unitary Model

Partly in response to problems inherent in the notion of a joint utility function, a group of economists turned to game theory in the early 1980s to develop bargaining models of the household (Manser and Brown 1980; McElroy and Horney 1981). In contrast to the unitary model, the bargaining framework envisages the household as composed of self-interested individuals whose preferences are separate from one another. The Nash formulation of the bargaining problem, which is the most widely used in household modeling, entails both conflict and cooperation, and it is this that makes it appear so relevant to household decisions. At the core of the Nash bargaining model is the notion of the 'threat point' or fall-back position, which represents the level of utility that each party will attain if they fail to cooperate, and hence the relative bargaining power of participants in the game. In formal renditions of the Nash problem, the threat point is defined in terms of exogenously given wages and prices, although more recently McElroy (1990, 1992) has proposed a broader set of 'extrahousehold environmental parameters' to capture relative differences in bargaining power between women and men.

Unitary and bargaining models not only provide very different interpretations of intrahousehold inequality; they also offer entirely different analyses of the effects of income subsidies or transfers. In the unitary model, it makes no difference who receives the subsidies since the household is a neutral medium through which policy actions pass in a way that maximizes the welfare of all its members. If, however, intra-household allocation is envisaged as a bargaining process, then the individual to whom resources are directed could make a great deal of difference to the way they are used.

The initial response of unitary modelers to bargaining models was basically dismissive. First it was argued that the alternative bargaining model has no different implications for empirical specification since it generates the same structural and reduced-form equations (Rosenzweig and Schultz 1984). In addition, it is analytically less tractable. The objection from the viewpoint of policy was that 'person-specific transfer programs that provide resources to an individual may not succeed in causing significant net redistribution of resources to that person because of family redistributive rules over which policymakers have no direct control' (Rosenzweig 1986, 236).

It was, in fact, only in the late 1980s that neoclassical economists began giving serious attention to the problems of intrahousehold conflicts of interest that had been posed in the early bargaining models. This rapidly developing literature has been made possible by the availability of increasingly sophisticated large-scale data sets, but it has not simply been data driven; a major impetus to move in this direction came from growing critiques of the unitary model during the 1980s by nonneoclassical economists (for example, see Sen 1983; Folbre 1986a, 1986b; Jones 1983, 1986; Berry 1984; Agarwal 1990), anthropologists (such as Guyer 1981, 1986; Guyer and Peters 1987; Whitehead 1981) and sociologists (such as Blumberg 1988; Dwyer and J. Bruce 1988), who buttressed their arguments with a rapidly growing body of evidence on intrahousehold inequality that is difficult to square with the unitary interpretation.[2] While accepting the general idea of the household as a site of both cooperation and conflict, many of these analysts were also quite critical of the economistic formulation of the bargaining model, and suggested a series of important modifications.

For example, several nonneoclassical economists maintained that defining relative bargaining power in terms of wage rates was excessively simplistic and called for a more rigorous understanding of the determinants of relative bargaining power (Folbre 1986a; Agarwal 1990). In the context of rural India, Agarwal (1990) identifies five factors that are important in determining the fall-back position of individual household members: private ownership and control over assets, especially arable land; access to employment and other income-earning means; access to communal resources such as village commons and forests; access to external social support systems such as kin networks; and access to support from the state and nongovernmental organizations (NGOs). The 'extrahousehold environmental parameters' (EEPs), proposed by McElroy (1990, 1992) to specify the empirical content of Nash-bargaining models, embody precisely the same arguments.

One of the fairly consistent patterns to emerge from a number of the small-scale studies conducted during the 1980s was that women and men spend income under their control in systematically different ways, with women typically spending a high proportion of their income on food, health, and other forms of child welfare, and men often retaining discretionary control over a higher proportion of their income for commodities such as alcohol, tobacco, and sometimes, 'female companionship' (see Kumar 1979; Guyer 1981; Tripp 1981; Pahl 1983; Acharya and Bennett 1981, 1982, 1983 [cited in Blumberg 1988]; Mencher 1988; Dwyer and J. Bruce 1988; J. Bruce 1989). According to the unitary model, it should not make any difference whether income (or ownership of the physical asset that produces it) is controlled by men or women since income is pooled and redistributed to maximize household welfare.

These findings were often dismissed as 'anecdotal'. In addition, it was pointed out, that in order to constitute a test of the unitary model, income under male and female control must be unaffected by other household decisions. The new wave of household studies based on large-scale survey data focuses on estimating whether or not unearned income in the hands of women and men is spent differently (Schultz 1990; Thomas 1990, 1993; Duraisamy 1992; Duraisamy and Malathy 1991).[3] These statistically representative studies concur with their small-scale counterparts that who controls income is indeed associated with different outcomes. Using Thai data, Schultz (1990) found that women's unearned income reduces fertility more than income held by men, and that the impact of nonlabor income on labor supply is significantly different for men and women. In his analysis of data from over 25,000 urban Brazilian households, Thomas (1990) reports that increments to nonlabor income controlled by women have a stronger positive effect on child health and household nutrient intakes than the same increments to income controlled by men. More recently he has used the same data set to show that, in addition to improvements in child health, income controlled by women is associated with increases in the share of the household budget spent on health, education, and housing (Thomas 1993). Studies in India by Duraisamy (1992), and Duraisamy and Malathy (1991) find that children are more likely to attend school and receive medical attention if the mother has more assets (cited by Strauss and Thomas 1993). Authors of these studies are careful to conclude that, although the results are inconsistent with the unitary model, they do not necessarily support the bargaining model.

Proponents of the unitary approach respond that these results do not, in fact, negate the unitary model because the measures of unearned income may in part reflect wages and productivity in labor market activity associated with human capital investments in the past (Behrman 1992, 75). The unitary model could only be rejected if income were randomly distributed and not associated with human capital either directly or indirectly (see Behrman and Deolalikar 1988, 638). In addition, as one of the discussants of an earlier version of the present paper argued, for empirical work it does not really matter which model one believes in because both models lead to the same reduced forms.

The most obvious problem with this argument is that different models come to quite different conclusions on policy questions, such as whether transfers should be made to the household or to individual members, and whether they should take the form of lump-sum or in-kind transfers. This ambiguity reflects a more basic problem—that a particular set of quantitative results is always subject to multiple interpretations, depending upon one's assumption about the underlying causal mechanism. This is essentially the point made by Chiappori and his colleagues (Bourguignon and Chiappori 1992, 360):

> While any evidence against income pooling falsifies the traditional approach [i.e. the unitary model], it certainly does *not* support any alternative model in particular. There are certainly hundreds of ad hoc assumptions that could explain the observed results within the traditional approach, and thousands of more or less funny alternative models that could justify them outside it.

The solution proposed by Chiappori and his followers is to generate testable restrictions rather than impose them on the data; under certain conditions, it is also possible to recover the sharing rules from the data. However, this approach is itself fraught with problems.

Collective Models of the Household

Collective models as conceived by Chiappori et al. are firmly within the orthodox neoclassical tradition, and represent a return to the individual as the unit of analysis. The chief limitation of the unitary model, in this view, is that it 'falls short of meeting the basic rule of neo-classical micro-economic analysis, namely *individualism*, which obviously requires each individual to be characterized by his (her) own preferences, rather than being aggregated within the ad hoc fiction of a collective decision unit' (Bourguignon and Chiappori 1992, 356).

Collective models describe the household as a group of individuals characterized by individual preferences among whom collective decision processes take place. They fall into two broad categories: cooperative models that conform to Pareto efficiency, and noncooperative models that allow for informational asymmetries and enforcement problems, and are generally not Pareto efficient. In the literature to date there are very few examples of noncooperative models; some are presented by Kanbur (1991), Lundberg and Pollak (1993), and Carter and Katz (1993). Non-cooperative models call for analytical and methodological approaches very different from those proposed by Chiappori and his colleagues; in effect, the collective approach developed thus far is synonymous with cooperative models based on Pareto efficiency.

The general class of cooperative models encompasses the unitary model, marked by income pooling and dictatorial decision making, which is in fact simply a special case of the Nash bargaining model. These models in turn are nested within a more general category of cooperative models that make no assumptions about the specific form of intrahouse-hold decision rules other than that they guarantee efficient outcomes.

The unitary model has thus been deposed from its preeminent position within neoclassical theory, and the possibility of a far wider array of intrahousehold arrangements has been opened up. In addition, debates cast in terms of 'unitary versus bargaining models' can now be seen as overdrawn; both are special cases of cooperative models, and are far more similar to one another than to noncooperative models that take account of informational asymmetries and enforcement problems.

Proponents of the collective approach point to several possible policy failures associated with the unitary model's neglect of intrahousehold decision processes (see Alderman et al. 1993; Chiappori et al. 1993; Haddad et al. 1993). First is the point raised earlier concerning the effect of public transfers; if, contrary to the unitary model, the identity of the recipient determines the way resources are used, policies that target the household rather than individuals are likely to fail.

Second, at the project level, the unitary model implies that it does not matter to whom policy initiatives are directed because knowledge as well as income is pooled within the household. Haddad et al. (1993, 9) point out, however, that the assumption that the self-declared head of the household has detailed knowledge of the activities of other household members will invariably lead to policy failure, such as (i) the nonadoption of particular policies (such as technologies that require lumpy inputs of female labor when women do not have the flexibility to adjust their work schedules); and (ii) unintended costs arising from policies that are adopted (for example, policies to retard environmental degradation that fail because women farmers have insecurity of tenure and are unable to make land improvements).

Third, Haddad et al. (1993, 9) note that 'perhaps the most important drawback of relying on the unitary model for policy guidance is that a number of powerful policy handles are disabled. Under the unitary model, policymakers affect intrahousehold resource allocation primarily through changes in prices. Some collective approaches suggest that additional policy handles, often with a very long reach, are available to the policymaker. Examples of these policy handles include change in access to common property resources, credit, public works schemes, and a general strengthening of legal and institutional rights.' The main thrust of these arguments is the need to channel resources directly to women —an argument that echoes longstanding themes in the literature on women in development.

Proponents of the collective approach acknowledge that their policy analysis is based on the shortcomings of the unitary model rather than an estimation of a specific collective model.[4] Accordingly, the question of whether or not the collective approach will prove useful in practice is becoming quite contentious.

The collective (or, more accurately, cooperative) approach pioneered by Chiappori and his colleagues is resolutely agnostic about the forms of intrahousehold relations; these are empirical issues that cannot be assumed a priori, and should not be imposed on the data. Instead, sharing rules have to be recovered from the data through a systematic testing process. These procedures, described with great clarity by Deaton (1994), entail nested tests, first, of efficiency, and then, of income pooling. If the efficiency condition holds, and at least one good is assignable to the consumption of a particular member or is exclusive to one person, then the household's income sharing rule can be recovered from the data. Deaton goes a step further, showing that a similar analysis can be carried out for any other variables—such as household composition—that exert an income effect on demand.

To date it appears that efforts to derive sharing rules governing the allocation of income from different sources consist of a set of studies of French and Canadian data by Bourguignon et al. (1993), and Browning et al. (1993). In both cases the efficiency assumption could not be rejected, whereas data were inconsistent with the income pooling assumption; hence, the burden of proof should shift onto those who would claim that the unitary model is the rule and the collective model the exception (Browning et al. 1993, 24). At the same time, the authors concede that they were not able to identify the location of the sharing rule.

In the context of developing countries, Deaton and others have tested the usefulness of the collective approach by estimating the effects of male and female children respectively on the consumption of adult goods.[5] The results consistently fail to show any evidence of gender discrimination. In the case of Thailand and Ivory Coast, where women's status is reasonably high, these results are perhaps not so surprising; the results for Bangladesh and Pakistan are far more problematic, because there is so much other evidence of gender discrimination that the collective approach based on expenditure survey data is failing to pick up. As Deaton (in chapter 2 of this volume) observes, a great deal of work needs to be done before these methods can be fruitfully used to investigate intrahousehold allocation.

Proponents of the unitary approach have reacted sceptically to the collective approach, although several of the drawbacks identified are also shared by the unitary model—including the static character of collective models and the tendency to ignore the role of unobserved heterogeneous endowments (Behrman 1992, 82). Other drawbacks identified by Behrman include the dependence on cardinal measures of utility to generate threat points in the Nash bargaining subset of models, and the abstraction from household production. The stage thus seems set for an intraneoclassical debate over whether it is the household or the individual that is the salient unit of analysis.

In fact, both approaches are deeply problematic. Collective modelers correctly point out that the unitary approach entails the arbitrary imposition of ad hoc institutional assumptions. Yet the institutional agnosticism of the collective approach is not the answer. Sharing rules cannot be unproblematically 'recovered' from aggregate survey data, because the way the data are collected will determine the conclusions that can be drawn from them. Household survey data collection exercises require predefined categories and assumptions about underlying relations, and it is these a priori assumptions and categories that are likely to be captured in any effort to recover sharing rules.

In short, economic models of the household have encountered the limits of economism. What is needed is a direct understanding of *relations* within and among households—and of the way these relations are structured in terms of gender.

Analyzing Relations Within and Between Households
Survey Data and Household Categories
For all the problems inherent in the collective approach, it does represent an important advance on the unitary model because it recognizes the varied forms that intrahousehold allocation can assume. On this level, there is a degree of convergence with the position of many anthropologists and other social scientists who have argued for some time that the

household should be viewed not as a natural, universal unit, but rather as a complex and variable set of relationships (for example, see Stack 1974; Yanagisako 1979; Harris 1981). Indeed, one of the major objections to the unitary model by anthropologists and others has been treatment of the household as a generic concept applicable across all societies. Africanist anthropologists have delivered particularly devastating critiques, pointing to the enormously complex and varied household forms, structures, and activities both within and across societies (see Guyer 1981, 1986; Guyer and Peters 1987). This critique is by no means limited to Africanists, however. White (1980), for example, observes that 'there is no clear-cut distinction between "sharing" and "not sharing", but rather a *range* of possible domestic arrangements in any society in which there are different *areas* of sharing, each with its own *degree* of sharing. These arrangements tend to become more complex (and it may be added, the degree of sharing less and the degree of tension and conflict about these arrangements greater) when the household contains adults in addition to, or instead of, the nuclear family' (White 1980, 16). Precisely because of this complexity and variability, the nature of household organization and relations cannot be assumed but must be investigated (Moore 1988, 59).

The question is, What conceptual framework will be used to guide empirical analysis and define research methods? The collective approach is, of course, firmly grounded in positivist methodology and the analysis of large-scale survey data. As pointed out earlier, what is most obviously problematic about collective modelers' strategy of recovering sharing rules from the data rather than imposing restrictions is that large-scale survey data collection exercises, themselves, embody predefined categories and assumptions about underlying relations. A basic dilemma confronting collective modelers is that the data that they need to follow through with their analysis requires a prior understanding of precisely the institutional rules they are seeking to recover from those data.

Even the apparently most basic question, What and where is the household? is in practice deeply problematic. In contemporary Asia, for example, in addition to huge variations in forms of domestic arrangements within and across societies, there is accumulating evidence that household arrangements are becoming spatially more dispersed. Instead of a straightforward process of rural-urban migration, systems of labor circulation seem to be taking hold in many parts of South and Southeast Asia, entailing complex transfers of resources over space and time in ways that are typically masked by aggregate survey and census data (Standing 1984; Hugo 1984; Fan and Stretton 1984; Chapman 1984;

Mukherji 1984; Shaw 1988; Dasgupta 1992). Another example is the emergence of 'aggregate families' in China—namely complex kin networks that span villages, small towns, and urban areas (Croll 1987). In short, the complexity of household formation and dissolution, together with the networks of resource flows that stretch across residential units, render any arbitrary definition deeply problematic.

There is indeed growing recognition, by those who rely on aggregate survey data, that answers to the question, What and where is the household? are far from self-evident (for example, Behrman 1990; Schultz 1990; Haddad et al. 1992; Strauss and Thomas 1993); the latter, for example, note that in most cases the definition of the household is dictated by survey data practice (such as a group of people who share a common cooking pot), but that it is far from clear that this is the appropriate definition if one is concerned with understanding key aspects of behavior.

In addition to problems surrounding definitions of 'the household', gendered norms and perceptions regarding what is 'deserved' and what is not (Sen 1990, 131) are likely to influence what is and is not captured in survey data. For example, particularly in heavily male-dominated settings, there may well be a tendency to understate women's morbidity, as well as their labor contributions (see also K. Bardhan 1993a, 1993b). Also, if particular household members—notably adult men—are in a better position than others to maintain independent control over resources, such person-specific income and expenditures may well be systematically understated.

In other words, recovering sharing rules from cross-sectional data presupposes that the data have been collected in such a way that captures key resource flows. Yet devising appropriate instruments requires understanding how and why these linkages and relationships are established and maintained in the first place.

Recognition of the limits of standard survey procedures has spurred renewed calls for collaboration between economists and anthropologists, and for a more multidisciplinary approach. As discussed earlier, these discussions typically revolve around questions of data collection—in particular, the way in which ethnographic field methods can contribute by quantifying qualitative variables, producing more refined quantitative data (such as on time allocation), and clarifying cultural norms (see Alderman et al. 1993; Gittelsohn 1992; Haddad et al. 1992; Paolisso 1992).

To frame the discussion simply in terms of data collection is, however, misleading because it evades the more basic question of the conceptual framework that guides both qualitative and quantitative empirical enquiries. The key question confronting the collective approach is, How can intrahousehold (as well as interhousehold) relations be conceptualized within a paradigm of individual decision making in order to define an appropriate research methodology? The basic problem is that the paradigm itself is inherently limited in its analytical capacity to address such questions.

Noncooperative Models of the Household and the Limits of Economism

A particularly ironic feature of the collective approach is that, in a putative effort to crack open the black box of the household and examine its inner workings, it has abandoned any sort of institutional analysis. The seemingly innocuous assumption of Pareto efficiency, which is shared by both the unitary and the Nash bargaining models, and, which is necessary to estimate cooperative models more generally, is in fact extremely powerful. In effect it treats the household as a solved political problem, and assumes away any issues of informational asymmetries, endogenous enforcement of claims, and the mutually conditioning effects of household members on one another. The orthodox neoclassicism of cooperative models of the household stands in sharp contrast to the non-Walrasian tools of the 'new institutional economics' that have been used to pry open other black boxes—notably the firm (see Williamson 1985) and agrarian institutions (see P. Bardhan 1989b; Stiglitz 1989).

Recent efforts to formulate noncooperative models of the household (such as Lundberg and Pollak 1993; Carter and Katz 1993) do indeed take institutional analysis seriously, and represent a major theoretical and methodological departure from the collective (or, more accurately, cooperative) approach advocated by Chiappori and his followers. In dealing with intrahousehold informational asymmetries and claim enforcement, these models are forced to confront both patriarchy (or the social construction of gender) and the limits of methodological individualism—the presumption that preferences and norms are exogenously given and unaffected by social context.

Both of these noncooperative models are rooted in the notion of 'separate spheres'. Lundberg and Pollak (1993, 990) distinguish their model from the Nash bargaining model in two key ways: First, the threat point is not divorce but a noncooperative equilibrium defined in terms of traditional gender roles and gender expectations. Second, the noncooperative equilibrium is not Pareto optimal, but may be the final one because of transaction costs. They go on to show how this model yields predictions of the distributional effects of child allowances and other family policies that differ from those of both the Nash bargaining and the unitary model. This model illustrates two particularly important points. First is the sensitivity of distributional outcomes to assumptions about intrahousehold institutions. Second is the awkwardness of the assumptions. The level of transfers in the noncooperative, 'voluntary contribution' equilibrium is 'maintained by social enforcement of the obligations corresponding to generally recognized and accepted gender roles' (Lundberg and Pollak 1993, 994). The authors concede that this ad hoc invocation of norms and enforcement mechanisms is a cop out.

The Carter-Katz model also elaborates the idea of a domestic economy comprised of separate gender-defined spheres, but provides a considerably more sophisticated analysis of how transfers are mediated. Carter and Katz envisage household members as being in possession of individual property rights as well as autonomous control over income and time allocation. Transfers of resources and labor are mediated by a conjugal contract (Whitehead 1981), and are enforceable only at some cost. The conjugal contract, in turn, is determined by 'voice'—the degree to which both partners can influence or bargain over net resource transfers—as well as their respective 'exit' options: As fundamentally social constructions, both voice and exit reflect a complex of attitudes, mores, and opportunities exogenous to the household that can be labeled the 'degree of patriarchy' (Carter and Katz 1993, 7.18).

The question of 'voice', in other words the capacity to *renegotiate* the rules or terms of exchange, represents a major advance on the Nash bargaining model in which the rules are given and relative bargaining power is determined purely by threat points (or 'extrahousehold environmental parameters' or 'exit options'). What it means in effect is that gender-biased shifts in policy or in economic opportunities not only have differential effects on different household members, but may also provoke a renegotiation of the rules governing access to and control over resources and labor. The dynamics of household formation and partition also hinge crucially on how the rules, rights, and obligations governing relations between women and men, as well as between elders and juniors, are renegotiated in relation to larger structures and processes.

Recognition of the endogeneity and negotiability of intrahousehold relations is actually the product of indepth ethnographic studies. For example, in her discussion of intrahousehold 'bargaining' in a Cameroonian rice-growing scheme, Jones (1986, 118) pointed out that:

> It is not only the rate of compensation and type of contractual agreement that are being negotiated but also the meaning of the contractual arrangement itself. Women are bargaining not only over the level of the "wage"

they are paid [by their husbands] but also over their right to be paid a certain amount based on the level of their labor input. In effect, they are challenging the husband's right to dispose of the product of his wife's labor, a right which was recognized heretofore by the transfer of bride-wealth cattle.

Similarly, Carney and Watts (1990) show how a project designed to intensify rice production in the Gambia provoked a renegotiation of labor and property rights between men and women that undermined the original intent of the project.

The Carter-Katz model is in fact an effort to formalize insights derived from ethnographic work in Africa. The key question is, How can one move forward with these insights, and apply them in other settings? Carter and Katz's 'degree of patriarchy' may be useful as a general description of some of the issues that need to be addressed, but does not provide analytical purchase on them.[6]

Rather it is the concept of gender—in the sense outlined below—that contains the key to understanding how intrahousehold relations are socially constructed and contested in relation to other economic and sociopolitical structures and processes. This particular conceptualization of gender is part of a more general recognition that struggles over resources and labor are simultaneously struggles over socially construct-ed meanings and definitions.

Gender and the Household: Elements of a Dynamic Analysis

In recent years, a number of anthropologists, sociologists, geographers, historians, and a small group of nonneoclassical economists have rejected Durkheimian notions of culture as a pre-given, coherent, and consistent set of rules and norms, and focused instead on the social construction of meaning as an ongoing process.

Rather than positing a set of structural rules to which people automati-cally adhere (as 'cultural dupes'), attention has shifted to understanding how socially constructed meanings both inform and are shaped by everyday practice (Bourdieu 1977). Since meanings—such as those associated with intrahousehold or intergenerational exchanges of goods and claims on productive resources—are often multiple, contested, and change over time, outcomes cannot necessarily be predicted from the official 'rules'. Instead, as Moore (1992) observes, conventions are best thought of as actual resources that are drawn on in the process of negotiation, rather than as norms that determine the outcome of negotiation.

This focus on the social construction and contestation of meaning carries major implications for ethnographic research. The question is not simply, *What* are the cultural norms that prevail in any particular setting? but rather, *How* are meanings—particularly those that define access to and control over resources and labor—negotiated and redefined in everyday practice? A crucial insight within this perspective is that 'people may invest in meanings as well as in the means of production —and struggles over meaning are as much a part of the process of resource allocation as are struggles over surplus or the labor process' (Berry 1989, 1993). Thus what appears as 'consumption' may in fact represent an investment in establishing or strengthening social relations, and hence the terms and conditions of access to resources.

This recognition of the fluidity of institutions and the multiple, contested meanings that mediate claims over material resources and labor vitiates any notion of methodological individualism and preference exogeneity. Gender is, of course, a central element in the construction of interests and identities, as well as the conditions of access to and control over resources. Sen (1990), for example, points out that the rules governing intrahousehold distribution are often made to appear natural and legitimate, even though in many cases they embody spectacular inequalities. Although gendered perceptions may appear to support and sustain such rules, these perceptions are not immutable: the process of politicization—including a political recognition of the gender issue—can itself bring about sharp changes in these perceptions (Sen 1990, 126).

Gender, in the sense of the social construction of biological difference, is not only a system of discrimination, but a key analytical concept for clarifying *how* socially constructed inequality is made to appear 'natural', the ongoing processes that reinforce or undermine particular gender definitions, and the conditions under which these meanings are called into question. In contrast to 'patriarchy', which connotes a rather monolithic and universal power relation between men and women, this conceptualization of gender focuses on the multiple, contested, and often contradictory meanings associated with male/female categories both within and across societies, and the way they are manifested in social relations and access to resources within and beyond the household.[7]

It is particularly important to emphasize that gender is not simply a 'household' phenomenon, but operates at multiple levels of economy and society and is a pervasive element in the way all institutions are constructed and the dynamics through which they change. As Folbre (1992), Elson (1991), and others have pointed out, implicit or explicit gender biases are embodied in public policies and in political and legal institutions, and are often a major *cause* of intrahousehold inequality. In addition, land, labor, and credit markets operate in ways that are inherently gendered and that influence intrahousehold processes. As discussed more fully below, the same policy or shift in employment conditions can have very different implications for intrahousehold distribution depending on renegotiations of gender relations both within and beyond the household. More generally, gender is crucial to specifying the interactions between intrahousehold processes and nonhousehold institutions, and hence the outcomes of policy and economic changes.

This type of gendered approach clearly entails a conceptualization of the household very different from either the unitary or collective models. Rather than a solitary unit or a collection of individuals with predefined preferences, the household is more usefully seen as a political arena constituted by particularly dense bundles of gendered rules, rights, and obligations governing relations between men and women, and elders and juniors (cf. Guyer 1981). The rules defining property rights, the division of labor, resource distribution, and so forth, are potentially subject to contestation, and must be constantly reinforced and reiterated. Accordingly, we need to ask not only, *What* are the rules? but also, *How* are they reinforced or redefined in daily practice? and, Under what conditions are they called into question? Ideologies of gender figure prominently in these struggles and negotiations, often in conjunction with conflicting notions of family unity (see for example Lem 1988; Carney and Watts 1990; Yanagisako 1990).

Intrahousehold relations are reciprocally linked with the relationships and networks that household members forge with those outside the household, and with the gendered organization of labor and conditions of access to resources in nondomestic institutions. As Berry (1984, 20) puts it, 'The questions we need to ask are not what do "households" decide and how, but rather how does membership in a household affect people's access to resources, obligations to others, and understanding of their options—and vice versa?'

In some circumstances, extrahousehold networks play a central role in resource flows and allocation. For example, as discussed more fully below, there are indications from different parts of Asia that poor women try to compensate for fractured kinship networks by forming non-kin groups with other women.[8] Different household members are differently placed in their capacity to construct and maintain extrahousehold networks. In the Muda region of Malaysia, for example, the women agricultural workers are far better able than men to form groups and act collectively (Hart 1991). Part of the reason has to do with women's exclusion from the political patronage ties that bind rich and poor men, and through which state support is organized at the local level. The social construction of gender meanings in Malaysian society, and their manifestation in state policy, is also crucial to understanding men's more limited capacity to organize collectively.

The creation and maintenance of extrahousehold networks typically requires ongoing investments of time and resources. Guyer (1993, 16) has recently extended the argument about investment as social process, pointing out that even poor women and men are actively engaged in creating and maintaining at least some goods and some relationships that are multipurpose, and that can veer from investment to consumption to status signifiers as needed. Accordingly, what at one point in time appears as an exogenous 'extrahousehold environmental parameter' is very likely to reflect past processes of investment—in other words, the threat point becomes variable over time, and present consumption or expenditure decisions express, confirm, or create a potential claim over the longer term (Guyer 1993, 19). The concept of investment in social relations also enables one to see how impoverishment is not just a question of declining income and assets, but the disintegration of social networks that can operate in very different ways for women and men.[9]

Conceptualizing the household in terms of how relationships are constructed and negotiated also provides analytical purchase on the question of spatially extended resource flows. Much of the neoclassical literature on remittances entails quite arbitrary invocations of altruism, that simply evade obvious problems of informational asymmetries and enforcement mechanisms.[10] To explain spatially extended resource flows one needs a direct and contextualized understanding of *how* rights and obligations are socially constructed and maintained in practice, and the conditions under which they disintegrate. The social relations that mediate spatially extended resource flows are frequently both objects of investment and determinants of resource allocation in sending and receiving areas (see, for example, Berry 1985). These reciprocal linkages between relationships and resource use can only be understood through indepth ethnographic research.

Attention to gendered relations within and among households is crucial to understanding dynamic processes. Changes in technology, market opportunities, or policy initiatives often affect different household members differently, altering the distribution of resources and/or the balance of power within the household, and in the process affecting the way household members allocate resources separately or together. Resource allocation within the household, or by different household members, in turn affects broader patterns of economic performance and change, but in complex ways, involving changing patterns of cooperation, conflict, exchange, and domination among individuals, households, and other social groups and institutions. An example of how this type of approach can illuminate dynamic processes comes from Yanagisako's (1990) study of the historical transformation of gendered interests in Italian family firms. She shows how as economic, political, and legal circumstances have changed, wives, sons, and daughters have redefined their interests: 'This transformation is leading them to pursue projects that challenge the collectivities to which fathers have been committed and the strategies of capital accumulation that have enabled fathers to achieve those projects' (Yanagisako 1990, 338). In short, this type of analysis enables us to see households as both channels and outcomes of broader processes (Guyer and Peters 1987).

This approach is capable of illuminating change and dynamics in part because it is methodologically rooted in longitudinal and historical analysis, combining indepth ethnographic methods with analysis of macroeconomic and political structures and processes. More fundamentally, it entails reconceptualization of 'the household' in relational terms, and an analytical as well as an empirical focus on the gendered micropolitics of negotiation, cooperation, and contestation in different but intersecting institutional arenas.

A closely related point is that ethnographic methods are not just an adjunct to large-scale survey data collection exercises.[11] Rather they are capable of addressing very different questions, but this entails a very different, and indeed incommensurate, conceptual and methodological orientation from neoclassical theory and positivist methodology. Despite the obvious differences, there are several ways in which the relational and processual approach outlined above could help to inform collective modeling and survey data collection. First, by illuminating the dynamics of household formation and dissolution it could help to specify salient categories for survey data collection. Second, it can function as a source of theoretical insight; as pointed out earlier, the Carter-Katz (1993) model is an example of an effort to formalize insights from theoretically informed ethnographic work. As discussed more fully in the next section, this type of approach can also provide a new angle of vision on issues of policy and practice.

Implications of a Gendered Approach for Policy and Action

As noted earlier, the shift from unitary to collective models of the household has been accompanied by a shift in policy emphasis from the household to the individual. Proponents of the collective approach point to the policy distortions associated with unitary views of the household, and emphasize policies that channel resources directly to individual women. In particular, they argue that policies that expand women's access to resources and economic opportunities can affect intrahousehold allocation of resources *indirectly*, and in ways not recognized by the unitary approach.[12]

The policy arguments put forward by collective modelers are in fact very similar to those that proponents of women in development have been advocating since the early 1970s. By and large, however, as Guyer and Peters (1987, 210) have noted, much of this work has proceeded in isolation from mainstream economic analyses of the household:

> Perhaps the most bizarre outcome of over-concretized thinking in develop-
> ment practice is that 'women' (or less often 'gender') and 'household' have
> been dealt with in separate domains of discourse and action. For example,
> in numerous donor agencies 'women's issues' are ensconced in a specially
> defined field of 'women in development', whereas households appear as
> units of analysis and social units addressed within substantive fields such
> as rural credit, agricultural development, small-scale enterprise, nutrition,
> and so forth. One of the regrettable consequences of this analytical and
> institutional separation has been the failure to integrate information on
> these two topics sufficiently well in policy and project development.

That it has taken more than 20 years to move toward such an integration is, perhaps, a remarkable testament to the intransigence of professional cultural norms and the practices that keep them in place.

At the same time, it is important to bear in mind that there now exists a huge body of accumulated experience with programs designed to channel resources to women. There are also incisive analyses of the assumptions behind the advocacy of direct assistance to women, the goals that are sought in providing such assistance, the means advocated for achieving these goals, and the reasons why outcomes are often at odds with stated intentions (see, for example, Kandiyoti 1990).

One of the central themes of recent rethinking of 'women in develop-
ment' is the importance of focusing on gender, rather than simply incorporating women within existing approaches. There are three particularly important ways in which an explicitly gendered approach that focuses on the social construction of intrahousehold and interhousehold relations contributes to reframing questions of policy and action. First, the salient units may be neither households nor individuals, but rather networks of relationships that cut across residential units. Second,

policies or expanded economic opportunities can have very different outcomes depending on the operation of gender both within the household and in nonhousehold institutions. Third, a gendered approach emphasizes the limits of top-down 'targeting' of either women or households, and underscores the importance of organizational capacity in different institutional arenas for redressing gender inequality and bringing about social change.

Practical Implications of Interhousehold Networks

Unitary and collective modelers may be locked in debate over whether and how the identity of the recipient of transfers or policy attention affects intrahousehold resource allocation, but they share the presumption of the household as a clearly bounded unit. What this presumption obscures are the networks of kin and non-kin relationships discussed earlier that stretch across conventionally defined households and that link members of different households to one another and to nonhousehold institutions. Interhousehold networks and organizations are enormously variable in their forms, functions, and modus operandi, even when they are composed exclusively of women.[13] In some circumstances, however, they could have significant potential as agents of change.

Interhousehold networks of cooperation and organization by poor rural women in many parts of Asia are probably far more pervasive than is often recognized. The widely acclaimed Grameen Bank in Bangladesh is one example of a policy initiative that built on such networks and groupings. A huge proportion of the Grameen Bank's loans are to landless women who are grouped on the basis of preexisting ties to one another. Despite the enormous attention devoted to the Grameen Bank, remarkably little is understood about these relationships. Ethnographic research would probably reveal multistranded ties constituted through prior and ongoing forms of investment in social relations. The activities of the Grameen Bank, which include direct efforts to influence gender relations, such as requiring borrowers to adhere to principles such as rejection of dowry, undoubtedly play into these relationships. The gendered forms and dynamics of extrahousehold networks and groupings probably go a long way toward explaining why peer monitoring seems to operate so effectively in the Grameen Bank case.[14]

Recent research suggests that collective work groups formed by women laborers operate in several different Asian settings yet in ways that are quite analogous (for example, Hart 1991; Kapadia 1993). In some cases these groups are fluid; however, particularly among women who use these groups to compensate for fractured kinship ties as well as to organize in the labor market, these relationships can often be quite enduring and entail multiple, ongoing resource transfers. There would seem to be considerable potential for these groups to form the basis not only of credit programs, but also agrarian reforms. In the Muda region of Malaysia, for example, women's labor groups could, in principle, significantly expand their income-earning capacity if they were able to rent and operate land collectively (Hart 1992). In practice, policies to support this kind of action require high levels of organized pressure from the beneficiaries themselves.

Gendered Renegotiations and Policy Outcomes

How one conceptualizes the household matters a great deal for the analysis of policy outcomes. Unitary modelers assume that intrahousehold reallocation in response to gender-specific shifts in prices and wages maximizes the welfare of the household as a whole. In the Nash bargaining model, which in practice informs much of the policy analysis of proponents of the collective approach, gender-specific changes in wages and prices generate shifts in relative bargaining power via their effects on the threat point or fall-back position of individual household members, and hence the relative weight of their preferences. Accordingly, gender-biased policies have a direct and differential impact on the welfare of individual household members.

The politicized approach to the household outlined in this paper suggests that intrahousehold reallocation in response to policy and employment shifts cannot simply be read off or deduced from changes in the fall-back position. Rather, a key determinant of policy outcomes is whether and how the terms of access to and control over resources and labor are renegotiated. Accordingly, a central question for policy-oriented research is, What are the conditions that enable or undermine women's capacity to negotiate a better deal within and beyond the household? To address this question, one needs precisely the type of ethnographic research outlined above.

There are a number of ways in which this type of research could help to clarify policy debates, and expand or redefine questions of practice. One example has to do with the effects and implications of gender-specific increases in employment, such as the rise in demand for female labor associated with the expansion of export production in sectors like textiles and electronics. Whether and to what extent young women benefit from the expansion of low wage employment is heavily debated. What is not often recognized in this debate is that the same pattern of employment and wages can have very different outcomes depending on the operation of gender within and beyond the household, as well as legal and institutional factors that determine workers' capacity to organize. For example, Wolf (1992) has shown how in a Central Java factory, daughters were able to maintain a substantial degree of control over their earnings, and to use their earning capacity (albeit meagre) to renegotiate a position of somewhat greater influence within the household. In Taipei,China, however, parents retained tight control over their daughters' earnings, which were often invested in sons' education, and relations of filial obligation were, in fact, reinforced. Wolf attributes these differences to the very different ways in which gender and kinship operate in the two contexts. Ong's (1987) research on export factories in Malaysia illustrates how restrictions on women workers at the point of production affects their capacity to exercise influence in other institutional arenas.

Another example of how a politicized view of the household can expand policy analysis concerns what collective modelers term policy handles with long reaches. For example, Haddad and Kanbur (1992b) draw on the logic of the Nash bargaining model of the household to suggest that policies that equalize access to resources and income-generating activities could have an important influence on intrahousehold allocation, even if these options are not taken up. Thus for example if women's access to a common property resource is made equal to that of men, intrahousehold equality may well improve if the income from improved access is above that which women could earn previously on their own; even if the income is less than that from cooperation and is not taken up, the existence of a credible and readily available option for women could improve intrahousehold resource allocation.

While this argument is interesting, there is a missing dimension that may in fact be quite important. If intrahousehold allocation depends not only on threat points but also on how negotiation takes place, then the effects of policy are likely to depend not only on the level of resources and the conditions of access to these resources, but also on discourses about the rights and needs of particular individuals originating at the level of the state or development agencies (see, for example, Fraser 1989; Moore 1992). Thus public policies that play into dominant gender representations may simultaneously undermine women's capacity to press their claims.

In addition, policies that channel resources to women on the assumption that women are more likely than men to use these resources to increase household welfare may well backfire. The official representation of women as 'good mothers' in effect shifts the burden of responsibility on to their shoulders. As Kandiyoti (1990) has pointed out, in areas where male responsibility for dependents is at least normatively present, women themselves are likely to put up fierce resistance to measures bypassing the male household head, even though in practice they may contrive ways of increasing their control over household resources. More generally, there is a need to move away from viewing women as passive recipients, and to recognize the importance of organizations within and through which women can define and articulate their needs and interests. The voices of those who have been excluded from access to resources and influence need to be heard not only in the household, but also in the policy arenas where macro allocations of resources are made.

Acknowledgments

The author is most grateful to Kalpana Bardhan, Jere Behrman, Jane Guyer, Lawrence Haddad, M. G. Quibria, and Duncan Thomas for sharing unpublished papers with her. Ananya Roy provided excellent research assistance. This paper has been informed by longstanding discussions with Bina Agarwal, Sara Berry, Carmen Deere, Jane Guyer, Carol Stack, David Szanton, Michael Watts, and Diane Wolf—although they are not in any way responsible for the results. The author has also benefited from comments by participants at the Second Asian Development Bank Conference on Development Economics, specifically Anil Deolalikar, M. S. Rao, and M. G. Quibria.

Notes

1. Empirical work on the household economy did not, of course, begin in the mid-1960s; see Deaton and Muellbauer (1980) for a discussion of earlier empirical studies.

2. For very useful recent reviews of Asian evidence on women's disproportionate representation in poverty groups and the extremely heavy labor burden of poor women, see K. Bardhan (1993a, 1993b) and Quibria (1993).

3. The latter two references are cited by Strauss and Thomas (1993).

4. In fact, several of these policy analyses are based on a Nash bargaining model of the household.

5. See Deaton (1994) for references.

6. See Deere (1990, 18) for a useful discussion of the conceptual limits of patriarchy.

7. It encompasses gender ideology or symbolism (the attribution of opposing qualities as male or female—strong/weak, generous/grasping, active/passive etc.), gender relations (such as the division of labor that defines tasks as male and female, gender-differentiated property rights, etc.), and gender identities (experiences of masculinities/femininities that intersect with other dimensions of identity such as race/ethnicity, class, etc.).

8. This is not necessarily or always the case. Kalpana Bardhan (1993b) points out that the splintered kinship networks and nuclear families of landless laborers in South Asia carry particularly harsh consequences for working women who are in need of alternative social safety nets.

9. Agarwal (1990), for example, argues that the disintegration of kinship networks during the 1943 Bengal famine had far more serious implications for women than for men.

10. In the context of South India, for example, Rosenzweig and Stark (1989, 905) argue that 'the marriage of daughters to locationally distant, dispersed, yet kinship-related households is a manifestation of implicit intrahousehold contractual relationships aimed at mitigating income risks and facilitating consumption smoothing in an environment characterized by information costs and spatially co-variant risks'. The obvious question is, What about enforcement and monitoring? Rosenzweig and Stark assert (1989, 909) that the presence in household i of a member of household j not only supplies household j with an incentive to contribute to consumption smoothing in i (altruism) but also introduces a verification and monitoring capacity. Precisely why daughter j who has been transferred by her natal kin to household i should be (a) willing or (b) able to perform a monitoring and enforcement function is far from clear. Further, if the observed resource flows are going to an individual rather than a unitary household, one would have to come up with a different set of causal explanations. Other efforts to come to grips with the question of resource transfers include Lucas and Stark (1985), and Stark and Lucas (1988); they experiment with an assumption of individual self-interest on the part of the migrant, but concede that the problem of dealing with enforcement mechanisms requires what are, in effect, quite arbitrary invocations of altruism.

11. See P. Bardhan (1989a) for a fascinating set of encounters and debates between anthropologists and economists. The argument of the present paper is that the key issues are theoretical rather than disciplinary. There are, for example, formalist anthropologists who operate in a basically neoclassical framework.

12. Unitary modelers will no doubt maintain that these claims are exaggerated, and/or that the policy implications of the collective approach are not significantly different from those of the unitary model. To the extent that the policy implications are different—such as Haddad and Kanbur's (1992b) contention that expanding women's access to resources will improve their position within the household even if these opportunities are not taken up—unitary modelers will argue that they rest on unsubstantiated claims about the validity of the Nash bargaining model. Given the methodological limitations inherent in efforts to implement the collective approach using aggregate survey data, this debate is likely to go around in circles for some time. In all probability, the impasse over whether the household or the individual is the salient unit of analysis will simply be reproduced in policy debates.

13. For example, as K. Bardhan (1985) points out, the networking that interests female laborers is fundamentally different from the networks that peasant women use; the former are directed toward protecting women workers vis-a-vis employers, whereas the latter tend to operate within the existing hierarchy of familial relationships.

14. Besley (1992), for example, argues that group lending entails both positive and negative effects, that the net effects are ambiguous a priori, and that even the performance of the highly touted Grameen Bank leaves unresolved issues—one of which is identifying what forms of group selection and management have been successful in practice.

References

Acharya, M., and L. Bennett, 1982. "Women and the Subsistence Sector: Economic Participation and Household Decision Making in Nepal." Staff Working Paper No. 526. World Bank, Washington, D.C.

Agarwal, B., 1990. "Social Security and the Family: Coping with Seasonality and Calamity in Rural India." *Journal of Peasant Studies* 17(3):341-412.

Alderman, H., et al., 1993. "Policy Issues and Intrahousehold Resource Allocation." In L. Haddad et al., eds., *Intrahousehold Resource Allocation in Developing Countries: Methods, Models, and Policy.*

Bardhan, K., 1977. "Rural Employment, Wages, and Labor Markets: A Survey of Research." *Economic and Political Weekly* 12, June 25, July 2, July 9.

———, 1985. "Women's Work, Welfare and Status: Forces of Tradition and Change in India." *Economic and Political Weekly* XX(51,52):2261-9.

———, 1993a. "Social Change and Gender in India: The Structure of Differences in the Conditions of Women." In A. Clark, ed., *Gender and Political Economy: Explorations of South Asian Systems.* New York: Oxford University Press.

———, 1993b. "Women and Rural Poverty: Some Asian Cases." In M. G. Quibria, ed., *Rural Poverty in Asia: Priority Issues and Policy Options.* Hong Kong: Oxford University Press.

Bardhan, P. K., ed., 1989a. *Conversations Between Economists and Anthropologists: Methodological Issues in Measuring Economic Change.* New York: Oxford University Press.

———, 1989b. *The Economic Theory of Agrarian Institutions.* New York: Oxford University Press.

Barnum, H., and L. Squire, 1979a. "An Econometric Application of the Theory of the Farm-Household." *Journal of Development Economics* 6:79-102.

———, 1979b. *A Model of an Agricultural Household: Theory and Evidence.* Baltimore: Johns Hopkins University Press.

Becker, G. S., 1965. "A Theory of the Allocation of Time." *Economic Journal* 75:463-519.

———, 1974. "A Theory of Marriage." *Journal of Political Economy* 81:813-46.

———, 1981. *A Treatise on the Family.* Cambridge: Harvard University Press.

Behrman, J. R., 1990. "Intrahousehold Allocation of Nutrients and Gender Effects: A Survey of Structural and Reduced Form Estimates." In S. Osmani, ed., *Nutrition and Poverty*. Oxford: Oxford University Press.

———, 1992. "Intrahousehold Distribution and the Family." University of Pennsylvania. Mimeographed.

Behrman, J. R., and A. Deolalikar, 1988. "Health and Nutrition." In H. Chenery and T. N. Srinivasan, eds., *Handbook of Development Economics*. Amsterdam: North-Holland Publishers.

———, 1990. "The Intrahousehold Demand for Nutrients in Rural South India: Individual Estimates, Fixed Effects and Permanent Income." *Journal of Human Resources* 24(4):665-97.

Benjamin D., 1992. "Household Composition, Labor Markets, and Labor Demand: Testing for Separation in Agricultural Household Markets." *Econometrica* 60(2):287-322.

Bernheim, B., and O. Stark, 1988. "Altruism within the Household Reconsidered: Do Nice Guys Finish Last?" *American Economic Review* 78:1034-45.

Berry, S., 1984. "Households, Decision-Making, and Rural Development: Do We Need to Know More?" Development Discussion Paper No. 167. Harvard Institute for International Development, Cambridge.

———, 1985. *Fathers Work for Their Sons: Accumulation, Mobility and Class Formation in an Extended Yoruba Community*. Berkeley: University of California Press.

———, 1989. "Social Institutions and Access to Resources." *Africa* 59.

———, 1993. *No Condition is Permanent: The Social Dynamics of Agrarian Change in Sub-Saharan Africa*. Madison: University of Wisconsin Press.

Besley, T., 1992. *Savings, Credit and Insurance*. Research Program in Development Studies, Princeton University.

Blumberg, R., 1988. "Income Under Female Versus Male Control: Hypotheses From a Theory of Gender Stratification and Data From the Third World." *Journal of Family Issues* 9(1):51-84.

Bourdieu, P., 1977. *Outline of a Theory of Practice*. Cambridge: Cambridge University Press.

Bourguignon, F., and P. A. Chiappori, 1992. "Collective Models of Household Behavior: An Introduction." *European Economic Review* 36:355-364.

Bourguignon, F., et al., 1993. "Do Households Pool Income? Some French Evidence." *Annales D' Economie Et De Statistique* 29.

Browning, M., et al., 1993. "Incomes and Outcomes: A Structural Model of Intra-Household Allocation." Mimeographed.

Bruce, N., and M. Waldman, 1990. "The Rotton-Kid Theorem Meets the Samaritan's Dilemma." *Quarterly Journal of Economics* 105(1):155-65.

Bruce, J., 1989. "Homes Divided." *World Development* 17(7):979-91.

Carney, J., and M. Watts, 1990. "Manufacturing Dissent: Work, Gender and the Politics of Meaning in A Peasant Society." *Africa* 60.

Carter, M., and E. Katz, 1993. "Separate Spheres and the Conjugal Contract: Understanding the Impact of Gender-Biased Development." In L. Haddad et al., eds., *Intrahousehold Resource Allocation in Developing Countries: Methods, Models, and Policy.*

Chapman, M., 1984. "Policy-makers and Circulation at the Grass Roots: South Pacific and South-east Asian Examples." In G. Standing, ed., *Labor Circulation and the Labor Process.* New Hampshire: Croom Helm.

Chayanov, A., 1966. *The Theory of Peasant Economy.* Illinois: The American Economic Association.

Chiappori, P.-A., 1992. "Collective Labor Supply and Welfare." *Journal of Political Economy* 100(3):437-67.

Chiappori, P.-A., et al., 1993. "Unitary Versus Collective Models of the Household: Time to Shift the Burden of Proof?" Paper presented for the American Economics Association Meetings.

Croll, E., 1987. "New Peasant Family Forms in Rural China." *Journal of Peasant Studies* 14(4).

Dasgupta, N., 1992. *Petty Trading in the Third World: The Case of Calcutta.* Brookfield: Avebury.

Deaton, A., 1994. *The Analysis of Household Surveys: Microeconomic Analysis for Development Policy.* Research Program in Development Studies, Princeton University.

Deaton, A., and J. Muellbauer, 1980. *Economics and Consumer Behavior.* New York: Cambridge University Press.

Deere, C. D., 1990. *Household and Class Relations: Peasants and Landlords in Northern Peru.* Berkeley: University of California Press.

Deolalikar, A. B., and W. P. M. Vijverberg, 1983. "The Heterogeneity of Family and Hired Labor in Agricultural Production: A Test Using District-Level Data from India." *Journal of Economic Development* 8(2):45-89.

Duraisamy, P., 1992. "Gender, Intrafamily Allocation of Resources and Child Schooling in South India." Economic Growth Center Discussion Paper No. 667. Yale University, New Haven.

Duraisamy, P., and R. Malathy, 1991. "Impact of Public Programs on Gender-Specific Earnings and the Human Capital of Children in Rural India." In T. Schultz, ed., *Population Research and Development Economics.* Greenwich: JAI Press.

Dwyer, D., and J. Bruce, eds., 1988. *A Home Divided.* Stanford: Stanford University Press.

Elson, D., ed., 1991. *Male Bias in the Development Process.* New York: Manchester University Press.

Fan, Y., and A. Stretton, 1984. "Circular Migration in South-East Asia: Some Theoretical Explanations." In G. Standing, ed., *Labor Circulation and the Labor Process.* New Hampshire: Croom Helm.

Folbre, N., 1984. "Market Opportunities, Genetic Endowments, and Intrafamily Resource Distribution: Comment." *American Economic Review* 74:518-20.

———, 1986a. "Hearts and Spades: Paradigms of Household Economics." *World Development* 14:245-55.

————, 1986b. "Cleaning House." *Journal of Development Economics* 22:5-40.

————, 1992. "Rotten Kids, Bad Daddies, and Public Policies." Paper presented at the IFPRI-World Bank Conference on Intrahousehold Resource Allocation: Policy Issues and Research Methods, Washington, D.C.

Fraser, N., 1989. *Unruly Practices: Power, Discourse and Gender in Contemporary Social Theory.* Minneapolis: University of Minnesota Press.

Gittelsohn, J., 1992. "Applying Anthropological Methods to Intrahousehold Resource Allocation." Paper presented at the IFPRI-World Bank Conference on Intrahousehold Resource Allocation: Policy Issues and Research Methods. Washington, D.C.

Gronau, R., 1973. "The Intrafamily Allocation of Time: The Value of Housewives' Time." *American Economic Review* 68:634-51.

————, 1977. "Leisure, Home Production, and Work: The Theory of the Allocation of Time Revisited." *Journal of Political Economy* 8:1099-123.

Guyer, J., 1981. "Household and Community in African Studies." *African Studies Review* 24(2/3):87-137.

————, 1986. "Intra-Household Processes and Farming Systems Research." In J. Moock, ed., *Understanding Africa's Rural Households and Farming Systems.* Boulder: Westview Press.

————, 1993. "Endowments and Assets: The Anthropology of Wealth and the Economics of Intrahousehold Allocation." In L. Haddad et al., eds. *Intrahousehold Resource Allocation in Developing Countries: Methods, Models, and Policy.*

Guyer, J., and P. Peters, eds., 1987. "Conceptualizing the Household: Issues of Theory and Policy in Africa." *Development and Change* 18(2).

Haddad, L., and R. Kanbur, 1992a. "Is There an Intrahousehold Kuznets' Curve: Some Evidence from the Philippines." *Public Finance* 47:77-93.

————, 1992b. "Intrahousehold Inequality and the Theory of Targeting." *European Economic Review* 36(2):372-8.

Haddad, L., et al., 1992. *Intrahousehold Resource Allocation: Policy Issues and Research Methods.* Washington: International Food Policy Research Institute.

————, eds., 1993. *Intrahousehold Resource Allocation in Developing Countries: Methods, Models, and Policy.*

Harris, O., 1981. "Households as Natural Units." In K. Young et al., eds., *Of Marriage and the Market: Women's Subordination Internationally and Its Lessons.* London: Metheun.

Hart, G., 1991. "Engendering Everyday Resistance: Gender, Patronage and Production Politics in Rural Malaysia." *Journal of Peasant Studies* 19(1):93-121.

————, 1992. "Household Production Reconsidered: Gender, Labor Conflict and Technological Change in Malaysia's Muda Region." *World Development* 20(6):809-23.

Hirschleifer, J., 1977. "Shakespeare Versus Becker on Altruism: The Importance of Having the Last Word." *Journal of Economic Literature* 25:500-502.

Hugo, G., 1984. "Structural Change and Labor Mobility in Rural Java." In G.

Standing, ed., *Labor Circulation and the Labor Process.* New Hampshire: Croom Helm.

Jones, C., 1983. "The Mobilization of Women's Labor for Cash Crop Production: A Game Theoretic Approach." *American Journal of Agricultural Economics* 65:1049-54.

———, 1986. "Intra-Household Bargaining in Response to the Introduction of New Crops: A Case Study from North Cameroon." In J. Moock, ed., *Understanding Africa's Rural Households and Farming Systems.* Boulder: Westview Press.

Kanbur, R., 1991. "Linear Expenditure Systems, Children as Public Goods, and Intrahousehold Inequality." Discussion Paper 104. Development Economics Research Center, University of Warwick.

Kandiyoti, D., 1990. "Women and Rural Development Policies: The Changing Agenda." *Development and Change* 21(1):5-22.

Kapadia, K., 1993. "Mutuality and Competition: Female Landless Labor and Wage Rates in Tamil Nadu." *Journal of Peasant Studies* 20(2):296-316.

Kumar, S., 1979. *Impact of Subsidized Rice on Food Consumption and Nutrition in Kerala.* Report No. 5. Washington: International Food Policy Research Institute.

Lem, W., 1988. "Household Production and Reproduction in Rural Languedoc." *Journal of Peasant Studies* 15:500-29.

Lindbeck, A., and J.W. Weibull, 1988. "Altruism and Time Consistency: The Economics of Fait Accompli." *Journal of Political Economy* 96:1165-82.

Lopez, R., 1986. "Structural Models of the Farm Household that Allow for Interdependent Utility and Profit-Making Decisions." In I. Singh et al. *Agricultural Household Models: Extensions, Applications and Policy.* Baltimore: Johns Hopkins University Press.

Lucas, R. E. B., and O. Stark, 1985. "Motivations to Remit: Evidence from Botswana." *Journal of Political Economy* 93(5):901-18.

Lundberg, S., and R. A. Pollak, 1993. "Separate Spheres Bargaining and the Marriage Market." *Journal of Political Economy* 101(6):988-1010.

Manser, M., and M. Brown, 1980. "Marriage and Household Decision-Making: A Bargaining Analysis." *International Economic Review* 21:31-44.

McElroy, M. B., 1990. "The Empirical Content of Nash-Bargained Household Behavior." *Journal of Human Resources* 25(4):559-83.

———, 1992. "Marriage Markets and Family Bargaining." Paper presented at the IFPRI-World Bank Conference on Intrahousehold Resource Allocation: Policy Issues and Research Methods, Washington, D.C.

McElroy, M. B., and M. J. Horney, 1981. "Nash-Bargained Household Decisions: Toward a Generalization of the Theory of Demand." *International Economic Review* 22:333-50.

Mencher, J., 1988. "Women, Work and Poverty: Women's Contribution to Household Maintenance in South India." In D. Dwyer and J. Bruce, eds. *A Home Divided.* Stanford: Stanford University Press.

Moore, H., 1988. *Feminism and Anthropology*. Minneapolis: University of Minnesota Press.

———, 1992. "Households and Gender Relations: The Modelling of the Economy." In S. Ortiz and S. Lees, eds., *Understanding Economic Process*. New York: University Press of America.

Mukherji, S., 1984. "The Process of Wage Labor Circulation in Northern India." In G. Standing, ed., *Labor Circulation and the Labor Process*. New Hampshire: Croom Helm.

Nakajima, C., 1969. "Subsistence and Commercial Family Farms: Some Theoretical Models of Subjective Equilibrium." In C. Wharton, ed., *Subsistence Agriculture and Economic Development*. Chicago: Aldine.

Ong, A., 1987. *Spirits of Resistance and Capitalist Discipline: Factory Women in Malaysia*. Albany: State University of New York Press.

Pahl, J., 1983. "The Allocation of Money within Marriage." *Sociological Review* 32:237-64.

Paolisso, M., 1992. "Methodological Contributions of Economic Anthropology to the Study of Intrahousehold Resource Allocation." Paper presented at the IFPRI-World Bank Conference on Intrahousehold Resource Allocation: Policy Issues and Research Methods, Washington, D.C.

Pitt, M., et al., 1990. "Productivity, Health and Inequality in the Intrahousehold Distribution of Food in Low-Income Countries." *American Economic Review* 80(5):1139-56.

Pollak, R. A., and M. L. Wachter, 1975. "The Relevance of the Household Production Function and Its Implications for the Allocation of Time." *Journal of Political Economy* 83(2):255-77.

Quibria, M. G., 1993. "The Gender and Poverty Nexus: Issues and Politics." Economics Staff Paper Number 51. Asian Development Bank, Manila.

Rosenzweig, M., 1986. "Program Interventions, Intrahousehold Distribution and the Welfare of Individuals: Modeling Household Behavior." *World Development* 14(2):233-43.

Rosenzweig, M., and T. P. Schultz, 1982. "Market Opportunities, Genetic Endowments and the Intrafamily Distribution of Resources." *American Economic Review* 72:803-15.

———, 1984. "Market Opportunities and Intrafamily Resource Distribution: Reply." *American Economic Review* 74:521-2.

Rosenzweig, M. R., and O. Stark, 1989. "Consumption Smoothing, Migration and Marriage: Evidence from Rural India." *Journal of Political Economy* 97(4):905-26.

Samuelson, P., 1956. "Social Indifference Curves." *Quarterly Journal of Economics* 70:1-22.

Schultz, T. P., 1990, "Testing the Neoclassical Model of Family Labor Supply and Fertility." *Journal of Human Resources* 25(4):599-634.

Sen, A.K., 1983. "Economics and the Family." *Asian Development Review* 1(2):14-26.

———, 1990. "Gender and Cooperative Conflicts." In I. Tinker, ed., *Persistent*

Inequalities: Women and World Development. New York: Oxford University Press.

Shaw, A., 1988. "The Income Security Function of the Rural Sector: The Case of Calcutta." *Economic Development and Cultural Change* 36(2):303-15.

Singh, I. et al., 1986. *Agricultural Household Models: Extensions, Applications and Policy.* Baltimore: Johns Hopkins University Press.

Stack, C. B., 1974. *All or Kin: Strategies for Survival in a Black Community.* New York: Harper and Row.

Standing, G., ed., 1984. *Labor Circulation and the Labor Process.* New Hampshire: Croom Helm.

Stark, O., and R. E. B. Lucas, 1988. "Migration, Remittances and the Family." *Economic Development and Cultural Change* 36(3):465-81.

Stiglitz, J. E., 1989. "Rational Peasants, Efficient Institutions, and a Theory of Rural Organization." In P. K. Bardhan, ed., *The Economic Theory of Agrarian Institutions.* New York: Oxford University Press.

Strauss, J., and D. Thomas, 1993. "Human Resources: Empirical Modelling of the Household and Family Decisions." In J. Behrman and T. N. Srinivasan, eds., *Handbook of Development Economics.* Vol. III. New York: North-Holland Publishers.

Thomas, D., 1990. "Intra-Household Resource Allocation: An Inferential Approach." *Journal of Human Resources* 25(4):635-64.

————, 1993. "The Distribution of Income and Expenditure within the Household." *Annales D'Economie Et De Statistique* 29:109-35.

Tripp, R., 1981. "Farmers and Traders—Some Economic Determinants of Nutritional Status in Northern Ghana." *Journal of Tropical Pediatrics* 27:15-22.

White, B., 1980. "Rural Household Studies: An Anthropological Perspective." In H. Binswanger, *Rural Household Studies in Asia.* Singapore: Singapore University Press.

Whitehead, A., 1981. "I'm Hungry Mum: The Politics of Domestic Bargaining." In K. Young, et al., eds., *Of Marriage and the Market: Women's Subordination Internationally and Its Lessons.* London: Metheun.

Williamson, O. E., 1985. *The Economic Institutions of Capitalist Firms, Markets, Relational Contracting.* New York: Free Press.

Wolf, D. L., 1992. *Factory Daughters: Gender, Household Dynamics and Industrialization in Java.* Berkeley: University of California Press.

Yanagisako, S., 1979. "Family and the Household: The Analysis of Domestic Groups." *Annual Review of Anthropology* 8:161-205.

————, 1990. "Capital and Gendered Interest in Italian Family Firms." In D. Kertzer and R. Sallers, eds., *The History of the Italian Family.* New Haven: Yale University Press.

Chapter Four

Income Distribution in Developing Economies: Conceptual, Data, and Policy Issues in Broad-Based Growth

Gary S. Fields

Introduction

The aim of economic development is to raise the standard of living of a country's people, especially its poor. Economic growth, particularly when broadly based, is a means to that end.

'Underdevelopment' can be defined as a state of severely constrained choices. When one is choosing from among an undesirable set of alternatives, the outcome will itself be undesirable. Standards of living will be low. If standards of living are to be improved, people must have a better set of alternatives from which to choose.

'Economic development' is the process by which the constraints on choices are relaxed. Based on ample evidence from microeconomic studies (see, for instance, the Nobel Prize winning research of T. W. Schultz 1980), we may be confident that when poor people in the developing world have better options from which to choose, the choices they make will lead them to enjoy better outcomes, hence raising standards of living. Accordingly, the task of economic development is to enhance the alternatives from which to choose, that is, the 'choice set'.

'Broad-based growth' means that the choice set is improved for all economic strata. There is good reason to expect that the upper and middle classes have many mechanisms at their disposal for benefiting from the growth process. These groups gain when economic growth takes place. It is less certain whether the poor are also reached by growth.

Income Distribution and Broad-Based Growth

The case can be made that the poor deserve special attention from development analysts and policymakers, because the poor have, or may be presumed to have, the greatest needs. Hence the marginal social valuation on their income is higher than it is for others. This argument justifies the so-called 'focus axiom', which suggests that we focus our attention on the poor (see Sen 1976).

One philosophical school of thought holds that the proper goal of a society is to maximize the well-being of the worst-off person. This criterion, called the 'maximin principle', has been developed fully by John Rawls (1971). Maximin adherents would accept gains for others, especially the rich, if and only if, such gains raise the well-being of the worst-off in society. Development agencies and some developing country governments, such as the government of India, have made antipoverty efforts the centerpiece of their development plans.

For political economy reasons, societies do not actually maximize the well-being of their worst-off members. In practice, the programs that benefit the poor must offer substantial enough benefits to the nonpoor so that they will support these programs, both financially and politically. These political economy considerations imply that even if the policy-makers, themselves, wish to mount propoor programs, there will inevitably be a certain amount of benefit accruing to the nonpoor.

In this connection, the late Arthur Okun (1975) suggested the metaphor of a leaky bucket. The bucket carries benefits directed toward target groups. Inevitably, there will be a certain amount of leakage, and others will thereby gain. Okun asked, How leaky must the leaky bucket be before it's not worth carrying the water?

The preceding points turn traditional development economics on its head. Rather than pursuing economic growth for its own sake and hoping that the benefits will be spread widely enough that the poor derive some gain, we might instead ask how development efforts might be directed toward the poor, through economic growth and other means such as government antipoverty programs and labor market policies. We want to be sure that the benefits of growth are broadly enough based that the poor participate. It would be tragic indeed if the have-nots are excluded from the growth process or, worse yet, impoverished by it.

In sum, broad-based growth means raising standards of living at all socioeconomic levels. As things are, the middle and upper strata probably do not need much help—they will benefit if growth takes place. It is the least well-off in society who require special attention. Therefore, broad-based growth is best operationalized to mean that development efforts are targeted on raising the standards of living of the poor.

Patterns of Income Distribution

Development analysts customarily measure standards of living in terms of household consumption or income. Ideally, these measures would include the value of goods and services provided or subsidized by the public sector (such as government housing, food, health care, and education), by employers (for instance, living accommodations for workers or on-the-job meals), and by others (such as nongovernmental organizations). In practice, though, the information at our disposal is often limited to cash income or expenditures only.

Suppose that we have such information on income or consumption for two or more points in time during which economic growth has taken place. By what criterion might we gauge how broadly based are the benefits of such growth?

One criterion is to see whether an economy has registered gains in real incomes or consumption for all groups. If this takes place, we would observe higher real incomes in all income quantiles (such as deciles or quintiles). So too absolute poverty, as measured by the poverty head-count ratio, the Sen index, or the P-alpha class, would be lower. In this case, the new distribution would be said to 'dominate' the old. For more on dominance results in poverty analysis, see Atkinson (1987), and Foster and Shorrocks (1988).

The criterion of absolute gains for each group, and hence falling absolute poverty, is a weak one. One reason for this is that although groups as a whole gain, there may be losses for certain individuals or households within those groups. Another reason is that if we find that there have been *some* gains for all groups this does not tell us whether particular target groups have benefited a lot or only a little.

The criterion for broad-based growth might be made more stringent by looking to see whether standards of living have been raised for *all* individuals or households. This, however, is probably *too* stringent a criterion: it is hard to imagine an economy in which there are *only* winners. Someone invariably loses. Looking on balance at the numbers and characteristics of winners compared with losers is more fruitful.

One way of doing this is to see whether an economy has achieved equiproportionate gains for all groups, in proportion to their original economic positions. A stricter criterion is to ascertain whether those with greatest need received disproportionately large gains. By the first of these criteria, growth would be judged to be broad based if inequality is constant, because then each group would have benefited proportionately. By the second criterion, we would require that inequality falls, because only then will the poor have benefited more than proportionately.

This suggests two workable criteria that might be used to help determine the distributional effects of economic growth: one absolute and one relative. One is to determine if real incomes have risen in all strata of the income distribution. If they have, then absolute poverty has surely fallen. The second is to determine whether income inequality has increased, decreased, or remained unchanged.

Data for Measuring Poverty and Inequality

One would think that the subjects of poverty and inequality are central to the assessment of the extent of economic development and that statistical offices of governments and development agencies would regularly publish such information. Alas, such data are not regularly published anywhere.[1]

Consider, for instance, the World Bank. The tables at the back of its *World Development Report* are probably the most consulted source for development data in the world. However, these tables contain nothing at all on income distribution for most of the low income and middle income countries. For those that are included, no information is presented on poverty, no calculation is made of summary measures of inequality such as the Gini coefficient, and no information is presented on changes in either poverty or inequality over time. What about other World Bank publications? The World Bank's *Social Indicators of Development* would seem a logical place to look. But unfortunately, this publication presents data on changing poverty rates over time only for two countries, Morocco and Pakistan, and no data at all on changes in inequality. Scattered bits of information can be found in other publications of the World Bank if one knows where to look (see chapter 3 of the 1990 *World Development Report* and the, as yet, unpublished work of Ravallion 1993). It simply shouldn't be so hard to find.

What about other international agencies? The United Nations' *Human Development Report* contains poverty head count ratios and Gini coefficients for a large number of countries, but no intertemporal data. *The State of the World's Children*, published by the United Nations International Children's Emergency Fund, has nothing on poverty and inequality, nor does the International Labour Organisation's *Yearbook of Labour Statistics*. However, *The Incidence of Poverty in Developing Countries: An ILO Compendium of Data* (Tabatabai 1993) contains much useful information that will inform the development community for years to come.

Researchers interested in measuring broad-based growth have not, until now, had access to the compendium of the International Labour Organisation, so have been forced to construct their own. In the data base constructed in Fields (1989), countries are included if they meet the following criteria:

(i) The data on income or expenditure must be derived from an actual household survey or census.
(ii) The surveys must be comparable over time.
(iii) The surveys must be national in coverage.
(iv) The data must be presented in enough categories so that reasonable calculations of poverty and inequality can be made.

Changing Poverty and Inequality in Various Countries' Experiences

Changes in Poverty Over Time

To be in 'poverty' means to experience a low living standard. 'Absolute poverty' means that the living standard is absolutely low, given the standards of the particular society in which one lives. In practice, a person or household falling below a specified income/expenditure amount is said to be 'poor'.

Poverty lines are set very differently in different countries—see, for instance, Drèze and Sen (1990), and Quibria (1993) for discussions in the context of Asian developing economies. In India, the poverty line was set in a scientific way. The caloric and nutrient values of various foods consumed by the poor were measured. The cost of an adequate diet was then calculated. To this was added the cost of shelter, clothing, and other basic necessities of life. Separate poverty lines were set for urban and rural India, reflecting differences in the cost of the basic market basket of goods. Each year, these poverty lines are increased in proportion to changes in consumer prices. Thus, the poverty line changes in nominal terms but is constant in real terms.

In the Republic of Korea, there is no poverty line. There is, however, a minimum wage. Although the Korean minimum wage is a convenient reference point, it has no scientific basis; it is determined by government in light of political considerations. Minimum wages in countries such as the United States and Brazil are determined in the same way. So in the absence of a scientifically determined poverty line for the Republic of Korea, the most practical thing to do is to define poverty relative to a reference year's minimum wage, adjusting that figure upward for inflation so that the poverty line used is constant in real terms.

Having defined a poverty line and determined whether a given individual or household is or is not poor, the next step is to determine how much poverty there is. The simplest poverty measure is the percentage of recipient units below the poverty threshold. This is called the 'poverty headcount ratio'. It would also be desirable to measure two other aspects of economic deprivation: the extent to which the incomes of the poor fall below the poverty line, termed the 'average income shortfall' and the extent of income inequality among the poor, as measured, say, by the Gini coefficient. Sen's poverty index and the P-alpha class include all three of these aspects. However, the available tabulations for developing countries do not report these measures or the additional data needed to calculate them, so as a practical matter, we are forced to rely on the poverty headcount ratio alone.

What do the poverty data show? The finding, shown in Table 4.1 (appendix), is a happy one. Nearly always, when economic growth, as measured by gross national product or Internationally Comparable Purchasing Power units per capita, has taken place, real incomes of individuals and households have risen and absolute poverty has thereby fallen. Using probit analysis, we find that the probability that poverty falls is a function of the economic growth rate: the higher the economic growth rate, the more likely poverty is to have fallen.

We find too that in most instances where poverty has risen, aggregate economic growth has been very small or even negative. This was true of India in the 1960s. Elsewhere, it was also true of Jamaica in the 1970s and of many Latin American countries in the 1980s. The same is thought to be true of many African countries as well, but because these countries lack household surveys for the beginning of the decade, this conjecture cannot be confirmed rigorously.

In the developing world, the outstanding exception to the generalization that poverty increases only in the absence of growth is the Philippines during the Marcos years. Data compiled by Mijares and Belarmino (1973) show that from 1961 to 1971, nominal income growth of the poorest 20 per cent in the Philippines was plus 79 per cent while consumer prices rose by 101.6 per cent over the same interval. This implies that absolute poverty rose, at least for the poorest 20 per cent. Balisacan (1993), in his study of the period between 1965 and 1971, also found a rising poverty headcount ratio in the Philippines. The most straightforward explanation—crony capitalism—may well be the right one.

The implication of these findings is that more growth can be expected to help *all* income groups including the poor. The poor have benefited absolutely when growth has taken place, even when that growth was based on a very unequal initial distribution of income. Of course, some *kinds* of economic growth would undoubtedly be more beneficial for the poor than others. When it is possible to stimulate such kinds of broad-based growth, this should indeed be done.

Some claim that in the absence of fundamental change, the poor will be rendered poorer by economic growth, and for this reason it is better not to grow at all. This claim is *not* supported by the bulk of the evidence. Even in very inegalitarian countries such as Brazil and Mexico, growth on the existing economic base has been better for the poor than no growth. Whenever possible, the first-best kinds of broad-based growth policies should be sought. But when political realities render the first-best unattainable, the second-best will probably still achieve growth.

Changes in Inequality Over Time

Another criterion for determining whether growth is broad based or not is the change in relative income inequality. Studying 'inequality' means comparing one group's income change relative to another's or to the average in an economy as a whole. When the comparison is made on the basis of income *ratios*, rather than income *differences*, the comparison is one of 'relative inequality'. Most often, income is the basis for such comparisons, although expenditures sometimes are used instead.

Ever since Simon Kuznets' pathbreaking work on economic growth and income inequality in 1955, relative income inequality measures have been the basis for comparisons. The most commonly used relative inequality measures are the income shares of particular quantile groups and Gini coefficients.

Kuznets himself, and many others who followed, used cross-sectional data to derive empirical inferences about the supposed relationship between inequality and economic growth. It was well understood that this was not the ideal methodology—looking over time within individual countries' development experiences would clearly have been better—but with the data then available, this could not be done. One investigator whose empirical work was extremely influential, Montek Ahluwalia (1976, p. 307), was quite explicit about this:

> The use of cross country data for the analysis of what are essentially dynamic processes raises a number of familiar problems. Ideally, such processes should be examined in an explicitly historical context for particular countries. Unfortunately, time series data on the distribution of income, over any substantial period, are simply not available for most developing countries. For the present, therefore, empirical investigation in this field must perforce draw heavily on cross country experience.

Kuznets suggested, and a long series of cross-section studies seemed to confirm, that inequality tends to increase in the early stages of economic growth and to decrease in the later stages.[2] But intertemporal studies of individual countries, including the work of Kuznets himself (1955), revealed no pronounced tendency one way or the other.[3] We know now that Kuznets' curve was an inverted-U shape because of the use of cross-sectional data; panel data methods turn the shape of the curve around to an ordinary U (Fields and Jakubson 1992).

Using the Gini coefficient as the inequality measure, data on inequality are presented in Table 4.2 (appendix). (As with the choice of the poverty headcount ratio to measure poverty, the choice of the Gini coefficient is on purely practical grounds: many countries publish Gini coefficients but not other inequality measures.) Taking the criteria discussed earlier, we might ask, How broad based is economic growth? Are the gains for the poor sufficiently large that the Gini coefficient falls? Do the poor benefit equiproportionately from economic growth, thus keeping the Gini coefficient unchanged? Or do the poor benefit less than the nonpoor, so that the Gini coefficient increases?

The evidence on Kuznets' curve and related hypotheses is decisively indecisive: there is *no* pattern to the observed changes. In fact, the testing of four hypotheses elicited the following results:

Hypothesis 1: Inequality tends to change systematically in developing countries.

Result: No pattern is found. Rather, inequality increases in half the countries' growth experiences and decreases in the other half.

Hypothesis 2: Inequality tends to increase in the early stages of economic development and to decrease in the latter stages.

Result: This hypothesis also is refuted. In cross-sectional data, inequality is higher for middle income developing countries than in those that are either richer or poorer. The developing countries were therefore divided into two groups: those with incomes below the turning point and those with incomes above the turning point. Kuznets' hypothesis would predict that the first group of countries would have inequality that rises with growth, and, the second, inequality that falls with growth. However, inequality rises as often in the lower income developing countries as it does in the higher income developing countries.

Hypothesis 3: Inequality is more likely to increase in fast-growing developing economies than in slow-growing ones.

Result: Again, the evidence fails to confirm the hypothesis. Instead, we find that the rates are the same: inequality rises with the same frequency in the fast-growing developing economies as in the slow-growing ones.

Hypothesis 4: A more unequal initial distribution of income leads to a faster subsequent rate of economic growth.

Result: False again. The initial inequality in the distribution of income has nothing to do with the subsequent rate of economic growth.

These results establish that when changes over time are measured, there is *no empirical tendency whatsoever* in the inequality-development relationship. If inequality does not tend to increase before it decreases, to fall with economic growth (or to rise), or to change systematically with the rate of economic growth, it must be that it is not the *rate* of economic growth, but rather the *type* of economic growth, that determines the extent to which the poor share in the growth process.

Furthermore, even when inequality *has* changed, the changes have almost always been small in magnitude. Thus, Brazil remains a relatively high inequality country, Costa Rica, a middle inequality country, and Taipei,China, a low inequality country. Maintaining present inequality levels means that for a very inegalitarian country like Brazil, the poorest quintile will get about 2 per cent of the benefits of growth and the richest quintile about 68 per cent. For a more egalitarian country, like the People's Republic of China, the corresponding figures are 6 per cent and 42 per cent (Chen, Datt, and Ravallion 1993).

For the poor to receive a larger share of the benefits of growth, reforms are needed, along the lines discussed below. These policies will not necessarily slow the economy's growth rate; indeed, the finding for hypothesis 4 above and other recent studies (Waldmann 1992; Alesina and Rodrik 1993; and Persson and Tabellini 1993) show that those countries with a more equal initial distribution of income grow *as fast or faster* than others. Growth being broadly based is good not just for the poor; it is good for growth too.

Broad-Based Growth in East Asia

For economic growth to have broad-based effects, there must be mechanisms for transmitting gains throughout the economy, especially to the poor. The single most important asset of the poor is their labor. It follows that economic growth can reach the poor if it increases the demand for their labor, increases the demand for the products of their labor, or provides complementary inputs with which to make their labor more productive.

The most outstanding examples of broad-based economic improvements over a sustained period of time are the newly industrializing economies (NIEs) of East Asia (Hong Kong, Republic of Korea, Singapore, and Taipei,China). Their labor market and income distribution experiences, presented in Appendix Tables 4.3 and 4.4, present a picture of extraordinary improvements.

In these economies, as firms expanded output, they also expanded their demand for labor. Labor-intensive growth first succeeded in leading to full employment in previously labor-abundant economies. When the Lewis-Fei-Ranis turning point was reached so that an additional supply of labor was no longer forthcoming at prevailing wage rates, firms that wished to expand output and employment further were forced to raise real wages in order to attract sufficient labor. They could have decided not to pay the higher wages, not to increase employment, and hence not to grow, and indeed some firms made exactly this choice—textile producers being perhaps the best known example. But so many other firms *were* willing to pay the higher costs that real labor earnings increased year after year in industry upon industry. Real wages *throughout* these economies rose apace with economic growth as a whole. See Table 4.5 (appendix). Unemployment rates of just 1 or 2 per cent prevailed for decades.

As labor markets tightened, the mix of employment improved: the fractions of workers in agriculture (a relatively low-paying sector) fell; wage employees, as a percentage of total employment, increased, as did the proportions of workers in the highest occupational categories. The educational levels of the employed population improved as well. The rapidly rising real wages and improved mix of jobs among a labor force with very little unemployment led to sharply falling rates of poverty and low to moderate levels of inequality.

There are arguments that the pursuit of broad-based growth through tightening labor markets leads to a dialectical contradiction: that the very act of stimulating labor demand raises wages and/or generates labor shortages, choking off the very growth it was designed to stimulate. So far, this hasn't happened—30 years of official and professional lamentation over wage increases notwithstanding. Perhaps developing economies have a lot of room for maneuvering before this becomes a problem.

In full employment economies, the only thing worse than rising real wages would be for wages *not* to rise. If wages are held below market-clearing levels, how would companies deal with the resultant labor shortages? Wouldn't economic growth be slowed? Wouldn't the rate of improvement of standards of living be curtailed? What is growth for?

The 'Asian Miracle' bears careful study, and indeed is receiving such study both from empiricists and from theorists.[4]

Policies Producing Broad-Based Growth

In a short paper such as this, space does not permit for more than a brief analysis of a few of the major factors that determine how conducive various types of growth have been to producing broad-based economic participation.[5]

The first points discussed in this section relate to labor returns directly. These include policies that favor the full utilization of labor and policies that affect what labor has to work with, namely land and education. The section continues to discuss two aspects of the economic environment that have proved central to determining how broadly based economic growth is: the interrelation between government regulation and private enterprise, and countries' trade and industrialization strategies.

Policies that Favor the Full Utilization of Labor

Two types of 'distortions' in labor markets are to be avoided (Fields 1993). The first involves policies to raise the returns to labor prematurely, before employers are ready to pay the higher labor costs. Unless we believe that labor demand curves are not downward sloping, we would have to expect that excessively high wages would reduce both employment and output. The other labor market distortion to avoid is labor market repression. Labor market repression is neither necessary nor desirable for economic growth, quite apart from the severe social consequences that it has. Policies that favor full utilization of labor should therefore be sought.

Because developing economies are labor abundant and because labor is the chief asset of the poor, it stands to reason that economic growth of a labor-intensive character would not only be efficient relative to capital-intensive development but it would also benefit the poor more than would capital-intensive growth. Indeed, the evidence presented earlier shows exactly that.

Labor-intensive growth has another advantage: prejudicial behavior becomes increasingly costly for employers. In the Far East, an important group of beneficiaries from tight labor markets was women, whose employment opportunities expanded greatly. Women have yet to attain economic and social equality with men in that part of the world, but the gap is narrowing.

This raises the question of how best to create more and better jobs. Real wages have plummeted in many countries in Latin America and Africa and yet employment has increased little. This suggests that developing countries may have little scope for increasing employment through wage cutting. It may be that a better way is to increase production and hence shift the derived demand for labor.

Distribution of Productive Assets: Education

As the *quantity* of labor demanded in the labor market is important, so is the *quality* of the labor process, that is, the skills workers bring to the labor market and the inputs they have to work with.

Education makes people more productive. Notwithstanding arguments about credentialism, screening, and low quality and inappropriate curricula, there can be no doubt that genuine human capital formation takes place in schools in developing countries.

Due to scarcity of resources, education in the developing world is neither universal nor free. Typically, the education ministry has a certain agreed-upon budget to be divided among various levels and qualities of educational inputs. As a result, more of one type of education necessarily means less of another.

How should education dollars best be spent? The most efficient allocation of resources would be the one that yields the highest social benefit per dollar spent. Typically, the social cost of a year of higher education is many times that of a year of primary education. Cost ratios of 20, 30, or 40 to 1 are not uncommon. One college graduate is probably not 20, 30, or 40 times as valuable to the society as one primary school graduate. So on efficiency grounds, resources would probably best be allocated to primary education. The egalitarian allocation of resources would be the allocation with the most equal possible outcome. Spending the marginal educational dollars on 20, 30, or 40 children who would otherwise be unschooled rather than on one person who already has a relatively high level of schooling would also be preferable on equity grounds.

This illustrates that in allocating resources to education, there may be no tradeoff between efficiency and equity: spending the marginal educational dollars on primary education rather than higher education may add more to the productive capacity of workers in the economy *and* spread the benefits of economic growth more widely.

More research is needed on the empirical effects of educational expansion. We need to know more about how labor markets adjust when more workers are educated. What kinds of jobs do the graduates get? How much more productive are they in those jobs with education than they or others might have been without the education? What happens to the less educated persons who are displaced by the better educated? What kinds of jobs do they get? After taking account of the possible reallocation of the labor force among jobs and the changes in productivity in each, how much is output enhanced when the labor force is better educated?

Distribution of Productive Assets: Land

As with the allocation of educational resources, there may be no tradeoff between equity and efficiency when land is considered. After labor, land is the next most important asset of people in developing countries. In the early post World War II period, both the Republic of Korea and Taipei, China had major land reforms. Singapore and Hong Kong, being city states, faced no significant inequality of land ownership. Thus, in all four of the East Asian NIEs, postwar economic development was based on a relatively egalitarian foundation.

An initially egalitarian distribution of land and other assets has three principal advantages. One is the direct effect of the assets in generating incomes, hence spreading the benefits of growth to those at the bottom of the economic scale. Second, ample research shows that small farms have higher yields per acre. Thus, on efficiency grounds, the presumption is that a more equal distribution of land would raise total agricultural productivity. The third advantage is political. Landed oligarchies can be extraordinarily powerful, often channeling public decisions toward their own personal gain rather than toward the larger social interest. It may well be because of the land reforms that the influence of landed oligarchies was much more limited in the Republic of Korea and Taipei,China than it was, and is, in the Philippines or Brazil.

Land reform can be a valuable ingredient in helping achieve broad-based growth in some cases, but not necessarily in all (see the paper by Rashid and Quibria in this volume for a more pessimistic view). But even when it is not possible to equalize the distribution of productive assets, growth will probably still be beneficial for the poor.

Government Regulation and Private Enterprise

There are two kinds of governments: those that mean well and those that don't. There are also two kinds of private enterprises: those that behave decently and those that will do whatever it takes to maximize the returns from their activities. Well-meaning governments often regulate their economies in the hopes of effecting better outcomes. At times, these regulations offer genuine protection against abuses that would otherwise occur. The question is how to strike the right balance between the legitimate interests of workers to earn fair wages and work in decent conditions, consumers to receive fair value for price paid, and businesses to earn profits.

To illustrate how such a balance might be struck, let us consider the regulation of labor markets. Most developing countries have abundant labor relative to other factors of production. When economic growth has *not* been labor intensive, it has often been because of efforts to legislate higher than market returns to labor. Among the mechanisms for doing this are minimum wages, encouragement of unions' wage bargaining efforts, public sector employment creation at above-market wages, and ambitious labor codes.

These efforts, though well intentioned, ignore the fact that higher wages for workers mean higher labor costs for employers, thus creating an incentive for firms to economize on the use of labor by not employing as many people. Some firms respond by substituting capital in place of labor. Others cut back on their output levels, using less of both capital and labor to produce less output. Others use less of one country's labor by moving offshore and hiring workers elsewhere.

Premature wage increases have predictable side effects. It is no accident that the forces leading to premature wage increases have been largely absent from the East Asian economies, which not only have achieved rapid economic growth but also rapidly rising real earnings. The labor market policies conducive to broad-based improvements in labor market rewards are those that *pull* the poor along when the economy grows, not those that *push* wages and working conditions up in the hope that the rest of the economy will somehow absorb these increases.

This is *not* an argument for a completely unregulated labor market. Far from it. Essential freedoms must be guaranteed and decent treatment assured. Labor markets must be regulated to prevent abusive practices. No person should have to endure such abuses as slavery, indentured servitude, restrictions on freedom of association or collective bargaining, unknowing exposure of workers to unsafe or unhealthy working conditions, or the employment of children for long work hours simply because they are cheaper to hire than adults. And no country should knowingly permit such abuses.

As a working rule, a very simple question may be asked, Is a particular way of doing things a socially acceptable *procedure* for undertaking economic activity? If the answer is no, as it is for slavery, for example, then that procedure is properly outlawed. But when the procedure is not inherently objectionable, the creative energies of the various participants may best be harnessed in a well functioning labor market.

Research is needed to determine when regulations have impeded *desirable* private enterprise adjustments and, equally importantly, when regulations have prevented private enterprise from engaging in socially *undesirable* actions. Regulations in labor markets would be a good place to start such research.

Trade and Industrialization Strategies

The evidence is compelling that outward-oriented trade and industrialization strategies are better than inward-looking strategies, not only for raising the rate of aggregate economic growth but also for achieving more broad-based economic growth. As discussed above, the most spectacular economic growth successes of the post-World War II period have been in East Asia: Japan, Hong Kong, Singapore, the Republic of Korea, and Taipei,China. These economies have low to moderate levels of inequality by international standards. They have all maintained essentially full employment and rapidly rising real wages. Poverty has fallen rapidly. And all achieved their successes through export-led growth.

The value of being able to sell profitably in foreign markets can hardly be questioned. Exporting is good for the export firms, for their suppliers, and for their workers. To be able to sell profitably in world markets means that the home-produced good is comparable in quality and price to the best foreign products (otherwise foreign buyers would buy elsewhere), and this means that domestic consumers also benefit. Using additional labor to produce for export brings about heightened competition in these countries' labor markets, thus spreading the benefits to workers in all parts of the economy, including those in nonexportables and agriculture.

When considering the benefits of exporting profitably, the word 'profitable' is the key. Why do some countries insist on exporting unprofitably? Yes, flying the national flag on a jumbo jet is a source of national pride, but isn't there a better way for man not to live by bread alone? Sociocultural factors aside, the only economically defensible reason to export unprofitably is as an investment in profitable activities for the future. Such investments might be warranted, at least temporarily, in order to learn by doing, to set up a marketing network, or to establish a reputation for quality. It was apparently for reasons such as these that the governments of Japan and the Republic of Korea *required* that companies increase their exports as a condition for maintaining licenses, access to foreign exchange, and other government-conferred benefits.

As has now become clear, the East Asian NIEs did *not* follow identical trade and industrialization strategies; some were much more dirigiste than others. What the East Asian economies did share was a belief that they could achieve rapid, broad-based growth by producing for the world market. Judging by the record, they were quite right.

One reason the East Asian NIEs succeeded is that they chose their trade and industrialization policies with careful attention to comparative advantage. Of equal if not greater importance is that those countries adapted their policies when comparative advantage shifted. Textile exports rose and then fell. So too did exports of heavy machinery and, more recently, of consumer electronics. It would be interesting to know more than we now do about how public policy fostered appropriate responses to changing comparative advantage.

Policy-Relevant Basic Development Research

Despite all that is known, more research is needed. Seven topics merit high priority for understanding development processes and formulating appropriate development policies, yet they may be lost amidst calls for research on other, more directly applied, topics.

1. *Additional Country Studies.* The experiences of the East Asian NIEs offer persuasive evidence to many, that growth can have very positive distributional effects. Yet, these are only four economies, and rather special ones at that. More country studies are needed, building, of course, on the many high quality studies that have already been carried out by researchers within the countries. A good place to start would be with those Southeast Asian economies (Thailand, Indonesia, Malaysia, and the Philippines) that aspire to be the 'next NIEs' to see how their income distributions and labor market conditions have changed. It would be interesting and worthwhile to compare the experiences of these econo-mies with the experiences of South Asian economies and select Latin American economies.

2. *Determinants of Constraints on Choices.* Basic economics courses teach that individuals make maximizing choices subject to constraints. While we have learned a great deal about the choices individuals make given the constraints they face, we know a great deal less about how the constraints are determined. The 'choice set' is the set of opportunities from which choices are made. Choice sets are determined by macroeco-

nomic conditions, public policies and strategies, markets, institutions, and the summation of individual behavior. But how precisely do these factors interact? More work is needed at the level of the market and intermarket analysis—what some now call the 'meso' level.

3. *Coping Strategies.* Over time, choice sets change. Individuals and households cope with these changes and reoptimize. How does behavior change with economic growth and decline? Are the adjustments symmetric, or do individuals and markets respond differently on the downswing than they did on the upswing? When macroeconomic conditions change or when policy reforms are undertaken, which institutional arrangements facilitate smooth adjustments? We need to know much more than we do about coping strategies and their determinants.

4. *Labor Market Functioning.* Labor market studies too often consist of descriptive information on rates of unemployment, employment patterns, labor supply, and earnings functions. We know too little about how labor markets actually function. How integrated or segmented are various countries' labor markets? What determines the amount of employment in each major sector or segment? What determines levels of earnings and changes in earnings in various parts of a country's labor market? How do education and labor markets interact? We need more behavioral studies of the labor markets of developing countries—in the best sense of the term—to 'get the story right'.

5. *Informal Sector.* Uncharacteristically of our profession, we talk a lot about the informal sector without having defined clearly what we mean by it. This term means many things to many people. A clear definition is needed. If the 'informal sector' consists of more than one tier, then we need to look at each tier separately and ask, Why are people in each part of the informal sector? What are the determinants of incomes in each? How might income opportunities be improved in each? Considering the costs, as well as benefits, is the solution to be found within the informal sector or outside of it?

6. *Dynamics of Growth.* After a long hiatus, economists are once again building formal theoretical models of economic growth. These models analyze various 'engines of growth' including technological change, positive externalities, human capital formation, quality upgrading, new product development, cost reductions, research and development, and international trade. Including these factors in formal models is a most welcome development. However, as with earlier formal growth models, the new models are emphasizing equilibrium growth paths, whereas the evolution of economies when they are out of equilibrium is of much more interest to development economists and policymakers. We need to adapt

these new models to the study of nonsteady state growth dynamics. We also need empirical case studies, including both successful instances of market penetration (such as textiles and electronics) and nonsuccesses. The insights from these case studies should then be used to guide further theoretical modeling efforts.

7. *Economic Mobility*. To supplement the data on changes in poverty and inequality, which give a series of snapshots, it is important also to know what happens over time to given individuals. To what extent do people move up or down within the income distribution? Which groups have higher rates of mobility than others? How much of the observed economic mobility can be accounted for by movements of individuals within a given income structure and how much by a change in the structure itself? Questions like these can be answered, but only with longitudinal data that, unfortunately, are not yet generally available for the developing countries of Asia or elsewhere. Therefore, such research must necessarily be postponed to the more distant future.

Conclusions

The main points of this paper may be summed up as follows:

• The concern with distributional aspects of economic development is motivated by a concern for broad-based growth. Measures for determining how broadly based growth has been fall into two categories: those that look at absolute changes in real incomes for the poor or other target groups, and those that compare one group's rate of income change with another's. Analysts need to decide first whether they are concerned primarily with changes in absolute poverty or in relative inequality, or whether they are equally concerned with both, for only then can they go to the available distributional statistics to see what has happened to the variables that concern them.

• The available evidence on the distributional effects of growth gives a completely different impression depending on which distributional approach is adopted. For reasons of intellectual history (such as Kuznets' pathbreaking work), economists and other social scientists devoted a great deal of attention to the effects of economic growth on relative income inequality. Notwithstanding Kuznets' hypotheses and subsequent cross-sectional evidence, we now know from current data that there is *no* relationship between economic growth and changing income inequality. Put in the terms used in the literature, not only does income distribution not *have* to get worse before it gets better, it does not even *tend* to. As for absolute poverty, the evidence is quite pronounced: nearly always when growth takes place, poverty falls; when poverty doesn't fall, it is because growth has not taken place.

• The rapid economic growth achieved by the newly industrializing economies of East Asia (Hong Kong, Republic of Korea, Singapore, and Taipei,China) has led to marked distributional improvements. These economies have had sustained records of full employment, improving job mix, rising real wages, falling absolute poverty, and low to moderate levels of income inequality. Their rates of improvement are the envy of the rest of the world.

• From country studies, we have learned that certain development policies are associated with better distributional outcomes than others. The key factors identified here are labor market policies, the distribution of education, the distribution of land, government regulation and private enterprise, and trade and industrialization strategies.

• More remains to be learned. High priority research areas are additional country studies, the determinants of constraints on choices, coping strategies of individuals and households, labor market functioning, the role of the informal sector, the dynamics of growth outside of the steady state, and economic mobility.

Acknowledgments

The comments of the participants at the Second Asian Development Bank Conference on Development Economics, in particular, Godfrey Gunatilleke, Ernesto M. Pernia, and Chalongphob Sussangkarn, are gratefully acknowledged.

Appendix

Table 4A.1

Change in Poverty and Rates of Growth, Spell Analysis

Part A: Change in Poverty and Growth Rate of GNP per Capita

Spell	Growth Rate of GNP per Capita (per cent)	Change in Poverty
Costa Rica, 1979-1982	−5.7	Poverty increased
Jamaica, 1973-1979	−5.3	Poverty increased
Bangladesh, 1966/67-1973/74	−2.3	Mixed evidence[a]
Pakistan, 1969/70-1979	1.4	Poverty decreased
Bangladesh, 1976/77-1981/82	1.6	Mixed evidence[a]
India, 1977/78-1983	2.0	Poverty decreased
Sri Lanka, 1963-1973	2.3	Poverty decreased
Sri Lanka, 1978/79-1981/82	3.0	Mixed evidence[a]
Sri Lanka, 1973-1978/79	3.0	Poverty decreased
India, 1973/74-1977/78	3.3	Poverty decreased
Mexico, 1969-1977	3.3	Poverty decreased
Malaysia, 1979-1984	3.8	Poverty decreased
Jamaica, 1968-1973	4.0	Poverty increased
Thailand, 1968/69-1975/76	4.0	Poverty decreased
Mexico, 1963-1969	4.2	Poverty decreased
Bangladesh, 1973/74-1976/77	4.3	Poverty increased
Korea, Republic of, 1976-1980	4.3	Poverty decreased
Indonesia, 1978-1980	4.5	Poverty decreased
Thailand, 1975/76-1981	4.6	Poverty decreased
Hong Kong, 1966-1971	4.8	Poverty decreased
Indonesia, 1970-1976	4.8	Poverty decreased
Thailand, 1962/63-1968/69	4.8	Poverty decreased
Indonesia, 1976-1978	5.0	Poverty decreased
Malaysia, 1976-1979	5.0	Poverty decreased
Malaysia, 1970-1976	5.2	Poverty decreased
Brazil, 1970-1980	5.7	Poverty decreased
Hong Kong, 1971-1976	6.2	Poverty decreased
Singapore, 1975-1980	6.8	Poverty decreased
Korea, Republic of, 1965-1970	7.0	Poverty decreased
Korea, Republic of, 1970-1976	7.2	Poverty decreased
Singapore, 1966-1975	8.4	Poverty decreased

(Continued next page)

Table 4A.1 *(Continued)*

Part B: Change in Poverty and Growth Rate of ICP per Capita

Spell	Growth Rate of ICP[b] per Capita (per cent)	Change in Poverty
Costa Rica, 1979-1982	−7.3	Poverty increased
Jamaica, 1973-1979	−4.0	Poverty increased
Bangladesh, 1966/67-1973/74	−1.7	Mixed evidence[a]
Sri Lanka, 1963-1973	−0.2	Poverty decreased
India, 1977/78-1983	0.8	Poverty decreased
Pakistan, 1969/70-1979	1.9	Poverty decreased
Mexico, 1958-1963	2.2	Poverty decreased
India, 1973/74-1977/78	2.5	Poverty decreased
Jamaica, 1968-1973	3.0	Poverty increased
Mexico, 1969-1977	3.0	Poverty decreased
Sri Lanka, 1973-1978/79	3.1	Poverty decreased
Bangladesh, 1973/74-1976/77	3.7	Poverty increased
Mexico, 1963-1969	4.0	Poverty decreased
Thailand, 1962/63-1968/69	4.0	Poverty decreased
Thailand, 1968/69-1975/76	4.1	Poverty decreased
Mexico, 1963-1968	4.2	Poverty decreased
Malaysia, 1979-1984	4.4	Poverty decreased
Hong Kong, 1966-1971	5.1	Poverty decreased
Indonesia, 1976-1978	6.0	Poverty decreased
Malaysia, 1976-1979	6.1	Poverty decreased
Brazil, 1970-1980	6.3	Poverty decreased
Indonesia, 1970-1976	6.5	Poverty decreased
Indonesia, 1978-1980	6.5	Poverty decreased
Hong Kong, 1971-1976	6.8	Poverty decreased
Singapore, 1975-1980	6.8	Poverty decreased
Malaysia, 1970-1976	7.8	Poverty decreased
Korea, Republic of, 1965-1970	8.0	Poverty decreased
Singapore, 1966-1975	8.6	Poverty decreased
Korea, Republic of, 1970-1976	8.8	Poverty decreased

[a] Poverty increased using one poverty line and decreased using another.
[b] International Comparison Programme.

Source: Fields, Gary, 1991. "Growth and Income Distribution." In George Psacharopoulos, ed., *Essays on Poverty, Equity, and Growth*. Oxford: Pergamon Press.

Table A4.2
Gini Coefficients in 35 Developing Economies

BAHAMAS
*Gini coefficient of income
among households*

1971	.435
1975	.523
1977	.481
1979	.625

BANGLADESH
Gini coefficient of household incomes

1968/69	.29
1973/74	.36
1976/77	.45
1981/82	.39

BRAZIL
*Gini coefficient of monetary income
among households*

1960	.53
1970	.59
1972	.61

*Gini coefficient of 'total gross personal
income' among households*

1976	.60
1978	.56
1980	.56
1983	.57

CHILE
Gini coefficient of family income

1968	.46
1971	.46

COLOMBIA
*Gini coefficient of income among
economically active persons*

1971	.57

COSTA RICA
*Gini coefficient of income
among households*

1961	.50
1971	.43
1977	.49
1979	.45
1982	.42

COTE D'IVOIRE
Gini coefficient of household income

1985	.553

EGYPT
Gini coefficient of household expenditure

1958/59	.42
1964/65	.40
1974/75	.38

EL SALVADOR
Gini coefficient of household income

1976/77	.40

FIJI
*Gini coefficient of income among
households, unadjusted*

1977	.425

HONDURAS
*Gini coefficient of income
among households*

1967/68	.62

HONG KONG
*Gini coefficient of one month income
among households:*

1966	.49
1971	.43
1976	.43
1981	.45

INDIA
*Gini coefficient of income
among households*

1975/76	.416

INDONESIA
Gini coefficient of per capita expenditure

1964	.333
1967	.327
1970	.307
1976	.318
1978	.348
1980	.318
1981	.309
1984	.308

(Continued next page)

Table A4.2 (Continued)

IRAN	1968/69 .335
Gini coefficient of annual	1969/70 .331
household income, unadjusted	1970/71 .321
1973/74 .46	1971/72 .340
	1979 .360

IRAN
Gini coefficient of annual household income, unadjusted
1973/74   .46

JAMAICA
Gini coefficient of wage inequality among wage earners
1968   .628
1973   .651
1980   .655

KOREA, REPUBLIC OF
Gini coefficient of income among households:
1965   .344
1970   .333
1976   .391
1982   .357

MALAYSIA
Gini coefficient of income among households
1957/58   .421
1970   .499
1976   .529
1979   .508
1984   .480

MEXICO
Gini coefficient of family income after tax
1958   .53
1963   .55
1969   .58
1977   .50

NEPAL
Gini coefficient of adjusted monthly household income
1976/77   .53

PAKISTAN
Gini coefficient of income among households
1963/64   .356
1966/67   .349

1968/69   .335
1969/70   .331
1970/71   .321
1971/72   .340
1979   .360

Gini coefficient of per capita household income
1979   .37
1984   .38

PANAMA
Gini coefficient of adjusted gross available income among households
1970   .57

PERU
Gini coefficient of per capita household consumption
1985/86   .31

PHILIPPINES
Gini coefficient of one month income among households
1957   .452
1961   .465
1965   .465
1971   .453
1975   .452
1985   .450

PUERTO RICO
Gini coefficient of family income
1953   .415
1963   .449
1969   .516
1979   .464

REUNION
Gini coefficient of monthly cash income among households
1976/77   .51

SEYCHELLES
Gini coefficient of gross monthly household income
1978   .46

(Continued next page)

Table A4.2 *(Continued)*

SIERRA LEONE	1972 .277
Gini coefficient of monthly	1980 .259
household income, unadjusted	1985 .271
1967/69 .59	*THAILAND*
SINGAPORE	*Gini coefficient of income,*
Gini coefficient of income	*recipient unit not reported*
among households	1962/63 .414
1972/73 .40	1968/69 .429
1977/78 .37	1975/76 .451
1982/83 .42	1981 .473
SRI LANKA	*TRINIDAD AND TOBAGO*
Gini coefficient of one month income	*Gini coefficient of monthly income*
among spending units	*among households:*
1953 .46	1971/72 .539
1963 .45	1975/76 .474
1973 .35	*TUNISIA*
1978/79 .44	*Gini coefficient of per capita*
1981/82 .45	*expenditure, adjusted*
TAIPEI,CHINA	1974/75 .404
Gini coefficient of income	*TURKEY*
among households:	*Gini coefficient of household incomes*
1953 .5 (approx.)	1968 .56
1964 .305	1973 .51

Source: Fields, Gary, 1991. "Growth and Income Distribution." In George Psacharopoulos, ed., *Essays on Poverty, Equity, and Growth.* Oxford: Pergamon Press.

Table A4.3
Changes in Labor Market Conditions and Income Distribution in Seven Small Open Economies

	Barbados		Hong Kong		Jamaica		Korea, Rep. of		Singapore		Taipei;China		Trinidad & Tobago	
I. Unemployment rate (%)	1960	12.0	1961	1.7	1960	13.5	1963	8.2	1957	5.2	1955	6.3	1970	13.0
	1966[a]	13.0	1971	4.4	1968	19.4	1967	6.2	1965	9.1	1963	4.3	1975	15.0
	1970	9.0	1976	4.3	1972	23.0	1971	4.5	1969	10.4	1972	1.5	1979	12.0
	1976	16.0	1980	3.7	1980	30.0	1976	3.9	1971	7.0	1981	1.3		
	1980	13.0					1981	4.1	1977	4.8				
									1980	3.5				
II. Employment composition														
A. Agriculture as a % of total employment	1970	21.3	1961	7.4	1972	33.4	1963	63.2	1957	6.9	1964	50.0	1970	22.7
	1975	9.9	1971	4.0	1979	33.6	1970	50.4	1970	3.5	1970	36.3	1977	13.4
			1976	2.5			1980	34.0	1979	1.5	1979	21.5		
			1980	1.4										
B. Employees as % of economically active population		—	1961	83.8		—	1963	31.5	1957	73.7	1956	36.8		—
			1971	87.3			1971	39.3	1970	76.5	1964	39.2		
			1980	89.4			1980	47.3	1979	83.5	1970	50.7		
											1979	63.7		
C. Professional & technical, administrative & managerial, clerical, and sales occupations as % of economically active population	1960	5.1	1961	27.5	1968	14.6	1963	16.9	1957	36.8	1964	22.4	1970	22
	1970	9.2	1971	26.8	1978	21.9	1970	22.9	1970	39.4	1970	26.9	1975	18
			1976	28.3			1980	29.5	1979	42.5	1979	30.0	1978	20
			1980	32.5										
D. % of employed workers with no schooling [% illiterate in brackets]		—	1961	20.2	1970	3.5	1960	44.7	1966	54.1	1965	[26.0]	1970	19.6
			1971	16.2	1979	1.7	1970	23.8	1972	20.6	1970	[20.7]	1975	21.9
			1976	13.9			1980	16.0	1977	35.2	1975	[15.9]	1979	9.2
			1980	10.4					1980	22.5	1980	[9.0]		

III. Real wages or earnings	1976 100.0[b] 1980 125.7	1960 105.0[c] 1965 157.0 1970 167.0 1975 194.0 1980 253.0	1980[d] Men 69.0 Women 76.0	1966 52.0[e] 1972 88.0 1978 154.0 1980 159.0	1966 100.0[f] 1975 100.0 1975 100.0[i] 1980 120.0	1954 100.0[g] 1960 102.0 1970 183.0 1979 400.0	1971 100.0[h] 1978 124.0
IV. Poverty	—	1966 18.0[l] 1971 11.0 1976 7.0	1968 70.0[k] 1973 72.0 1979 80.0	1965 41.0[l] 1970 23.0 1976 15.0	1966 37.0[m] 1975 29.0 1980 18.0	1964 35.0[n] 1972 10.0 1964 80.0[p]	1971/72 8.0[o] 1975/76 94.0 1971/72 19.0[q]
VI. Inequality, as measured by Gini coefficient among households [Gini coefficient among individuals in brackets]	— 1981 0.447	1966 0.487 1971 0.411 1976 0.435	1968 [0.628] 1973 [0.651] 1980 [0.655]	1964 0.34 1970 0.33 1976 0.38	1966 [0.499] 1975 [0.452] 1980 [0.455]	1950[r] 0.50 1972[s] 0.30 1978[t] 0.27	1971/72 0.5339 1975/76 0.47

— = Time series information not available.

[a] Figure for period 1965-66.
[b] Index of average real wage, 1976 = 100.
[c] Index of average real manufacturing wage, 1948 = 100.
[d] Index of average real wages, 1975 = 100.
[e] Index of real earnings, 1975 = 100.
[f] Index of real income per worker, 1966 = 100.
[g] Index of real manufacturing earnings, 1954 = 100.
[h] Index of real weekly earnings of production workers, 1971 = 100.
[i] Index of real weekly earnings, all industries, 1975 = 100.
[j] % of households with annual incomes less than HK$3,000, in constant 1966 HK$.
[k] % of labor force with weekly incomes less than J$20, in constant 1973 J$.
[l] % of households with incomes below a constant real poverty line.
[m] % of persons with incomes below S$200 per month in 1975 prices.
[n] % of households with incomes below specified figure in specified year: NT$20,000.
[o] Average income of specified group in constant 1971/72 TT$: Poorest quartile.
[p] NT$40,000.
[q] Median.
[r] Figure for early 1950's.
[s] Figure for period 1968-72.
[t] Figure for period 1976-78.

Source: Fields, G. S., 1984. " Employment, Income Distribution, and Economic Growth." *The Economic Journal* 94 (March): 74-83.

Table A4.4
Changes in Labor Market Conditions and Income Distribution
in Four Newly Industrializing Economies in the 1980s

	Hong Kong	Korea,Rep. of	Singapore	Taipei,China
I. Unemployment rate (%)				
1980	3.8	5.2	3.1	1.2
1981	3.5	4.5	2.9	1.4
1982	3.8	4.4	2.6	2.1
1983	4.1	4.1	3.2	2.7
1984	3.8	3.9	2.7	2.4
1985	3.3	4.0	4.1	2.9
1986	2.6	3.8	6.5	2.7
1987	1.9	3.1	4.7	2.0
1988	1.5	2.5	3.3	1.7
1989	1.4	2.6	2.2	1.6
1990	1.7	2.4	2.0	1.7
II. Employment composition				
A. Agriculture as a % of total employment				
1980	–	34.0	1.75	19.5
1981	2.0	34.2	1.49	18.8
1982	–	32.1	1.35	18.9
1983	–	29.7	1.34	18.6
1984	–	27.1	1.08	17.6
1985	–	24.9	1.11	17.5
1986	1.8	23.6	1.20	17.0
1987	–	21.9	.87	15.3
1988	–	20.7	.72	13.7
1989	–	19.5	.71	12.9
1990	–	18.3	.32	12.8
B. Employees as % of total employment				
1980	–	47.3	85.0	64.4
1981	88.5	47.2	85.1	64.3
1982	–	47.6	84.7	64.1
1983	–	49.5	84.3	63.8
1984	–	52.9	84.4	64.4
1985	–	54.1	84.4	64.1
1986	87.4	54.4	84.4	64.7
1987	–	56.2	84.2	66.7
1988	–	57.0	85.4	67.1
1989	–	59.1	85.6	67.4
1990	–	60.2	87.5	65.6

(Continued on next page)

Table A4.4 (Continued)

	Hong Kong	Korea,Rep. of	Singapore	Taipei,China
C. Professional & technical, administrative & managerial, clerical, and sales occupations as % of total employment				
1980	–[a]	29.0	42.9	31.8
1981	30.8	29.2	42.8	32.7
1982	–	30.6	44.2	33.1
1983	–	32.1	45.5	33.4
1984	–	32.9	46.5	33.7
1985	–	34.3	46.5	34.2
1986	37.9	34.3	46.2	34.3
1987	–	34.1	47.0	35.1
1988	–	34.6	46.1	37.2
1989	–	35.4	46.8	38.5
1990	–	36.2	60.0[b]	39.8
D. % of employed workers with no schooling				
1980	–	51.3[c]	25.2	9.8 [6.7][d]
1981	–	49.9	24.5	9.4 [6.5]
1982	–	45.7	24.9	8.9 [6.3]
1983	–	43.2	23.3	8.9 [6.5]
1984	–	39.6	20.7	8.6 [6.2]
1985	–	37.7	22.8	8.2 [6.0]
1986	–	35.6	22.1	8.0 [5.6]
1987	–	33.7	23.1	7.1 [5.1]
1988	–	31.7	19.5	6.2 [4.3]
1989	–	30.3	19.4	5.7 [3.9]
1990	–	29.3	–	5.1 [3.6]
III. Real wages or earnings				
1980	100.0[e]	100.0[f]	100.0[g]	100.0[h]
1981	102.0	98.9	105.5	102.0
1982	107.0	105.9	116.9	108.7
1983	106.0	114.6	125.9	114.1
1984	114.0	120.7	134.1	124.0
1985	119.0	129.7	146.6	129.5
1986	132.0	137.8	151.1	141.6
1987	140.0	149.0	152.9	154.8
1988	147.0	165.6	158.4	169.5
1989	155.0	195.3	170.4	186.0
1990	160.0	215.8	179.8	202.7

(Continued on next page)

Table A4.4 (Continued)

	Hong Kong	Korea,Rep. of	Singapore	Taipei,China
IV. Poverty				
1980	–[i]	4.8[j]	–[k]	30.7[l]
1981	28.5	5.3	–	32.9
1982	–	8.6	31.2[m]	32.6
1983	–	7.3	–	29.0
1984	–	6.2	–	24.9
1985	–	5.6	–	23.9
1986	18.3	5.3	26.1[n]	20.8
1987	–	5.7		18.5
1988	–	5.5		15.2
1989	–	5.6		13.4
1990	–	5.3		–

V. Inequality, as measured by Gini coefficient of income among households

	Hong Kong	Korea,Rep. of	Singapore	Taipei,China
1980	–	.3891[o]	–	0.277
1981	.414	–	–	0.281
1982	–	–	.418[p]	0.283
1983	–	–	–	0.287
1984	–	–	–	0.287
1985	–	.3449	–	0.290
1986	.388	–	–	0.296
1987	–	–	.402[q]	0.299
1988	–	–	–	0.303
1989	–	–	–	0.303
1990	–	.2886	–	0.312

[a] Hong Kong total employed includes unemployed who have previously held jobs.
[b] 1990 figures include service workers.
[c] % illiterate.
[d] % with preliminary school.
[e] Index of average real manufacturing wage.
[f] Index of average real monthly earnings in mining and manufacturing.
[g] Index of average real monthly income.
[h] Index of average monthly manufacturing earnings.
[i] % of households with monthly income less than HK$2,000, in 1981 prices.
[j] % of livelihood protection persons in total population.
[k] % of households with monthly income less than S$1,000 in 1982/83 prices.
[l] % of households with monthly income less than NT$200,000 in 1986 prices.
[m] Figure for 1982/83.
[n] Figure for 1987/88.
[o] Gini coefficient of urban income.
[p] Figure for 1982/83.
[q] Figure for 1987/88.

Source: Fields, Gary, 1993. "Changing Labor Market Conditions and Economic Development in Hong Kong, Korea, Singapore, and Taiwan." Paper prepared for the East Asian Miracle Project. Revised version. World Bank, Washington, D.C.

Table 4.5
Economic Growth and Earnings Growth in Four
Newly Industrializing Economies in the 1980s

	Growth of Real GNP or GDP Per Capita (per cent)	Growth of Real Earnings (per cent)
Korea, Republic of, 1980-90	+121.8[a]	+115.8[c]
Tapei,China, 1980-90	+88.0[a]	+102.7[d]
Hong Kong, 1980-90	+64.2[b]	+60.0[d]
Singapore, 1980-90	+77.5[b]	+79.8[e]

[a] GNP growth.
[b] GDP growth.
[c] Mining and manufacturing.
[d] Manufacturing.
[e] All industries.

Source: Fields, Gary, 1993. "Changing Labor Market Conditions and Economic Development in Hong Kong, Korea, Singapore, and Taiwan." Paper prepared for the East Asian Miracle Project. Revised version. World Bank, Washington, D.C.

Notes

1. Readers interested in learning about this topic are invited to consult Fields (forthcoming).

2. See Fields (1980, 59-77), Adelman and Robinson (1988), and Bourguignon and Morrisson (1990) for reviews of this literature.

3. See also Ahluwalia, Carter, and Chenery (1979, 466-468), Fields (1980, 77-98), and Bourguignon and Morrisson (1990).

4. See Krueger 1981; Krause 1985; Bradford 1986; Scitovsky 1986; Amsden 1990; Young 1992; World Bank 1993; and Lucas 1993.

5. For recent indepth policy studies, see the World Bank's Study: *East Asian Miracle: Economic Growth and Public Policy* (World Bank 1993), and the Asian Development Bank's rural and urban poverty studies (Quibria 1993; ADB forthcoming).

References

Adelman, I., and S. Robinson, 1988. "Income Distribution and Development." In H. Chenery and T. N. Srinivasan, eds., *Handbook of Development Economics.* Amsterdam: North-Holland Publishers.

Ahluwalia, M., 1976. "Inequality, Poverty and Development." *Journal of Development Economics* (September).

Ahluwalia, M., N. Carter, and H. Chenery, 1979. "Growth and Poverty in Developing Countries." In H. Chenery, ed., *Structural Change and Development Policy.* New York: Oxford University Press.

Alesina, A., and D. Rodrik, 1993. "Distributive Politics and Economic Growth." Harvard University and Columbia University. Mimeographed.

Amsden, A., 1990. *Asia's Next Giant: South Korea and Late Industrialization.* New York: Oxford University Press.

Asian Development Bank, forthcoming. *Urban Poverty in Asia.* Manila.

Atkinson, A., 1987. "On the Measurement of Poverty." *Econometrica* 55(4):749-64.

Balisacan, A. M., 1993. "Urban Poverty in the Philippines: Nature, Causes and Policy Measures." Paper prepared for the Asian Development Bank, Manila.

Bourguignon, F., and C. Morrisson, 1990. "Income Distribution, Development and Foreign Trade: A Cross-Sectional Analysis." *European Economic Review* 34(6):1113-32.

Bradford, C., 1986. "East Asian 'Models': Myths and Lessons." In J. P. Lewis and V. Kallab, eds., *Development Strategies Reconsidered.* Washington: Overseas Development Council.

Chen, S., G. Datt, and M. Ravallion, 1993. "Is Poverty Increasing in the Developing World?" Policy Research Working Paper Series WPS 1146. World Bank, Washington, D.C.

Drèze, J., and A. Sen, 1990. *Hunger and Public Action.* London: Oxford University Press.

Fields, G. S., 1980. *Poverty, Inequality, and Development*. New York: Cambridge University Press.

———, 1989. "A Compendium of Data on Inequality and Poverty for the Developing World." Cornell University.

———, 1991. "Growth and Income Distribution." In G. Psacharopoulos, ed., *Essays on Poverty, Equity, and Growth*. Oxford: Pergamon Press.

———, 1993. "Changing Labor Market Conditions and Economic Development in Hong Kong, Korea, Singapore, and Taiwan." Paper prepared for the East Asian Miracle Project. Revised version. World Bank, Washington, D.C.

———, forthcoming. "Data for Measuring Poverty and Inequality Changes in the Developing Countries." *Journal of Development Economics*.

Fields, G. S., and G. H. Jakubson, 1992. "New Evidence on the Kuznets' Curve." Paper presented at the Conference on Growth and Income Distribution. Paris.

Foster, J., and A. Shorrocks, 1988. "Poverty Orderings." *Econometrica* 56(1):173-7.

International Labour Organisation (ILO), annual. *Yearbook of Labour Statistics*. Geneva: ILO.

Krause, L. B., 1985. "Introduction." In W. Galenson, ed., *Foreign Trade and Investment*. Madison: University of Wisconsin Press.

Krueger, A., 1981. *Trade and Employment in Developing Countries*. Chicago: University of Chicago Press for the National Bureau of Economic Research.

Kuznets, S., 1955. "Economic Growth and Income Inequality." *American Economic Review* (March).

Lucas, R. E., Jr., 1993. "Making a Miracle." *Econometrica* 61(2):251-72.

Mijares, T. A., and L. C. Belarmino, 1973. "Some Notes on the Sources of Income Disparities Among Philippine Families." *Journal of Philippine Statistics* (September).

Okun, A. M., 1975. *Equality and Efficiency: The Big Tradeoff*. Washington: Brookings Institution.

Persson, T., and G. Tabellini, 1993. "Is Inequality Harmful for Growth?" Working Paper Number 3599. Revised version. National Bureau of Economic Research, New York.

Quibria, M. G., ed., 1993. *Rural Poverty in Asia*. Hong Kong: Oxford University Press.

Ranis, G., 1989. "The Role of Institutions in Transition Growth: The East Asian Newly Industrializing Countries." *World Development* 17(9):1443-53.

Ravallion, M., 1993. "Growth, Inequality and Poverty: New Evidence on Old Questions." World Bank, Washington, D.C.

Rawls, J., 1971. *A Theory of Justice*. Cambridge, MA: Harvard University Press.

Schultz, T. W., 1980. "Nobel Lecture: The Economics of Being Poor." *Journal of Political Economy* 88(4):639-51.

Scitovsky, T., 1986. "Economic Development in Taiwan and South Korea, 1965-1981." In L. J. Lau, ed., *Models of Development*. San Francisco: ICS Press.

Sen, A. K., 1976. "Poverty: An Ordinal Approach to Measurement." *Econometrica* 44(2):219-31.

Tabatabai, H., 1993. *The Incidence of Poverty in Developing Countries: An ILO Compendium of Data*. Geneva: International Labour Organisation.

Waldmann, R., 1992. "Inequality and Economic Growth in a Cross Section of Countries." Paper presented at the Conference on Growth and Income Distribution, Paris.

World Bank, 1993. *The East Asian Miracle: Economic Growth and Public Policy*. Washington: World Bank.

———, annual. *Social Indicators of Development*. Washington: World Bank.

———, annual. *World Development Report*. Washington: World Bank.

Young, A., 1992. "A Tale of Two Cities: Factor Accumulation and Technical Change in Hong Kong and Singapore." *NBER Macroeconomics Annual*:13-54.

Chapter Five

Rural Credit and Interlinkage: Implications for Rural Poverty, Agrarian Efficiency, and Public Policy

Kaushik Basu

Introduction

This paper is concerned with the modern theory of agrarian economic relations. Unlike most other areas, this subject developed from related findings generated by anthropologists and empirical economists, and from nonspecialist accounts from the field. The theory of agrarian economic relations has advanced rapidly during the last decade or so and is one that has many interesting open questions.

The aim of this paper is to survey the field, especially relating to rural credit and interlinkage. The survey, however, will not be an evenhanded one, but somewhat idiosyncratic, focusing on ideas where there is something new to say or where there are interesting open questions. These will be interspersed with observations from the field.

Over the last several years, I, along with some colleagues and students specializing in development, made short visits to Nawadih, a village in Bihar in eastern India. The eminent anthropologist, M. N. Srinivas once lost all of his field notes in a fire. The detailed footnotes, statistics, and data, which he had collected for a book, were all gone. What emerged was a seminal book in anthropology, *Remembered Village* (Srinivas 1976). Since one cannot always rely on fire, in Nawadih, we took no notes, or hardly any. Our aim, however, was not one of producing any major work; we treated the trips as a form of immediate exposure for the students and casual empiricism for us. We had no plans of sharing our experience with anyone. Yet, it is impossible to resist doing so altogether. During these visits we had long conversations with one small landlord—Sukur Mia.

Sukur has two *bighas* of land and being blind has no option but to treat himself as an absentee landlord. He 'chose' to lease out his land on a share-tenancy contract. It struck me that since we already knew the reasons for share tenancy given by Newbery and Stiglitz (1977), Cheung (1969), and Allen (1982, 1985)[1] it would be interesting to find out Sukur's reason since he had practiced what Newbery, Stiglitz, Cheung, and Allen had written about. The conversations turned out to be extremely instructive and drew our attention to the importance of 'limited liability' in backward agriculture and was the basis of the paper, Basu (1992).

Among the themes that run through the literature on agrarian relations, the most important must be the credit market. Its failure has been the inducement for a variety of institutions and practices. Credit has also been the instrument for monitoring other factor inputs and this has resulted in the practice of 'interlinkage' in rural markets.

As a starting point of this discussion it is useful to begin with a benchmark model. Hence, a model of interlinkage as a form of monitoring labor inputs will be presented. This gives us a lead into the credit market and allows a variety of questions to be raised.

Interlinkage as an Instrument of Monitoring

Markets are said to be interlinked if the prices of two products are determined simultaneously and agreement to buy or sell one is predicated upon the agreement to buy or sell the other. If a landlord provides employment and credit to a laborer and the wage and interest are simultaneously agreed upon then the labor market and credit market are said to be interlinked. As evidence accumulated of the great importance of interlinkage in backward markets from anthropological sources (see Bardhan 1980 for a survey) and empirical economic research (Bharadwaj and Das 1975; Bardhan and Rudra 1978), the theoretical question as to why interlinkage occurs also began generating papers (Braverman and Srinivasan 1981; Braverman and Stiglitz 1982; Basu 1983, 1987; Gupta 1987; Banerji 1993; Bose 1993).

One of the earliest theoretical ideas viewed interlinkage as an instrument for minimizing moral hazard associated with labor.[2] As is well-known, share tenancy has the moral hazard problem of the tenant trying to use less inputs, such as labor, than efficiency warrants and also than the landlord would want. Under circumstances, such as these, it is natural for the landlord to look for instruments to monitor the labor input used by the tenant. A number of economists (notably Braverman and Stiglitz

1982; and Mitra 1983) have argued that interlinkage may be one such instrument. Hence this may be a rationale for the existence of factor-market linkage.

The essential idea behind the model of Braverman and Stiglitz (1982) is not difficult to convey. Suppose that output, X, from a plot of land depends on the amount of effort, e, used, and a stochastic variable, θ, which has expected value equal to 1. For simplicity, this can be treated as a multiplicative risk. Thus

$$X = \theta f(e), \; f' > 0, \; f'' < 0 \tag{1}$$

Hence, if e is the amount of effort used, the expected output is $f(e)$.

In this region, we shall assume, the prevalent tenurial arrangement is that of share tenancy, where the landlord's share of output is $(1-\alpha)$ and this is fixed by custom. As we have already seen, in a situation such as this the landlord would like to coax the tenant to use more effort. However, it is reasonable to assume that effort cannot be directly monitored by the landlord, nor can it be deduced from the level of output. The latter is true because of the stochastic element in the production function, which means that a low output may be the consequence of low effort or poor weather resulting in a low θ.

There is, however, an indirect method of control that the landlord can adopt. If the tenant can be induced to take a lot of credit, then the tenant may be forced to work harder in order to repay the debt and, in the process, contribute more to the landlord's rental income. But to induce the tenant to borrow more, the landlord may be compelled to lend money to the tenant, for instance, at a subsidized rate. And hence, the result is a model of interlinkage.

To illustrate this formally, assume there are two periods. The first is the lean period where the tenant's (or laborer's) only consumption is whatever is borrowed. In period two, the tenant keeps the designated share of the output, repays debts, and that determines consumption. Thus, a tenant's utility function is

$$u = u(c_1, c_2, e)$$

where c_i is consumption in period i and e is the effort put in. If B units are borrowed at an interest rate i, then we could write the utility function more specifically as

$$u = u(B, \alpha\theta f(e) - (1+i)B, e) \tag{2}$$

Since the objective is to show that under some parametric configurations interlinkage may occur, there is no harm if we work with a special utility function. I therefore assume that (2) takes the following form:

$$u = \sqrt{B} + \alpha\theta\sqrt{e} - (1+i)B - ke \quad \text{where } k > 0 \tag{3}$$

It is assumed throughout that the tenant will always expect to be able to repay the debt in period two. That is, the tenant will choose e and B so that

$$\alpha\sqrt{e} - (1+i)B \geq 0 \tag{4}$$

Hence, in the long run the tenant is able to repay the debt. This may be justified by the implicit assumption that there are suitable penalties for nonrepayment of debt.[3]

If we assume that individuals can borrow money freely (the source is not important) at an interest rate of i, then the tenant's problem is to maximize the expected value of (3) by choosing B and e, subject to (4). To solve this, first ignore (4) and maximize (3). This gives us the following first order conditions:

$$\frac{1}{2\sqrt{B}} - (1+i) = 0 \tag{5}$$

and

$$\frac{\alpha}{2\sqrt{e}} - k = 0 \tag{6}$$

(5) and (6) imply

$$B = \frac{1}{4(1+i)^2} \tag{7}$$

and

$$e = \frac{\alpha^2}{4k^2} \tag{8}$$

Inserting (7) and (8) in (4) we see that (4) would be binding if i is such that

$$2(1+i)\alpha^2 - k < 0 \tag{9}$$

Hence if (9) were true then (4) would hold as an equality and $B = \alpha\sqrt{e}/(1+i)$. Inserting this in (3) we get

$$u = \sqrt{\frac{\alpha\sqrt{e}}{1+i}} - ke$$

Maximizing this with respect to e we get the following first order condition:

$$B = \left(\frac{1}{4k}\right)^{2/3} \left(\frac{\alpha}{1+i}\right)^{4/3} \tag{10}$$

and

$$e = \left(\frac{1}{4k}\right)^{4/3} \left(\frac{\alpha}{1+i}\right)^{2/3} \tag{11}$$

Hence, if (9) were true, the tenant's choice of B and e would be given by (10) and (11); and if (9) were not true, B and e would be given by (7) and (8). The above sentence sums up the tenant's behavior. Hence the landlord has to take account of it in making decisions.

Let us assume that there is a competitive credit market from which anybody can borrow and lend at an interest rate r. It is being assumed here that there is no default and no individual can influence r. In order to focus on this interesting case, we shall also assume

$$2(1+ r)\alpha^2 - k < 0 \tag{12}$$

Now the landlord has to take a decision whether to offer a simple tenancy contract or a tenancy-cum-credit contract, that is, an interlinked contract. The purpose of this model is to demonstrate that under certain conditions the tenant will prefer the latter.

To work out what the landlord would choose, let us determine the profit to be gained if an interlinked contract is offered. Suppose that for entering an agreement, the landlord offers a potential tenant the opportunity to borrow as much money as needed, at an interest rate of i, from the landlord. Of course, i has to be no greater than r because otherwise no tenant would borrow from the landlord. Hence the landlord's profit is

$$\pi(i) = (1-\alpha)\sqrt{e} - (r-i)B, \tag{13}$$

where e and B are given by (10) and (11) and not by (7) and (8), because $i \le r$ which implies that (9) must be true (since (12) is true).

The landlord's aim is to maximize $\pi(i)$ by choosing any $i \le r$. Using (10) and (11) we get

$$\pi(i) = \left[(1-\alpha) - (r-i)\frac{\alpha}{1+i}\right]\sqrt{e}$$

$$= \frac{1+i - (1+r)\alpha}{(1+i)^{4/3}} \cdot \frac{\alpha^{1/3}}{(4k)^{2/3}}$$

Hence,

$$\frac{\partial \pi(i)}{\partial i} = 0 \text{ if and only if } (1+i) = 4\alpha (1+r) \qquad (14)$$

If $\alpha < \frac{1}{4}$, then $i < r$ in equilibrium.

Note from (13) that the profit that the landlord would earn if a pure tenancy contract was offered is the same as the profit that would have been earned from an interlinked contract with $i=r$. Hence $\pi(r)$ is the landlord's profit from a pure tenancy contract. Assume $\alpha < \frac{1}{4}$. Hence if $i^* = argmax \ \pi(i)$, then $\pi(i^*) > \pi(r)$ and $i^* < r$. Hence the landlord *prefers* to offer an interlinked contract.[4]

By offering an interlinked deal the landlord gives credit at subsidized rates and thus makes a loss in this. But this loss is more than made up for by the extra effort that the landlord manages to eke out of the tenant by using this method.

There are enough assumptions in the model of Braverman and Stiglitz. We have added more to these in order to simplify the analysis and to bring out the essential idea. Some of the features, like (4), could have been changed but at the cost of greater complexity. What the above rendering does is to bring out an important general point. In a general equilibrium it may at times be in the interest of some agents to have compulsions imposed on them that prevent moral hazard. In other words, even though laborers would choose to work less, if they had the option, they may prefer to be forced to work more, because they end up better off (through the workings of the market).

Worker Sovereignty and Worker Welfare: A Digression

The final observation of the previous section is important and has policy ramifications that go beyond agrarian markets. This section is a digression meant to elaborate on the observation and to bring out its general policy importance.

Consider a competitive labor market. Purely for reasons of algebraic simplicity, we assume that there is only one landlord or employer and mimic competition by simply assuming that the landlord/employer is a wagetaker.[5] If n workers are employed and each worker puts in an effort of c units, the employer will get a total output of X, given by

$$X = g(ne), g' > 0, g'' < 0,$$

where g is the production function.

Suppose there are N identical workers who always prefer to be employed rather than unemployed. Hence labor supply is inelastic at N. A laborer can choose to put in any amount of effort e from within the feasible interval $[\underline{e}, \bar{e}]$. If $e' > e''$, we say that at e' the laborer is working harder than at e''. Effort or hard work here does not refer to the hours of work, which may be assumed to be fixed. It refers to the amount of efficiency or initiative that is put into the work.

The laborer's welfare depends on the effort put in and the wage received. Hence,

$$u = u(e, w), u_e < 0, u_w > 0$$

The landlord's aim is to maximize profit $g(ne) - wn$.

In this model, a laborer's effort is observable but, for social and political reasons, it may not be enforceable. Suppose, for instance, that the only way to force a worker to work harder is to use the threat of discharge. Now, if discharging workers is prohibited by law or custom then this threat is ineffective and clearly each worker will put in only $\underline{e}$ units of effort. Consider first the case where the landlord or the employer cannot enforce workers to put in specified levels of effort. Then his problem is the following:

$$\underset{n}{Max}\ g(n\underline{e}) - wn$$

From the first order condition we get

$$g'(n\underline{e})\underline{e} = w \tag{15}$$

Hence $n = n(w)$. In the final equilibrium, demand for labor $n(w)$ must be equal to the supply of labor. Hence, w must be such that

$$g'(N\underline{e})\underline{e} \equiv \underline{w} \tag{16}$$

Thus in equilibrium each laborer's welfare level is $u(\underline{e}, \underline{w})$.

Suppose now that employers are allowed to *force* workers to work harder. At first, this looks like an antilabor change. But actually this may benefit the workers and workers may *want* to relinquish their freedom to indulge in moral hazard. Suppose employers compel workers to put in e' units of effort where $\underline{e} < e' \le \bar{e}$. Then, in equilibrium the wage would be w', given by

$$g'(Ne')e' = w' \tag{17}$$

And each laborer's welfare would be $u(e',w')$. This may well be greater than $u(\underline{e}, \underline{w})$. To see this, assume that

$$g(ne) = ane - \frac{b}{2}(ne)^2$$

with $a, b > 0$.

Hence,

$$g'(ne) = a - bne$$

Since in equilibrium e and w are connected by the following

$$g'(Ne)e = w,$$

we have

$$ae - bNe^2 = w$$

This is given by the inverted-U curve in Figure 5.1.

Figure 5.1

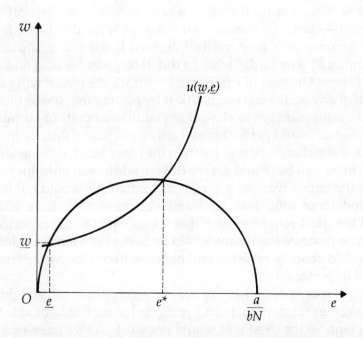

Let $\underline{e}$ be as shown in the figure. Then $\underline{w}$ is easily read by going vertically above $\underline{e}$ until the inverted-U curve as shown in the figure is reached. Clearly then, as e is raised to e' the workers' welfare rises above $u\,(\underline{w}, \underline{e})$ as long as $e' < e^*$. If $\bar{e}$ happens to be less than e^*, then allowing the employer to raise worker effort to as high as feasible, to wit $\bar{e}$, benefits the workers. It results in the reduction of poverty. This exposes a policy dilemma, with worker sovereignty and worker welfare pulling in different directions.[6]

The advantage of the monitoring model discussed above, apart from its power of explaining interlinkage, is that it gives us a preview of many of the most important topics in agrarian economic relations—share tenancy and credit markets for example.

Tenancy

In the model of Braverman and Stiglitz (1982), the tenurial arrangement between the landlord and the laborer is *assumed* to be one of share tenancy or sharecropping. That makes sense because a perusal of this sharecropping literature suggests that explaining why share tenancy exists, instead of simply assuming it to exist, may indeed be a hazardous venture for a researcher. Yet the question is important and, as a result, has generated a large literature.[7]

Hence, it is useful to bring information from the field and to record recent theoretical work that explains the assumption in the model of the previous section. Let us therefore return to where we left off in the introduction—the conversation with Sukur of Nawadih. Being familiar with the arguments of economists, I decided to ask Sukur, a practicing 'share landlord', why he did what he did. If he gives his land on a share-tenancy contract instead of a fixed-rent contract, the tenant will get only a fraction of any additional output. So if by putting in more fertilizers or labor the tenant manages to eke out ten additional units of output from the land, Sukur would get for himself only a fraction of this, for instance, five units, if the share rent was half. On the other hand, if the tenant was paying a fixed rent he would get the full ten additional units for himself. Hence, if the tenant were on a fixed-rent contract, he would put in more inputs and innovation into land and get more output. So if Sukur adjusted the fixed-rent level such that it was equal to the expected rent under share tenancy, the tenant would be better off. Hence, under fixed rent, he could actually raise the rent higher without losing the tenant so he would be better off.

Sukur's response was that this was a region prone to droughts and general weather fluctuation. In bad years, no tenant would be able to pay the fixed rent. So the fixed rent would not work. As we cross-examined him further, no doubt leading him to believe that our immense interest in this 'pointless' subject was evidence of some pathology on our part, it became clear that what he was pointing to was similar to the 'limited liability' clause in the finance and banking literature (see, for example, Stiglitz and Weiss 1981). In years of drought, if the tenant's financial position drops too low then the landlord cannot collect what is contractually due to him or, in other words, every contract was underwritten by a limited liability clause.

In Basu (1992), I assumed this to be true, and then, checked which tenurial form was dominant from the landlord's point of view. Interestingly enough, sharecropping turned out to be the preferable option.

This has important implications for policy, but before going into that we want to briefly question whether 'limited liability' is a reasonable assumption in agrarian economics. The use of this axiom is in no sense a novel one. Beside Basu (1992), Kotwal (1985) and Shetty (1988) have used it in an agrarian context. But how real is the assumption?

This is difficult to answer because there is little systematic data on this, one way or the other. Since many of our empirical interests arise out of prior theoretical interests and since limited liability in agrarian theory is a relatively recent idea, it is not surprising that no systematic data is readily available. However, whatever piecemeal evidence I have been able to collect, either by conversing with farmers or through reading, seems to confirm that landlords or moneylenders do forego their dues when the tenant or the borrower falls on real hard times. The pressure of custom seems to compel landlords and moneylenders to do so and rent or repayment remission are not acts of occasional altruism.

There is also reason to believe that the limited liability axiom has also been historically valid. Recent research by Atchi Reddy (1990) has unearthed a large number of tenancy contracts from the Nellore district dating back to the first half of the nineteenth century. This data source lends support to the belief that limited liability and bankruptcy clauses are not primarily the preserve of twentieth century industrialized nations but were often formally written into tenancy contracts in rural India.

Two examples from Atchi Reddy's rich data source may be cited. On 21 November 1834, Konderaju Parvathamma signed a tenancy agreement, *maktha kaul*, to lease her land to Badela Pitchivadue. After specifying little details like 'you should cart the paddy to my residence in Nellore town for which the hire charges are Rs 1.00,' the landlady goes on to state, 'In cases of total failure of the crops due to lack of rains or floods, the tenant need not pay the rent but only the land revenue Rs 9.00'.[8] Likewise when in 1868, Mula Anki Reddy leased out his 20.5 acres to Malireddy Ramireddy, the tenancy agreement said that 'He [the tenant] need not pay anything in years of severe famines . . . .'

Crossing over from Nellore in the early eighteenth century to Hereford-shire around the same time one finds evidence of concessions in times of distress. To quote from the dissertation of Eric Jones (1962, 389-90):

In spells of agricultural distress most landowners preferred to remit a proportion of their farm rents or to grant allowances designed to raise the productivity of the farms rather than reduce the nominal level of rent. This, they believed, would serve to placate the tenants, help them to ride out the depression and also have the advantage of appearing as a gratuity, the more prized because it might be withheld.

Again (Jones 1962, 392),

> The next spate of remissions began in 1829. From early that year until early in 1831 there were reports of landowners remitting some of their rent, usually 10%, sometimes 20%, and in the case of a single farm at Much Marcle, 30%. These allowances were specifically made as compensation for the low prices of 1828, '29 and '30.

These are just a few from a variety of such examples quoted in Jones' thesis. Before moving on, observe one difference between Herefordshire and Nellore. In the former, the rent remissions seem to be discretionary whereas in Nellore they appear to be contractual. The difference is, however, not as sharp as it appears at first blush since in the Nellore contracts terms like 'severe famine' and 'total failure of crops' are not well-defined, thereby giving the landlord the discretion of deciding whether a crop failure is quite 'total'.

Now assume that the limited liability clause underlies all contracts. That is, no matter what contract is used, the tenant has the right to renege on making payment if the harvest fails totally. Notice that, given such an assumption, the tenant will have a tendency to select riskier projects because the failure of a project does not hurt the tenant as much as it would in the absence of the limited liability axiom. Since such risk taking will go against the landlord's interest, the landlord will try to devise a contract that steers the tenant to choose less risky projects and thereby minimizes the tension between the landlord's and the tenant's interests. If we consider the spectrum of contracts from share tenancy to fixed-rent tenancy, via all mixtures of the two, it can be shown that it is share tenancy that minimizes this tension.

From this explanation of share tenancy some testable propositions emerge.

1. Share tenancy is more likely in areas where output is relatively weather dependent, that is, where irrigation and flood control does not mitigate the severity of exposure to the fluctuations of the weather.
2. It will also be more likely in areas where technology is relatively fixed in coefficients, that is, there is not much scope for substitution between land and other factors.
3. Share tenancy will tend to wither away as a region becomes well off, because the limited liability clause will then not have much bite since everybody will have enough buffer wealth not to be able to invoke the bankruptcy cover in the event of harvest failures.

Arguments based on limited liability also have important implications for poverty. Though this is not clear from the examples cited above it is arguable that the question of rent remission arises only when the tenant is sufficiently poor. In other words, even during times of drought a sufficiently well-off tenant would not be allowed to forego his contractual payments. If this were so, it seems possible that it is the wealthier tenants who would be more coveted because the landlords would not have to forego rents as easily with them as with the poorer tenants. This is not an argument without pitfalls because a poorer tenant may try to offset this disadvantage by offering a higher rent. But to the extent that rent variations are not always practically feasible, the poor may indeed be at a disadvantage. Tenancy, instead of mitigating the problem of poverty, may well magnify the inequities of the system.

The availability of credit can, it seems, offset some of these inequities of the market. However, a closer analysis of credit markets, in particular interventions in rural credit markets, suggests that there is a lot more that can be done on this front.

Credit

Credit is a subject that is closely related to limited liability and was an integral part of the model of Braverman and Stiglitz. In fact, the credit market and its distortions lie at the heart of a variety of rural practices and institutions.[9]

It is not difficult to see why credit markets function poorly. There is one important way in which credit transactions are different from other transactions and exchange. By its very nature, in a credit transaction the exchange is protracted over a long stretch of time. Unlike in the market for potatoes where with one hand you give the money and with the other you collect the potatoes (assuming that the readers are potato buyers rather than potato sellers), in the credit market the buyer of credit first gets the desired good (such as credit) and then after a certain lapse of time, which could be a few months or even a few years, pays the supplier the price (that is, the principal plus interest). Hence, the implicit assumption in much of economics—that individuals adhere to contracts— becomes particularly questionable in credit markets where the borrower has scope for reneging on the contract and not repaying.[10] This has to be kept in mind when commenting on rural credit markets.

One of the more enduring features of rural credit markets is that a formal loan, or what is alternatively called organized credit, typically tends to elude the poorest people. There is now much systematic evidence on this (see, for example, Sarap 1991) and it stood out starkly during our field visits to the village of Nawadih. Nawadih is a village where one sees some presence of government. There are farmers who have taken government loans and sunk wells or, in the case of two households, obtained gobar gas plants. There are some skeleton medical facilities available in the nearby town of Suriya. Yet, what stands out as soon as one begins to get familiar with village life is that all of these services seem to be for the relatively better-off people. The poorest farmers live *as if* there were no government.[11]

Unlike the wealthier farmers, the poor ones are always borrowing money from private moneylenders with interest rates varying between 5 and 10 per cent per month. There are two reasons for this. Formal lenders, like bank officials need to show on paper what the borrower's permanent address is, what collateral the borrower is able to offer, and other evidence of the loan being safe.[12] These are difficult to justify in the case of footloose, landless, or near landless laborers and so bankers are unwilling to give credit because repayment is difficult to guarantee.

On the other hand, the local moneylender or landlord uses personal links and relationships to ensure that the borrowers, even the poor ones, will not be able to renege on repayment and are therefore willing to lend to the poorest. The second reason why the poor do not get organized sector credit is more surprising—they do not want it. This came out clearly in Nawadih and, after repeated questioning, it became clear that the bureaucratic hurdles and corruption involved in getting official credit is what thwarted the poor farmers from approaching the organized sector. Using data collected by Sarap (1991), we have tried to show else-where (Basu 1990) how bureaucratic red tape is shorter for richer farmers. The reason for this involves issues complicated by triadic interactions.

This phenomenon—the poor relying on the free market and the better off using the facilities provided by the government—plays a major role in exacerbating problems of equity. Official data released by the Reserve Bank of India show that the share of organized credit in the rural sector has grown rapidly in India over the last few decades.[13] Given that this credit is available at interest rates as low as 10 per cent or even 6 per cent *per annum* and that it is quite common all over India for the poor to get their credit at much higher rates of 5 to 10 per cent *per month*; this means an effective subsidy for the middle and upper class farmers. Bangladesh's experience suggests that if we want cheap credit not only to reach the rural sector, but also the poorest sections of the rural sector, then much more grassroots activism is needed.

Triadic Relations

In models of interlinkage, a landlord transacts with a laborer on two fronts—labor and credit—and the terms of each one depends on the other. There is, however, another way in which different markets can get linked together. Suppose a landless person or a marginal farmer sells personal labor to a landlord and borrows money from a moneylender. On the face of it, these are two separate transactions and there is no reason to expect any connection between the prices of the two transactions, to wit, the wage rate and the interest rate.

However, in small village communities, where everybody knows everybody, it may be possible for the landlord to use personal influence over the moneylender to threaten the laborer. For example, a laborer who turns down the landlord's offer will lose out with the moneylender as well, because the moneylender will refuse to lend. The landlord can make this threat effective either by threatening to cut off trading relations with the moneylender if the moneylender lends money to the laborer after the laborer turned down the landlord's employment offer, or by simply relying on the goodwill among the rich.

In such a situation, the labor market deal and the credit market deal do get linked, not via the normal interlinkage argument but via the mediation of a third person—in the above example, the moneylenders. Since such phenomena cannot occur if all interactions are two-person interactions and hinge crucially on there being a third (and possibly more) persons, such interactions are described as *triadic* interactions (Basu 1986, 1990; Platteau and Abraham 1987).

Unlike in our textbooks, triadic interactions are, in reality, extremely important. When the United States threatened Bangladesh that it would not transact with Bangladesh unless Bangladesh ceased to trade with Cuba (as happened in 1974), this was a case of triadic interaction. In international relations one sees repeated instances of this.

Likewise, this is a common phenomenon in village societies. It is easy not to recognize this occurrence because the threats are often such a part of everyday life that they do not need to be articulated and seldom have to be carried out; but as we tried to argue in Basu (1986), they do influence prices.

To understand this, suppose the landlord offers a wage of w for a fixed amount of work. Will the worker accept this? The answer depends on what we believe will happen if the worker rejects it. In a standard model, if a worker rejects the wage offer, there is no interaction with the landlord and that is what determines the worker's reservation utility. In a triadic model, a worker, by rejecting the landlord's offer, risks losing out not just on the transaction with the landlord but with others, such as the moneylender, who wishes to please the landlord. Hence, the worker reaches a lower utility than would be reached in a textbook model. Since the landlord knows this, w will be set very low knowing that the worker will take it since the consequence of rejecting it is so drastic.

Hence triadic interactions allow for greater extortion by the rich and the powerful. This could also help us understand why rich borrowers get a better deal from banks and the officials of organized sector credit. Even if the village bank official has no other dealings with the village landlord except the giving and taking of credit, there may be 'third persons' with whom both the landlord and the bank official have dealings. This could be the local doctor, the headmaster of the school, or the village merchant. The bank official could get hurt via these people if the landlord is displeased. The interest rate cannot be varied because it is generally fixed by a faraway government, but the bribes can be lowered, the red tape cut, and the enforcement of loan repayment relaxed.

In terms of policy, the conclusions must be drawn carefully. Given the aberrations of the market, it would be worthwhile if government can intervene with optimal policies. However, one has to keep in mind that the government officials who have to administer and deliver the goods will themselves come under the pressures of the market and, depending on the circumstances, they could curb inequity and increase efficiency, but the opposite could happen as well. Government clearly cannot shake off its responsibility and has a major role to play in backward rural areas. But in designing its intervention it is important for government to realize that it is not immune to the bugs that caused the original distortion. Such awareness will improve the chances of success.

Acknowledgments

The author is grateful to Angus Deaton, Jean Drèze, Raul Fabella, Eric Jones, Mokhtar Tamin, and M. A. Taslim for helpful comments.

Notes

1. For surveys of the sharecropping literature, see Singh (1989) and Taslim (1992).

2. For surveys of other kinds of motivation for interlinkage and the nature of contractual arrangements, see Basu (1990), Bell (1988), and Binswanger and Rosenzweig (1984).

3. If (4) holds as an equality, 'consumption' in period two is zero. This may

trouble some readers but we simply need to define 'consumption' as consumption over and above subsistence. Hence zero 'consumption' means subsistence consumption on the right-hand side of (4). If an equivalent correction is then made in (2) the entire algebra remains unchanged.

4. It is often claimed that in reality $\alpha = \frac{1}{2}$. First, this is empirically contestable (Sharma and Drèze, 1990). Secondly, numbers, like $\alpha < \frac{1}{4}$, should not be taken literally. This was chosen in the model for algebraic simplicity and not for empirical realism. It is easy to see that the model can be reconstructed to get empirically realistic solutions.

5. More accurately, we assume the landlord to be a taker of the workers' reservation utility, u (defined below). When e is fixed, this amounts to wage-taking behavior.

6. Fields (1993) discusses a very similar problem.

7. Apart from the references already cited, see Rao (1971), Otsuka and Hayami (1988), Quibria and Rashid (1984), Eswaran and Kotwal (1985), and Bardhan (1984).

8. This is not exactly the same as the assumption that says that only that part of the rent will be foregone that allows the tenant to have some predetermined level of consumption. The author is grateful to Angus Deaton for this observation.

9. Bangladesh's successful 'credit scheme', the Grameen Bank project, was founded on precisely this understanding that rural credit is central to what happens in rural economies and to solve 'the problem of credit' would amount to improving overall living standards. It must, however, be pointed out that the Grameen Bank, as conceived by Mohammed Yunus, is more than a credit program; it combines some minimal effort at raising literacy, community development, and improving the status of women.

10. In Basu (1983) this is called 'potential risk' and interlinkage is explained as a direct response to this. This is also the reason for the widely observed phenomenon of market fragmentation in credit markets (see, for example, Swaminathan 1991).

11. The one exception is the employment program, Jawahar Rozgar Yojana. The JRY is the new name for the National Rural Employment Program, which in turn was the revised name of the Food for Work Program started on an all-India basis from 1977. The frequent changes in the name of this program is testimony to the fact that it has met with some marginal success and hence each new government, by restarting it under a new name, tries to create the illusion that it has initiated the program. In Nawadih, one sees the poorest people working on roadmaking projects under the JRY. These roads are usually so poorly constructed that each year after the rains the same job is once again available.

12. This need not mean that the loan *is* safe. The table below, consisting of data pertaining to formal credit, and constructed out of a larger table of Sarap (1991), confirms what Lipton (1976) had earlier reported from other parts of the world, that the largest borrowers are the largest defaulters.

The table suggests that default behavior is U-shaped with the smallest and largest farmers being the big defaulters, which, at least on the face of it, seems to support Bhaduri's (1983) thesis of how the poor and the rich behave similarly to each other and differently from the middle class, with the poor being compelled to do what the rich choose to do.

Size of borrower's land holdings (in acres)	Overdues as % of total loan outstanding by group	% of loan defaulted by the group to total loan defaulted
Up to 2.5	76	11
2.5-5	54	16
5-10	19	11
10 and above	81	62

13. The share of organized credit among all rural credit in India was 14.87 per cent in 1961, 29.2 per cent in 1971, and 61.2 per cent in 1981.

References

Allen, F., 1982. "On Share Contracts and Screening." *Bell Journal of Economics* 13(2):541-47.

———, 1985. "On the Fixed Nature of Sharecropping Contracts." *Economic Journal* 95(377):30-48.

Atchi Reddy, M., 1990. "Tenancy in Nellore District: 1833-1984." Hyderabad. Mimeographed.

Banerji, S., 1993. "Interlinkage, Investment and Adverse Selection." Jadavpur University. Mimeographed.

Bardhan, P. K., 1980. "Interlocking Factor Markets and Agrarian Development: A Review." *Oxford Economic Papers* 32(1):82-98.

———, 1984. *Land, Labour and Rural Poverty.* New York: Columbia University Press; Delhi: Oxford University Press.

———, ed., 1989. *The Economic Theory of Agrarian Institutions.* Oxford: Clarendon Press.

Bardhan, P. K., and Rudra A., 1978. "Interlinkage of Land, Labour and Credit Relations: An Analysis of Village Survey Data in East India." *Economic and Political Weekly* 13 (February).

Basu, K., 1983. "The Emergence of Isolation and Interlinkage in Rural Markets." *Oxford Economic Papers* 35(2):262-80.

———, 1986. "One Kind of Power." *Oxford Economic Papers* 38(2):259-82.

———, 1987. "Disneyland Monopoly, Interlinkage and Usurious Interest Rates." *Journal of Public Economics* 34(1):1-17.

———, 1990. *Agrarian Structure and Economic Underdevelopment.* Chur: Harwood Press.

———, 1992. "Limited Liability and the Existence of Share Tenancy." *Journal of Development Economics* 39(1):203-20.

Bell, C., 1988. "Credit Markets and Interlinked Transactions." In H. Chenery and T. N. Srinivasan, eds., *Handbook of Development Economics*. Amsterdam: North-Holland.

Bhaduri, A., 1983. *The Economic Structure of Backward Agriculture*. London: Academic Press.

Bharadwaj, K., and P. K. Das, 1975. "Tenurial Conditions and Modes of Exploitation: A Study of Some Villages in Orissa." *Economic and Political Weekly* (Annual Number) 10 (February).

Binswanger, H., and M. Rosenzweig, eds., 1984. *Contractual Arrangements, Employment and Wages in Rural Labor Markets in Asia*. New Haven: Yale University Press.

Bose, G., 1993. "Interlinked Contracts and Moral Hazard in Investment." *Journal of Development Economics* 41(2):247-73.

Braverman, A., and T. N. Srinivasan, 1981. "Credit and Sharecropping in Agrarian Societies." *Journal of Development Economics* 9(3):289-312.

Braverman, A., and J. E. Stiglitz, 1982. "Sharecropping and the Interlinking of Agrarian Markets." *American Economic Review* 72(4):695-715.

Cheung, S. N. S., 1969. *The Theory of Share Tenancy*. Chicago: Chicago University Press.

Eswaran, M., and A. Kotwal, 1985. "A Theory of Two-Tier Labour Markets in Agrarian Economies." *American Economic Review* 75(1): 162-77.

Fields, G. S., 1993. "Income Distribution in Developing Economies: Conceptual, Data and Policy Issues in Broad-Based Growth." Delta and Cornell University. Mimeographed.

Gupta, M. R., 1987. "A Nutrition-Based Theory of Interlinkage." *Journal of Quantitative Economics* 3(2):189-202.

Jones, E. L., 1962. "The Evolution of High Farming, 1815-65 with Reference to Herefordshire." D. Phil. diss., Oxford University.

Kotwal, A., 1985. "Consumption, Credit and Agricultural Tenancy." *Journal of Development Economics* 18(2-3):273-95.

Lipton, M., 1976. "Agricultural Finance and Rural Credit in Poor Countries." *World Development* 4(7):543-53.

Mitra, P., 1983. "A Theory of Interlinked Rural Transactions." *Journal of Public Economics* 20(2):167-91.

Newberry, D. M. G., and J. Stiglitz, 1977. "Risk-Sharing, Sharecropping and Uncertain Labour Markets." *Review of Economic Studies* 44(3):585-94.

Otsuka, K., and Y. Hayami, 1988. "Theories of Share Tenancy: A Critical Survey." *Economic Development and Cultural Change* 37(1):31-68.

Platteau, J. P., and A. Abraham, 1987. "An Inquiry into Quasi-Credit Contracts: The Role of Reciprocal Credit and Interlinked Deals in Small-Scale Fishing Communities." *Journal of Development Studies* 23(4):461-90.

Quibria, M. G., and S. Rashid, 1984. "The Puzzle of Sharecropping: A Survey of Theories." *World Development* 12:103-14.

Rao, C. H. H., 1971. "Uncertainty, Entrepreneurship, and Sharecropping in India." *Journal of Political Economy* 79(3):578-95.

Sarap, K., 1991. *Interlinked Agrarian Markets in Rural India*. New Delhi: Sage.

Sharma, N., and J. Drèze, 1990. "Sharecropping in Palanpur." Working Paper 30. London School of Economics, London.

Shetty, S., 1988. "Limited Liability, Wealth Differences and Tenancy Contracts in Agrarian Economics." *Journal of Development Economics* 29(1):1-22.

Singh, N., 1989. "Theories of Sharecropping." In P. K. Bardhan, ed., *The Economic Theory of Agrarian Institution*. Oxford: Clarendon Press.

Srinivas, M. N., 1976. *Remembered Village*. Berkeley: University of California Press.

Stiglitz, J., and A. Weiss, 1981. "Credit Rationing in Markets with Imperfect Information." *American Economic Review* 71(3):393-410.

Swaminathan, M., 1991. "Segmentation, Collateral Undervaluation and the Rate of Interest in Agrarian Credit Market." *Cambridge Journal of Economics* 15(2):161-78.

Taslim, M. A., 1992. "A Survey of Theories of Cropshare Tenancy." *Economic Record* 68(202):254-75.

Chapter Six

Is Land Reform Passé?
With Special Reference
to Asian Agriculture

Salim Rashid and M.G. Quibria

Introduction

Of the approximately one billion people who live in absolute poverty, some 750 million live in rural Asia.[1] In a rural economy, the most important asset is land and a major policy instrument to alleviate rural poverty is land reform. In the immediate post World War II era, the United States encouraged land reform in the Republic of Korea and Taipei,China, for example, and in the 1970s, Latin American land reform plans aroused major interest. Today, however, we find land reform to be a minority, if not minor, vision. Were the earlier economic arguments for land reform incorrect or were they based on an inadequate understanding of the political process? Why have texts on economic development relegated land reform from a major participant in the process of societal development to one of the 'also-ran'? Has a deeper understanding of economic and political realities led to land reform becoming passé? In any issue of public policy a multiplicity of considerations is involved. Weighing the relative importance of each aspect is a vital part of any policy recommendation. We shall argue that the earlier arguments were not so much incorrect as incomplete—both in terms of economics and of political economy. If land reform is to gain importance as public policy, the case has to be made anew.

The term, land reform, has been used in many different senses. For our purpose, we shall define it to encompass both land distribution and tenancy reforms. (Land consolidation and land titling or colonization will not be considered.) Land reform in the former sense entails the distribution of land from households with landholdings higher than a stipulated upper limit to households owning little or no land, or the granting of ownership rights to the current tillers. Land reform in the latter sense entails changing the terms and conditions defining the tenancy contract. While the primary, and older, sense refers to the redistribution of land, the secondary sense, which refers to changes in agricultural tenancy laws, has, since the 1950s, become closely associated with the older meaning. Both uses have now become standard.[2]

Land reform, especially in the sense of redistribution of land, involves interference with the most basic feature of capitalism—the sanctity of private property. If one is willing to go back far enough in time, it can be argued that virtually every collection of property rights currently considered legal can be traced to the use of force. If land reform is seen as a way of redressing recent usurpations of land, let this be handled directly as a police matter. If the goal is to effect a transfer of political power, then land reform is undoubtedly a potent policy. Indeed this is suggested by the plentitude of references to 'feudal and semi-feudal relations of production' in the literature. Our concern is primarily with the economic arguments.

The main arguments for these reforms are to improve the efficiency of agricultural production and to ensure equity in the distribution of income. It is widely presumed that small farms are more efficient than large farms and that share tenancy is inefficient vis-a-vis other modes of organizing farm production; hence land reform contributes to efficiency. In this connection, some would go so far as to argue that land reform is an essential prerequisite for growth.[3] However, what is not explicitly stated is how land reform, and, more broadly, agricultural growth feeds into the general process of economic growth.[4] Finally two further issues, which are likely to be of greater significance in the future—women and the environment—have been cited as reasons for undertaking land reform. However, the impact of land reform on either of these issues is far from conclusive.

While the equity aspects of redistributive land reform are quite apparent and require little elaboration, theory and practice differ. As experience shows, land reforms in many countries have contributed little to equity, and even less to efficiency. On the contrary, efforts at land reform have, in several instances, led to consequences that are unfavorable to the poor. If equity is the overriding concern, then the political economy of public policy will suggest that an equally effective way of obtaining the desired results is by taxation. Since confiscation can be usefully equated to a prohibitive tax, no policy option is lost. However, taxation is a normal part of capitalist economics and it is a continuous variable; land reform, on the other hand, is much more discrete and hence liable to arouse more heated feelings, at once raising too many hopes and fears. The brutal facts are the following: If a State is too weak to enforce justice and legislate appropriate taxes, it is too weak to enact effective land reform; if a State is strong enough to uphold the law and enforce its taxes, it can achieve all the goals claimed for land reform through other, less interventionist, means.

Land Reform and Economic Development: A Prologue

The impetus for land reform after World War II arose both from a fear of communism as well as from positive arguments indicating the desirability of agrarian change. Perhaps the first such focal study was one by the United Nations in 1951 entitled *Land Reform*, with the indicative subtitle 'Defects in Agrarian Structure as Obstacles to Economic Development'. In 1955, Doreen Warriner, one of the leading proponents of land reform, delivered an influential lecture in Egypt on the same topic. In 1961, the Punta del Este Charter of the Organisation of American States called on Latin America to pass antifeudal reform laws. A study by the Canadian International Development Agency found the latifundio-minifundio holding system in several Latin American countries to blame for backward technology and rural unrest.

Throughout the 1950s and 1960s an economic case for land reform was steadily developed. No doubt much land reform had already taken place, but a great deal of it can be said to have been politically motivated, either from fear of domestic peasant violence, or of communist agitation, sometimes both. This case, argued in the 1950s, was built upon a few salient observations. First, employment was a major problem for the less developed countries (LDCs) and economic policies were needed to combat widespread unemployment. Secondly, adequate food supplies were critical, not only for political stability, but also to conserve scarce foreign exchange for investment goods. The strategy of growth thus focused upon a labor-intensive, capital-saving approach that would maximize employment potential while relying on yield-increasing technological innovations to provide more food.

Land reform would solve two problems simultaneously. On the one hand, land productivity on small farms was usually much higher than that on large farms—so much more food could be grown with smaller farms—and the smaller farms also used more labor—thus providing employment and deterring the large flows of rural-urban migration that led to slums and overloaded the educational, sanitary, and transport infrastructure of LDC cities. The confidence of agricultural and development economists in the efficacy of land reform reached a peak around 1970, when it was publicized in the *AID Review of Land Reform*.[5]

That land reform will become a live issue in the near future is not improbable given the fact that 46 out of 63 countries subjected to International Monetary Fund/World Bank adjustment policies during the periods of 1970-71 and 1979-85 suffered a decline in food production per head. The somber effects of this decline have been depicted as follows (El-Ghonemy 1990, 72-3):

1. A fall in employment in the food sector of agriculture and a corresponding fall in productivity and the earnings and consumption levels of peasants.
2. Widening inequality in incomes between food producers, on the one hand, and export crop producers and agricultural inputs importers, on the other.
3. An increasing share of imported food in total calorie supplies (this increased between the average of 1970s and 1980-4 from 6 per cent to 13 per cent in Africa and from 8 per cent to 15 per cent in Latin America (FAO 1985c, 15).
4. A greater demand on their scarce foreign exchange to import food (usually paid by earnings from agricultural exports).

The basic premise of the reform argument is that labor efficiency is affected by income—higher incomes lead to better nutrition and medical care, hence richer workers are more efficient workers. Dasgupta and Ray (1986, 1987) argue that the landless (or, more generally, the assetless) are the most vulnerable group in the labor market. This vulnerability stems from the fact that potential employers would find those with positive nonwage income more attractive as employees, as, in efficiency terms, they can offer cheaper labor. On the other hand, those who do not enjoy nonwage income will be expensive as workers and can be undercut by those with nonwage income. The asset advantage gets translated into employment advantage for those with some land. In this context, partial land reform, which implies transfer of land from the landed gentry (that is, those who do not enter the labor market because of their higher reservation wage) to those who are involuntarily unemployed because of relatively higher wage due to lack of landholdings, contributes to increased employment (in efficiency terms) and output. In short, decline in food availability, with its consequent impact upon the efficiency wage, will provide additional grounds for land reform. It is further notable in this context that if we separate out 11 countries (subject to the above adjustment policies) according to their concentration of land ownership, then those countries with a more equal distribution of land were also found to have suffered the least loss in their growth rates.[6]

Table 6.1
Poverty and Landholding in Bangladesh, 1978-1979

Landholding Class (acres of land owned)	Percentage of Total Households in Class	Mean Income (taka per month)	Mean Landholdings (acres)	Headcount Index (percentage of population)
Landless	7.1	508	0	93
0.0 - 0.5	36.1	560	0.1	93
0.5 - 1.0	10.5	711	0.7	84
1.0 - 1.5	8.9	783	1.2	78
1.5 - 2.5	12.1	912	2.0	68
2.5 - 5.0	13.8	1,163	3.5	45
5.0 - 7.5	5.7	1,516	6.0	23
7.5+	5.8	2,155	14.0	10
Total	100.0	865	2.1	70

Source: World Bank, 1990. *World Development Report 1990*. Oxford: Oxford University Press.

The Agrarian Structure

Most Asian countries are characterized by high population density and small farm size.[7] In Bangladesh, Indonesia, the Republic of Korea, and Sri Lanka, the average farm is about one hectare; but two thirds of the farms are less than one hectare. In India, Philippines, and Thailand, the average farm size is somewhat larger and varies from about 2 to 4 hectares. In these countries, farms exceeding three hectares constitute about 20 to 40 per cent of all farms and 50 per cent of aggregate farm land. Table 6.1 presents some data on poverty and landholdings in Bangladesh. One cannot but be struck by the degree of (negative) correlation between rural poverty and landholdings. Tenancy provides a mechanism through which more equal access to land is obtained.[8] Many landless and marginal farmers become tenants by leasing land from the land-abundant households.

Despite redistributive land reforms, the distribution of farm lands is much more unequal in India, Philippines, and Sri Lanka as compared to other Asian countries. In India, farms exceeding ten hectares occupy about 25 per cent of the land. In the Philippines, land reform has abolished the large rice-producing haciendas, but sugar cane and plantation haciendas are still pervasive. In Sri Lanka, large farm estates constitute more than one quarter of the farm land. In India, Philippines, and Sri Lanka, the Gini coefficient of land concentration exceeds 0.6, which is higher than in other Asian countries.

Given the relatively small farm size, owner cultivation rather than tenancy is the most common way of organizing farm production in developing Asia. However, tenant farming occupies a significant portion of total farm land, although its importance varies from country to country. In Bangladesh, owner-cum-tenancy is the most common, while in the Philippines, pure tenancy is quite pervasive.

Among tenancy contracts, share tenancy is most common in Bangladesh and the Philippines, and in Sri Lanka, share tenancy is pervasive in the peasant sector. In Indonesia, share tenancy is relatively common despite the land reform law, which tried to suppress its incidence; while in India, share tenancy is underreported, being officially prohibited. Thailand is one of the few countries where fixed-rent tenancy is more prevalent than share tenancy. This is partly explained by the relatively better economic status of the tenants and their ability to shoulder risks.

In view of the considerable variation in ownership and tenancy patterns, the potential importance of redistributive and tenancy reforms varies from country to country, depending on the agrarian structure of the country. Any attempt at land reform should, therefore, start with an analysis of the distribution structure, as well as considerations of the political economy of land reform. Without such a detailed analysis, any hasty reforms might be counterproductive.

While there is considerable variation in the tenancy and ownership structure among Asian developing countries, it is less dramatic as compared to Latin American countries. In Latin America, empirical studies point to the following features (Shaw 1974, 124-25):

> (i) inadequate credit and highly exploitative pricing and marketing arrangements impede possibilities of higher incomes on minifundios, (ii) the landless employee class is fraught with conditions of surplus labor, unstable land tenure rights, and a general lack of nonagricultural employment possibilities, and (iii) the latifundista typically operates back from a profit-maximizing position on his production possibility curve, seldom farms land intensively, exploits resident employees and occasional labor, reinvests very small proportions of farm profits, and is, very often, an "absentee landlord".

Many of the features described above for Latin America are not true for Asia. If these phenomena are not true for Asia, why should the same policy apply?[9] If, however, one looks at historical studies on this issue, one finds the emphasis to be somewhat opposite. In their excellent study, Berry and Cline (1979) try to use their studies on Latin America as guides to land reform in Asia. In the present paper, we do just the opposite—use Asia to guide Latin America.

Tenancy reform, the theoretical rationale and empirical evidence leading to such reform, and the results of intervention will now be discussed. The traditional case for redistributive land reform, which views this reform in a favorable light, will be presented, followed by a closer look at this favorable case with the introduction of practical issues. These will be illustrated with the experience of land reform. The conclusion gathers together our reasons for considering land reform to be passé.

Tenancy Reform: Underlying Rationale

Theoretical Issues and Case Studies

The economic justification for prohibition of share tenancy derives from a Marshallian (1956 [1890]) argument that share tenancy is inefficient. The inefficiency of sharecropping as embodied in the Marshallian tradition[10] is built upon a simple point, Why should the tenant work as hard when receiving only a share of the output as he would when receiving the whole amount?

The Marshallian tradition was built on the implicit assumption that the share contract refers to only one variable. However, as pointed out by Gale Johnson (1950), and subsequently developed by Cheung (1979), a contract need not contain only one variable. Several real-world contracts (such as those found in Taipei,China) specify such items as the amount of land to be cultivated, and nonlabor inputs to be supplied, in addition to the rental share. Marshallian analysis could well be misleading for this case. By incorporating this new feature one can show the Pareto-efficiency of sharecropping, since the landlord will simply stipulate the efficient level of labor-intensity.

The efficiency of sharecropping has now come to rest squarely on whether the labor-intensity stipulation can be enforced. For many parts of the world, this does not seem to be a realistic assumption. Indeed, even when the share contract explicitly states the labor-intensity on a given piece of land, one still has to ask how such a contract might be enforced. After all, if the landlord has to constantly watch the sharecropper to enforce the desired labor-intensity, he might as well employ wage labor.

Georgescu-Roegen (1969) had suggested earlier that the assumption of a competitive labor market may not be appropriate, but Zaman (1973) appears to be the first to examine sharecropping under the condition of a dual labor market. If this sort of duality exists in the economy, then sharecropping is not necessarily inefficient. The crucial assumption behind this analysis is the postulate of a dual labor market whose existence needs to be tested in any specific empirical context.[11]

It seems that the incentive problem associated with sharecropping stems from the difficulty the landlord faces in observing and monitoring the tenant's effort. As it is often very costly for the landlord to observe the tenant's effort, one suggested solution to overcome the disincentive effect is cost sharing, a practice widely observed in many developing countries. Another solution is to offer a short-term lease. If the tenant has no long-term security of tenancy, then the tenant will work hard to keep up to the average standard. In most agrarian economies, social interactions are constant and all information is virtually public. Even if the landlord is not in a position to monitor shirking and cheating by the tenants, the neighbors of the tenant can, through *peer monitoring*, often detect dishonest behavior. The defaulter can suffer loss of reputation and any future contracts will likely be extremely difficult to obtain. Finally, in many poorer economies where unemployment is widespread, tenancy is a reliable source of employment. As there is no unemployment insurance, the tenants are not likely to shirk, because it might imply the ignominious fate of being unemployed.

Sharecropping is not as inefficient as is widely perceived; on the contrary, it has certain advantages vis-a-vis other types of tenures, including risk sharing between landlords and tenants. There is no insurance market in most rural economies. It is argued that sharecropping provides a mechanism to make an optimal combination of incentives and risk sharing. In a fixed-rent contract, there is perfect incentive, but the tenant has to absorb all of the risks; in a wage contract, on the other hand, there is no incentive to work, unless the workers are closely monitored and the landlord absorbs all of the risks. It is also argued that in the face of imperfect capital markets, sharecropping provides the mechanism to economize the cost of capital. Whether we view the tenancy process as one of long-term learning or as a tournament, in both cases sharecropping shows no significant inefficiency (Banerji and Rashid 1994).

If these arguments are correct, there is hardly any justification for banning sharecropping as some countries have attempted to do. However, it is easier to describe the many virtues of sharecropping than to test them empirically. Indeed, the persistence of sharecropping in the face of so many adversaries may be taken as an indirect vindication of those virtues.

There have been many studies of tenancy in South and Southeast Asia. These studies compare the average output and input per unit of land among different tenure classes, usually in the production of rice and wheat. They usually control quality of land and factor market imperfections by classifying data according to the presence of irrigation and the size of the farm. The studies on the efficiency of sharecropping have been more or less inconclusive. Bell (1977), and Shaban (1987) found significant Marshallian inefficiency in areas where long-term share tenancy was not practiced. Both studies compared the relative efficiency between owned and sharecropped plots for the same farmer. Similar conclusions were reached in a number of studies in Bangladesh including that by Hossain (1977). The strongest results for the purported inefficiency of sharecropping come from the work of Shaban (1987). However, as Shaban himself indicates in his footnotes, his data come from areas where landlords have to obtain tenants constantly under the shadow of 'land-to-the-tiller' legislation. As a result, no effective constraints can be brought to bear on the sharecroppers.

While noting the care shown by the above studies in separating out pure Marshallian inefficiency, one should also point out that analysis of a wider spectrum of cases leads one to remark upon the absence of widely documented quantitative significance. In summarizing the results of some 25 studies, Otsuka and Hayami (1988, 50) noted that the distributions of percentage differences in crop yields per hectare between share and fixed-rent tenancies and between share tenancy and owner farming were bell shaped with their means not statistically different from zero at conventional significance levels. (Similar results were obtained from comparisons of labor days and other inputs per hectare.)

The fact that no significant Marshallian inefficiency is detected is perhaps not due to the fact that the share contract can be enforced without cost. It may be due to a combination of countervailing factors. First, in most rural economies, cost sharing is widely practiced; this has become even more widespread with the advent of the high yielding varieties (HYV). Second, in many of these economies, involuntary unemployment of the landless is widespread; this may act as a disciplinary device for the share tenant. Finally, there may be a 'self-selection' process at work here. Only those landlords who have a mechanism to monitor the tenant and enforce the contract may adopt sharecropping. In fact, it is commonly observed that it is the small and medium resident landlords who use share tenancy while large absentee landlords prefer fixed-rent tenancy. If landlords select contracts, based on their ability to monitor tenants' work effort, it is then only expected that Marshallian inefficiency will not be observed.

The above discussion is concerned with the static inefficiency of sharecropping when identical technology is obtained for all the different types of tenures. This abstracts from the dynamic issues of growth, accumulation, and technology change. While the issue of static Marshallian inefficiency has been the subject of a voluminous literature, the question of dynamic efficiency has received relatively scant attention.

In a provocative paper, Bhaduri (1973) sought to highlight the relationship of tenurial relations to technological change by a model that showed that landlords who provided credit to tenants would not wish to adopt technological innovations because a richer tenant would break free from the bonds of indebtedness. In the subsequent controversy, it has been shown that Bhaduri's assumptions are empirically unrealistic —while tenants do borrow, the landlord does not occupy an important role as creditor—and the theoretical predictions are also seen to be sensitive to Bhaduri's particular assumptions. As Newberry (1977) remarked, a landlord who had the power to prevent adoption of an innovation would also have the power to extract the surplus after adopting the innovation.

Whatever the merit of the theoretical arguments, the possibility of dynamic inefficiency does not seem to have much empirical support. In a recent survey of literature on technology adoption in developing agriculture, Feder, Just, and Zilberman (1985) concluded there was no consistent evidence to prove that share tenancy is characterized by lagged adoption of innovations as compared to other types of tenures.

Effects of Intervention in Agrarian Contracts in Developing Asia

In many countries the rationale behind agrarian reform has been a desire to give the ownership to the tiller. Such reforms have the aspect of redistributive land reform as land is taken away from the landlord and given to the tenant. By insisting that only the owner can till the land such laws also act to prohibit tenancy. Hence they are also an effective form of tenancy reform. Whenever such legislation is discussed, it, of course, gives an impetus to landlords to show that they directly cultivate their own lands; hence even the anticipation of such reform leads landlords to those actions that suggest direct cultivation, that is, to prefer wage labor and to discourage tenancy. In the short run, land-to-the-tiller legislation is an act of redistributive land reform; in the long run, it is more effectively viewed as tenancy reform.

Land reform in the Republic of Korea took the form of a land-to-the-tiller program and was relatively successful. It had at least two important weaknesses however, one of which had long-term consequences. First, tenants who were given land had to contribute 30 per cent of their produce toward the purchase of land for five years and to pay an agricultural tax that ranged from 8 to 25 per cent of output. In addition, poorer tenants had to borrow their working capital at high interest rates. Because of these financial pressures, some of the tenants who were given land later lost it. Second, the reforms created far too many small holders whose farms were not viable and who became a burden in the 1980s, inhibiting needed agricultural transformation and openness to imports and world agricultural markets. The restrictions on tenancy and inadequate land markets apparently precluded sufficiently rapid consolidation of holdings through such markets.

Many studies, especially in South Asia, have revealed an inverse correlation between farm size and the value of output per hectare, even after one controls for land quality. Some say that this is largely explained by the higher supervision costs of the large farm. In South Asia, it is often observed that large farmers employ permanent workers for a crop season or longer. These permanent workers are paid fixed wages at the end of the season, with consumption credit in the interim period to support their consumption needs. The use of permanent workers instead of tenants requires explanation. Why do land-abundant households not lease out the land to small farmers or landless tenants and provide the credit needed for efficient cultivation rather than incur the increasing cost of supervision?

The existence of the long-term, as opposed to short-term, fixed-wage contract is attributed to the lower cost of monitoring farm tasks performed by permanent workers. In return, the landlord offers better wages to permanent workers, and there is always an excess supply of permanent labor, along with a pool of casual laborers. But, will wage labor ever be chosen if tenancy is permitted? If tenancy provides more incentives, then land productivity will be lower under the permanent labor contract than under the tenancy contract. According to Otsuka (1991), the inefficiency of large farms can be explained by the inefficiency of permanent labor contracts, as the incidence of permanent labor contracts is higher for larger farms. In South Asia, particularly India, where the prohibition of tenancy contracts has led to the adoption of labor contracts by large owner-cultivators, the principal explanation for the inverse relationship between farm size and productivity may lie in the existence of the permanent labor contract.

Many tenancy reform efforts were based on an erroneous perception that share tenancy is inefficient while the labor contract is efficient. This perception has led to the following policy initiative: Owner cultivation with hired labor is exempted from land reform while share tenancy is subject to regulation. If tenancy is prohibited, legally or otherwise, the permanent labor contract becomes the common mode for organizing land cultivation. As a result, the permanent labor contract is more common in South Asia than in Southeast Asia. In South Asia, the exemption of land under 'personal cultivation' from land redistribution has had the unintended consequence of converting the tenants into permanent laborers. As a result, in India, the incidence of farms employing permanent labor increased from about 14 per cent in 1953/54 to about 20 per cent in 1970/71. There have been similar observable tendencies in other South Asian countries.

In Southeast Asia, land reform has not been implemented with much seriousness except in the Philippines. As Otsuka (1993) notes, since the late 1970s the permanent labor contract, similar to South Asia, has emerged slowly in irrigated areas of Central Luzon; the ratio of permanent laborers among landless laborers in Central Luzon increased from a very negligible level in the 1970s to about 20 to 30 per cent in the 1980s. As land reform beneficiaries or the landlords are not allowed to lease out land, permanent labor contracts are on the increase.

Tenancy reform has thus precluded a better contractual opportunity for landless tenants and has led to a substitution of a superior contract by an inferior one. According to the evidence presented by Otsuka, Chuma, and Hayami (1992), yields and residual profits per hectare are much lower on farms with permanent labor than farms without. Thus, restrictions on tenurial choice under the Philippine Land Reform Regulations have had an adverse impact on both equity and efficiency.

In Sri Lanka, share tenancy is permitted. However, the share-rental rate for the landlord has been fixed at one fourth, which is much lower than the conventional rate of one half. As a result, landlords have resorted to eviction of tenants as well as to the cancelation of the tenancy contract with one-half share.

In Bangladesh, earlier land reform laws prohibited fixed-rent tenancies. Consequently, even absentee landlords and widows, who are comparatively disadvantaged at monitoring tenants' work effort, were forced to adopt share tenancy vis-a-vis fixed-rent tenancy. Otsuka (1993, 77) argues that 'significant Marshallian inefficiency is naturally expected to arise in such an institutional environment'.

If one may summarize the thrust of both theoretical and empirical results on sharecropping in the last half century, it would be to emphasize the phrase 'endogenous institutions'. Whenever certain rules and procedures have been imposed upon agriculture, there has been a tendency on the part of the agricultural community—meaning landlords, farmers, and peasants—to seek out productive adaptations to their felt problems. For societies with long historical records, such as the People's Republic of China, the process can be traced, at least in outline, for several centuries (Chao 1983). While such adaptations need not be optimal, one should avoid the traditional presumption that 'ignorant' peasants necessarily produce inefficient agriculture. A lack of sensitivity to the power of local knowledge has led well meaning agronomists such as Rene Dumont (1957) to criticize sharecropping as 'a system which bars every avenue of progress'.

Redistributive Land Reform: Underlying Rationale

Theoretical Issues and Empirical Evidence

The major issue propeling discussion of land reform has been the purported higher productivity of smaller plots of land. However it is also incumbent upon us to raise a few more queries, Will population growth negate the benefits of land reform? Will small farmers adopt new technology? Do the rice economies of Asia have any special features requiring attention? Are there any new issues that the literature has yet to study?

The Size-Productivity Debate

The modern debate on economies of scale in agriculture began with publication of the Indian farm management data—first used by Amartya Sen (1964) to point out that output per acre is inversely related to the size of operational holding. This clearly suggests that small farms are more efficient—in the sense that dividing up larger farms into smaller private plots would increase total agricultural production. The explanation most commonly offered for the difference in productivities, a feature that has been subsequently verified in many other countries, is that small farms make intensive use of family labor. This happens due to the existence of a dual labor market where a differential in cost exists between family and hired labor arising out of the prospect of unemployment (Berry and Cline 1979). As a result, labor intensity is much higher on small farms and causes the higher observed productivity.

The value productivity of small farms can be caused by four factors: (1) higher percentage of cultivated to owned area, (2) higher cropping intensity on cultivated land, (3) higher value product mix in the cropping pattern, and (4) higher yields per acre for a given crop. Of the four, physical productivity or yields per crop is now seen to be of minor importance. The first factor, or proportion of land owned given to cultivation, has varied importance in different parts of the world. It appears to be of considerable importance in Latin America but of minor significance in Asia, where land is generally intensely cultivated. This leaves cropping intensity and choice of crop as two of the chief reasons for higher labor inputs (and productivity) on small farms.

A second explanation for the differences in land productivity is based on the notion that the land of smaller farms simply is more fertile, hence its greater productivity is no surprise. While some suggestions have been given to explain why small farmers have disproportionately more fertile land (such as the sale of least fertile lands first during distress sales), no conclusive evidence has been brought to bear on this issue. In particular, it is not clear how much of the original productivity of the land can be assessed independently of the labor input that has been invested in it.

The explanation that is analytically most tractable is based on the difficulty of supervising hired labor. Gershon Feder (1985) has modeled the suggestion that the supervision of hired labor is so important that it is entrusted only to family members. Even if large and small farms have families of equal size, the small farms clearly have more supervisors per acre, and hence can engage more profitably in labor-intensive cultivation. The inverse size-productivity relationship is thus seen as a consequence of labor supervision problems in agriculture.[12]

In assessing the empirical importance of this issue, Binswanger et al. (1993, 30) find support for the following generalizations:

> (1) The productivity differential favoring small firms relative to large ones is proportional to the relative size differences between small and large farms. It is therefore larger where the inequalities in land holdings are greatest, in the relatively land-abundant countries of Latin America followed by relatively land abundant Africa, and is smallest in land scarce areas with relatively equal farm size distributions like Asia. (2) The highest output per unit area is often achieved not by the smallest subfamily or part time farmers, but by the second farm size class which includes the smallest full time farmers, perhaps suggesting that the smallest farms be particularly credit constrained.

Other Theoretical Arguments

The first point requiring clarification in assessing the potential of land reform is the motivation of the peasantry; however for Asia as a whole, and for South and East Asia in particular, there is little debate that the peasants are hard-working, self-conscious maximizers.

If land reform is to succeed over time then one of the crucial variables that will determine its success is the growth of population. If peasants respond to the new accession of land solely by having larger families, then it is easy to envision all the benefits of land reform being wiped out in a generation. The simple arithmetic of per capita incomes tells us that a larger denominator—population—will mean that per capita income declines. However, this argument assumes that the numerator—income—remains constant. The compulsion to work harder and longer in order to maintain larger families may lead to changes in work habits, which would then raise overall productivity; furthermore, the greater population density enables a further refining of the division of labor, thereby permitting economies of specialization. These effects are most apparent when they induce changes in the infrastructure, particularly in transport and education. In addition, it is only when people have a standard to maintain that they begin worrying about the impact of additional children upon that standard and begin to consider family planning. A careful study by James Boyce (1987, 153) argues that 'population growth in West Bengal and Bangladesh has had a positive effect upon agricultural growth, contrary to the predictions of the Neo-Malthusian school'.

The adoption of innovations is a particularly complex issue. The most viable generalizations that we appear to possess are those provided by Ruttan (1977):

1. The new wheat and rice varieties were adopted at exceptionally rapid rates in those areas where they were technically and economically superior to local varieties.
2. Neither farm size nor tenure has been an important source of differential growth in productivity.

The phrase, land reform, has also been misleading in focusing on only one of several rural markets. The markets for labor, credit, and output are intimately linked with the land market in any productive economy. If a major change occurs in any one market we may expect repercussions in several. One may call the policy of giving all freed black slaves in the US South 'Forty acres and a mule', a policy of land reform: a study of the failure of this policy to provide economic emancipation for the blacks provides an interesting study in interlinked markets and power relations. The interlinkage of markets has encouraged the formation of cooperatives. It should be noted that while cooperatives have had virtually no success in organizing direct production, they have been quite successful in handling ancillary credit and marketing (Dovring 1965).

The general case for land reform is not altered by considering the specifics of rice economies. It seems clear that as long as adequate and timely water, fertilizer, and seeds can be provided, rice cultivation is clearly suitable for the family farm and makes a strong case for land reform. The fact that water is a public input leads one to wonder how far it can be fully privatized—a suggestion that has been made in some quarters. Nonetheless, highly successful systems of irrigation water supply do exist, as in Taipei,China. A combination of political pressure, together with the social contacts between members of the irrigation associations and the farmers make for a very workable system. Water being a critical input does not therefore require large farms and continues the thrust toward land reform.

New Issues: Gender and Environment

Two issues virtually ignored by the traditional analysis of land reform are assuming ever greater importance—gender and environment. We know very little about the impact of land reform on either issue, a fact that ought to give us pause.

Female Rural Poverty

In many countries, women seem to be more disadvantaged than men in the land market. This is evident from the fact that among the poor in South Asian countries, the percentage of landless women is higher than the percentage of landless men. This has much to do with the inheritance law of many of these countries, where male children inherit most of the family land. But it may also reflect the bias toward men in the working of the tenancy market.[13]

Faced by a lack of research directed specifically at the status of women under regimes of land reform, we are led to speculate on the status of women in peasant societies when the family is faced with a sudden increase in wealth, as envisaged by programs of land reform. In the case of Bangladesh, we find that material prosperity is followed by social conservatism. Frequently, womenfolk are withdrawn from the labor force. It is well-established that richer farmers have larger households.

While a part of the increased household size may be due to extended family members, some of the increase is due to larger families. In other words, children are a normal good while labor is an inferior good. Hence prosperous families reduce female labor and grow larger. Private volunteer organizations (PVOs) have found strong support from the poorest class of women. Being all too painfully aware of the rigors of poverty, they are the first to perceive the benefits of new organizational forms. While the organized credit market has provided very little support to such poor women, the Grameen Bank has done very well in being supported by women. The very poverty of such women has, in a sense, liberated them from social constraints and leaves them free to explore new potentialities. So the direct effects of land reform will probably be the opposite of the commonly perceived notions of gender equity—at least by Western standards.

Environment

Since the confident days of the sixties and seventies, the newest issue to come up with land reform is that of the environment. And yet, as William Thiesenhusen (1991) points out, there has been virtually no research conducted on this issue. In developing economies, environmental problems arise not so much from industrial or chemical pollution as from the pressure of population and the problems of adequate food production (Hansen 1993). We see an overuse of firewood leading to the use of dung for cooking instead of fertilizer; this in turn promotes land overuse and degradation and forces family members to seek nonfarm jobs, thereby making such labor unavailable for conservation practice. How does the system of land tenure mediate between environmental degradation and the agricultural population?

It is the Latin American scene that raises the strongest link between land ownership patterns and the environment. The large latifundios occupy most of the good lands and use them inefficiently; this leaves the poor with insecure titles to land and discourages conservation. For example, in Honduras, short-term contract renters had insecure tenure on very small plots and exhibited the poorest conservation practices—clearing all trees, burning crop residues, using steep lands, and growing mostly annual crops. This is one case where tenancy reform appears an appropriate conservation measure. What we need is some guidance on how conservation measures differ systematically between large and small farms, and this is precisely what the literature has not yet modeled.[14]

Significant externalities make conservation a particularly complex case to handle. The usual solution to externalities is to internalize them by assigning private property rights. Due to the long span of time involved, however, it is not at all clear that such privatization will work. Models show that farmers who fully own a resource will engage in suboptimal behavior when their discount rate does not coincide with the social discount rate; furthermore, it can clearly be optimal for a poverty-stricken farmer to deplete a resource to extinction if this strategy will ensure survival. Whether such actions become more or less likely with redistributive land reform is the critical unanswered issue.

This review of the salient features influencing land reform suggests that the traditional argument based on the greater productivity of small farms has considerable force. Nor is this case weakened by looking at population growth, technology, or the staple Asian grain, rice. However, the absence of systematic inquiry into the effects upon women or upon the environment can turn out to be a serious lacuna.

Biting the Bullet: Redistributive Land Reform

Practical Issues and Experience

The decision to undertake redistributive land reform requires a peculiar blending of economic and political considerations. That inequalities will be generated by a market economy has long been understood and egalitarian societies have often seen the need to intervene to maintain equality. A policy of repeated redistribution of land was practiced among tribal societies, for instance, the jubilee of the Jews. No one has revived such a suggestion nowadays. So the question is, Can a one-time change in the ownership of land have permanent beneficial effects?

How does one justify interfering with the sanctity of property in a capitalist system? Alfred Marshall generalized the concept of rent from a land-based income to all forms of income by defining rent as any excess above opportunity costs. Since rent could arise from any property, Marshall (1956 [1890], 495) took the properly cautious step about land reform.

> ... confiscation even of true rent, would be such a shock to general security that it would discourage accumulation even more than a moderate special tax on any kind of profit or quasi-rent.

Marshall's fear that discussions of expropriation disrupt faith in the system can be illustrated by the case of Indonesia. A land reform program introduced in September 1960 was intended primarily to eliminate the dualism that long existed between the legal system based on Western legal concepts and the traditional *adat* system of religious and customary law that governed agrarian issues. However, the program also intended to provide every farm household with at least two hectares of land. The pre-1965 government embarked on a land redistribution program after establishing ceilings that varied (from 5 to 20 hectares per family) depending on regional population density and irrigation availability. A major problem was the overestimation of excess land likely to become available, so the ceilings were lowered. Nevertheless, they were evaded by landholders through subdivision among family members. The post-1965 government gave up the whole program regarding it as 'communist inspired' and Indonesia has subsequently grown rapidly without effecting agrarian reform (Tjondronegoro, Soejono, and Hardjono 1994).

If land reform is agreed upon, the practical issues crucial to its success are compensation, speed of execution, and retention of government control. It will be convenient to discuss compensation here and leave the other issues until we examine the experience of some countries with land reform. Should the State aim for full compensation of landowners? This is implicit in programs such as Zimbabwe's 'willing buyer, willing seller' law, designed to amicably transfer land from landowning whites to landless blacks. However, now that the least desirable land has been sold by whites, there does not appear to be many willing sellers and the State is considering forcible redistribution. If a policy of full compensation is to take place, there will be very little aggregate redistribution if the tax increases to pay for the compensation are properly discounted (Ricardian Equivalence proposition). Therefore it is when the redistribution does not involve full compensation that we find real equity transfers. Such a policy, with incomplete compensation, can equivalently be termed partial confiscation.

In this connection, it is rather surprising to note that the literature on taxation has not been integrated into the discussion of land reform. The purported goals of the optimal taxation literature are exactly those of land reform proponents—equity and efficiency. When Stiglitz (1987, 494) claims that 'if one has a well-designed income tax, adding differential commodity taxation is likely to add little, if anything, to the ability to redistribute income', such a claim would appear to indicate that suitable redistribution of incomes can be achieved via income taxes—add a scheme of partial property value taxation and we may be able to achieve a desired redistribution of wealth. Of course any tax diminishes one's wealth, but the important point as far as peoples' expectations are concerned is that there is no direct attack upon the inviolability of property.

Lessons from the Experience of Land Reform

Success in Taipei,China

It is essential to learn from the experience of successful land reforms if further land redistribution is advocated as economic policy. The experience of Taipei,China is instructive. After Japanese occupation in 1905, a reform was undertaken whereby the Chinese system of dual titles —one by a 'superior' landlord and the other by an 'inferior' or working landholder—was eliminated (with compensation in ten-year bonds). When Chiang Kai Shek took over in 1949, the specter of communism spreading over from the mainland was very real. It was vital to reorganize Taipei,China so that Chiang Kai Shek's dream of retaking mainland China was made feasible: A stable and prosperous peasantry was an important military requirement—moreover nothing was owed to the existing landlords. Nonetheless, the reform that eventually took place in Taipei,China occurred in three decisive steps, with no provision for the eventual outcome.

In 1949, rents were reduced to a maximum of 37.5 per cent of the normal yield on the main crop for all tenants. This was decided by democratically elected representatives from each class of society and was only possible because the Japanese had established excellent cadastral surveys. These surveys classified the land into 26 productive categories and had been revised in the 1930s. The farmers had been used to this system and the accuracy of the data was widely agreed upon. The rent reduction act provided some tenants with rich lands, which they immediately tried to sublease, actions that the government had to immediately ban. Between April and August 1949, new titles confirming current landlord-tiller status were provided. In 1951, public lands were sold with the intention of raising a fund for land reclamation. This land was cheaply sold with a ten-year payoff period. It was so successful that several more such sales were undertaken, and by 1953 the government finally saw its way to complete a land-to-the-tiller program of land reform. Such a thought was not new to the Kuomintang, it had been part of their ideology since the early days of Sun Yat Sen (who in turn was considerably influenced by the American single-tax movement of Henry George). The program called for compulsory sales to the tillers at two-and-a-half times the 'normal yield'—a figure obtained by again going back to the Japanese infrastructure. Fear of inflation led the landlords to ask for 70 per cent of the payment to be in kind and the remaining 30 per cent was given as stock in government corporations. The maximum payment by tenants was limited to the rent they were already paying, so the tiller really had nothing to lose by purchasing the land. This reform enthused the rural populace. Many of the landholders took increased interest in education for their children and even older institutions, such as the cooperatives set up by the Japanese, were now infused with a new spirit of mutual help.

In the Taipei,China case, the situation was most favorable politically in that the government was a military one with no dependency upon the landlord class, but also the landlords themselves were intimidated by the prospect of communism sweeping in from the mainland. Despite this extremely favorable circumstance, it should be emphasized that the final reform of 1953 had not been planned. Events led to it, but no one foresaw it—otherwise a more concerted opposition could have developed. Even without the overt opposition of any class, the land redistribution would have been a bureaucratic nightmare had not the accurate cadastral surveys of the Japanese been available and agreed upon. Nor could the government completely ignore post-reform intervention, otherwise a new class of absentee landlords would have arisen directly after the rent reduction of 1949.

Doubts in Bangladesh

Let us contrast the situation in Taipei,China with that in Bangladesh, where land reform was initially seen as an integral part of the program of socialist Bangladesh. From Table 6.1 it can be seen that Bangladesh not only has very little land, but the general distribution shows hardly any concentration. Only 5 per cent of the households have more than 7.5 acres of land. The average farm size has declined from 1.23 acres in 1960 to .93 acres in 1984. As a subsistence holding requires about 2.5 acres, most holdings are not viable. The striking feature of land scarcity in Bangladesh is that a fully egalitarian redistribution of arable land would provide each household with a nonviable holding of 2.27 acres.

If less radical land reform is contemplated then we can expect that larger farms, which typically have more members per household, will distribute their land among family members during the debate preceding reform. So the excess land would have to come, for example, from farmers owning an excess of 15 acres. This would provide about 508,900 acres of land, which if redistributed in subsistence size holdings would benefit only 5 per cent of the landless laborers. The gain in agricultural output, assuming small farms to be 20 per cent more efficient than large farms, would be under 2 per cent while the loss of marketed surplus, since the poorer households have a much higher propensity to consume agricultural products, could be as high as 30 per cent! In an economy where the cities hold all real power, one may be sure that such a shortage would never be allowed to materialize, with the most likely outcome being considerable imports of food and loss of foreign exchange.

A *sine qua non* for any land reform, and especially for a country with as litigative a history as Bangladesh, is a set of accurate and agreed-upon land records. Unfortunately existing records are highly suspect with land being held *benami* or pseudonymously in many cases. Nor is the bureaucracy of such competence and disinterestedness as to handle the flood of protests that are sure to come in when the reform acts are publicized. Under these circumstances a serious attempt at meaningful land reform is likely to produce serious conflict and large scale destruction of rural assets. Since land reform is a one-shot change, which is bound to be diluted in one generation due to the Muslim law of equal inheritance among sons, one may wonder about the long-run benefits of such a change. Indeed, if the political will, the bureaucratic expertise, and the necessary data can all be acquired, one wonders whether there may not be some other policy change, less disruptive and more long-run, that is of greater benefit to Bangladesh.

Political Economy

One can distinguish between land reform 'by grace' and land reform 'by leverage'. With land reform 'by grace', the upper classes, either out of compassion or out of self-interest, provide the reform 'from above'. By contrast, when the peasants succeed in organizing themselves, acquiring a position of strength and bargaining therefrom, we have land reform 'by leverage'. If peasants wish to maintain the benefits to be gained from land reform it is essential that they continue their political activities. In the nature of things, this appears highly unlikely.[15]

Any land reform will bring about benefits in a nonneutral fashion among the various segments of the society. Those who will lose are the landed class, who are usually politically and economically powerful, numerically small, and therefore more organized—or easy to organize. Those who gain are the small farmers or the landless peasantry who are usually politically and economically weak and too numerous for cohesive organization. This potential beneficiary class is usually disorganized—or is difficult to organize. In a democratic regime, the voting power of the poor is diminished by their lack of organization and means, while the voting power of the rich is magnified by their organizational unity and financial resources. It is highly improbable that a society that displays wide income inequalities and where widespread logrolling takes place can easily legislate land reform—let alone implement it. This perhaps explains why nonlegislation of land reform laws is the rule rather than the exception in agrarian societies.[16]

It is widely recognized that three factors necessary for effective land reform are speed, compensation, and retention of government control. In democratic regimes, the requirement of adequate public discussion makes speedy actions impossible. An examination of the historical evolution of the land reform debate shows that in the course of the argument, reform provisions are diluted and loopholes provided. As a result, when land reform by grace, that is, with the benevolence of the upper classes, does occur, one is hard pressed to find any long-run impact of such reforms. It is notable that when forceful and effective reforms have happened, external agencies, such as the United States in the case of East Asia, or Sweden in the case of Ethiopia, have given active, if quiet, support for such moves (Ellis 1980). In the current climate of perestroika and glasnost, neither the United States nor the World Bank nor any other powerful international agency appears prepared to support the interventionist strategies that they themselves supported in the fifties. It is hard to disentangle the mix of motives for earlier US policy—whether it be the ideals of agrarian populism of Jefferson and Lincoln, or the fear of anticommunism, or the desire to see a stable rural society as the basis for democracy—but it suffices to note that none of these motives have much force today.

Any realistic land reform must therefore rely on force, or the threat of force, if it is to have the impact suggested by economic theory. However, this brings us back to the experience of the Soviet economy during collectivization. Is it realistic to think that those who have lived to see the demise of communism will peacefully accede to the loss of their land? Will it not lead to the same destruction of agricultural capital that the Soviets had to suffer?

> Stock was slaughtered every night in Gremyachy Log. Hardly had dusk fallen when the muffled, short bleats of sheep, the death-squeals of pigs, or the lowing of calves could be heard. Both those who had joined the kolkhoz and individual farmers killed their stock. Bulls, sheep, pigs, even cows were slaughtered, as well as cattle for breeding. The horned stock of Gremyachy was halved in two nights. (Quoted in Nove 1969, 174.)

The other option is to compensate the landowners for the loss of their land. How is this to be achieved? No LDC has a budgetary surplus and it is improbable in today's world economy that the money would be provided by a donor agency. The sale of industrial bonds of long maturity can only be plausible if the country already has a credible industrial development plan. But this runs into the circular problem that one of the important reasons for the land reform is to establish such a credible program. Where compensation has been paid—typically below market value—as in Taipei,China and in the Republic of Korea, there has been a military presence to enforce the reform. How far reforms are possible under democratic regimes is the difficult question we have to answer.

The need for alternatives to redistribute land reform is also suggested by a survey of the results of several extant policies. As Powelson and Stock (1987, 3) note pessimistically

> If the peasants sometimes do benefit, often their gains are temporary. What the state gives, the state can take away—and will take away, when it comes under political or economic pressure.

In neglecting the peasant, there does not appear to be much to distinguish capitalist from socialist states. There are many high-minded bureaucrats in capitalist countries and there are many calls to peasants to sacrifice 'for the revolution' in socialist states (Powelson and Stock 1987, 284). Furthermore, with the passage of a few years, the management of reform passes over to bureaucrats and this appears to be just as, if not more, deadening than landowners' rapacity (Ibid.).

> Worse yet, state officials believe they can manage agriculture. Until recently, bureaucrats in Cairo determine what would be planted on each farm in Egypt, when it would be planted, what fertilizers and seeds would be used, and when and where it would be sold. With little left for them to decide, farmers *on their own land* are but low-level employees of the state. In Egypt, agricultural output per capita has *decreased* at an *average* annual rate of 0.4% per year for nineteen years!

Conclusion

This review of the factors affecting the success of land reform suggests different sorts of conclusions for tenancy than for land redistribution. There appear to be no sound reasons, either theoretical or empirical, for passing tenancy legislation. Tenants, particularly share tenants, who comprise the great majority of agricultural tenants, work hard, maintain the land, and adopt new practices quickly. When laws force tenancy to be avoided, the landlord has to engage in cultivation with wage laborers and there is reason to believe that this is a less efficient option. This leads us to conclude that tenancy regulations should be eliminated to allow a wider contractual choice and to induce larger farms to lease out more land to the landless. To make the tenancy option attractive to the larger landowners and to ensure economic success for the tenants, the latter should be provided public support in the form of easy access to capital and technical know-how on farm management. If the tenancy market can be made to function efficiently, it will contribute to both the equity and efficiency of the rural economy. In particular, tenancy deregulation will open up for the landless tenants the agricultural ladder out of poverty, which has been denied to them by insensible tenancy regulations.

As for land reform proper, in the sense of redistribution of land, theoretical economics points quite favorably to such a policy. There appears to be no significant economies of scale in agriculture, so one cannot have any general presumption against small farms. For the rice economies of Asia, that we are particularly concerned with, the skill-intensive and scale-neutral nature of rice cultivation makes the case for land redistribution even stronger. While small farms are at a slight disadvantage in perceiving and adopting new technology, this difference is of no significance empirically. Indeed, the receptiveness of small farmers to extension services dilutes most objections to small farmers. The fragmented and oligopolistic nature of the land market in most LDCs further strengthens these general considerations.[17]

From an economic point of view, land reform would certainly improve distributional equity and appears to have many strong arguments in its favor regarding efficiency. Whether it be an efficiency wage argument, which leads to better health and a more effective labor force, or a labor-absorption argument based on the greater labor intensity of small farms, none of the traditional arguments can be faulted. While the impact of land reform on gender equity or on the environment are uncertain, there is certainly no presumption against land reform on these grounds. Why then is land reform not more popular?

The Asian evidence provides a simple answer. In Taipei,China land reform was conducted efficiently by an alien military power—a precedent that carries no force for democratic regimes. In the Republic of Korea, land reform was instigated by a military government and succeeded in bankrupting the existent landlord class. No agricultural surplus was generated to help toward industrialization, and the Republic of Korea's industrial success came over a decade later, out of seemingly unrelated circumstances. In Thailand, land reform has affected marginal farmers, yet the economy has grown quite well; in Indonesia, no land reform at all has taken place and yet the economy has shown enormous vitality. Why then is land reform considered to be so critical?

How far can the Taipei,China factors be duplicated? First, we come up against the data problem. Considering the Indian subcontinent, for example, Verma and Bromley (1987, 795) point out that,

> The problems with farm size as an explanatory variable have been emphasized by Krishna. He found that the same farm management survey data on which most of the empirical work was based would support the finding that holdings between 13 and 16 acres yield both the maximum and the minimum gross output per acre and that holdings of 1-3 acres yield both the maximum and minimum output per unit of input cost.

The inverse size-productivity relationship, on which so much of the argument rests, has been severely challenged by Usha Rani.

> This controversy of relationship between the size of farm and yield per acre was based on the aggregated data of FMS and on disaggregated data from some other sources, but the results were not put to statistical tests. After taking care of these factors, the conclusion which emerges from the present exercise is that the whole controversy and all the explanation offered to prove the different observations had a very weak statistical basis. (Quoted in Verma and Bromley 1987, 795.)

So neither facts nor inferences appear to be generally agreed upon.

Turn now to the specific benefits provided by land reform. If poverty alleviation is the goal, this can be tackled through land-contingent poverty alleviation schemes (Ravallion 1989). If commercial and export farming is the goal, systems of contract farming can be encouraged (Glover and Kusterer 1990). If economies of scale are the desired goal, then administrative agencies (Moore 1989) or associative farming may be used (Meyer 1991). Farmers have shown their innovativeness in evolving property rights by using a system of shares that are transferable and salable, thus mimicking some of the operations of a stock market (Heston and Kumar 1983, 202). Finally, while there is a need for gender-focused policies to alleviate female poverty, it is found that appropriate macroeconomic policies and accelerated growth can be conducive to alleviation of poverty including female poverty. In many countries, where export-oriented policies have been pursued successfully, women have benefited greatly. For example, in Bangladesh, success in garment exports has a beneficial fall out in the form of employment for 300,000 women. This has perhaps done good for more women than any other single gender-oriented policy in the country.

Nor has the theoretical literature addressed the issue of technological change adequately. The optimal farm size can be expected to change with ongoing technological change. How can we expect to redistribute land and maintain an efficient land ownership pattern as the desirable size of the efficient farm changes? The traditional literature has built a solid case by neglecting the impact of trade and by failing to incorporate land reform within questions of taxation. Successful land reform must fit within a vision of economic growth and such a vision has not been provided.

A major political decision, such as to introduce significant land reform, obviously entails winners and losers. The political calculus suggests that land reform is desirable if the energy, organization, and costs involved in a successful land reform project cannot be alternatively used for some other measure or measures that will provide greater benefits. Even if noneconomic goals such as education are to be encouraged, this can be directly done through fostering compulsory education. In other words, the critical question is: Could the same political resources be put to better use? When the question is posed in this way, one is left wondering whether land reform possesses any unique advantages other than making effective a transfer of political power.

Even if there were no difficulties in implementing land reform, it does not offer a panacea for poverty eradication. To improve the economic status of the poor, whose principal asset is labor power, it is critical that there are sufficient productive employment opportunities in the economy. As the experiences of East Asia attest, such employment opportunities can be fostered by an overall acceleration of growth driven by an outward-oriented strategy of development.

Acknowledgments

The authors wish to acknowledge the helpful comments of Pranab Bardhan, Sutanu Behuria, Partha Dasgupta, Mahabub Hossain, and S. M. Naseem. However, none of the above should be implicated in either the viewpoints or the remaining errors.

Appendix

It may help to gain perspective by looking at an issue where there seems to be no grounds for controversy—the consolidation of agricultural lands. As early as 1917 the disadvantages of scattered plots were listed as follows:
1. Waste of labor and cattle power,
2. Waste of land in hedges and boundary marks,
3. Waste of manure, etc,
4. Watching of crops impracticable,
5. Wells cannot be sunk economically,
6. Labor-saving implements cannot be used,
7. Difficulty of roads, water channels, etc.,
8. Change in cultivation inconvenient,
9. Increase in cost of production, etc., and
10. General backwardness of agricultural conditions.

(Quoted in Heston and Kumar 1983, 212.)

When land consolidation was encouraged by the Government of India it was found that an average of 12 to 15 per cent increases in productivity were obtained on the consolidated holdings. Nonetheless, in seeking to facilitate voluntary consolidation, the Kapoor Committee reports that consolidation was objected to by farmers because they believed their lands to be of better quality, or their own lands were more even or better located plus a variety of sentimental and miscellaneous reasons (Heston and Kumar 1983, 210). Even the voluntary consolidation that did take place required that the village lands be valued relative to each other—farmers objected strongly to 'objective' measures of valuation brought in by experts. In short, the facts on the ground are not only more complex, they also need to be appeased, before successful policies can be implemented.

Notes

1. According to the *World Development Report 1990*, the rural poor as a percentage of total poor constitute about 79 per cent in India, 90 per cent in Indonesia, 80 per cent in Malaysia, 67 per cent in the Philippines, and 80 per cent in Thailand.

2. Alain de Janvry (1981), for example, illustrates how readily both meanings are coupled.

3. It is surely suggestive that one of the chief proponents of land reform in Latin America, Alain de Janvry, has seen the dynamism of Latin American agriculture in the 1980s as grounds for a new strategy that no longer considers land reform as critical.

4. If the absence of land reform is said to retard growth because it leads to local oligopolies, it is not clear why such noncompetitive forces are not more

effectively removed by better transportation and the dissemination of information. If it is said that the rich will grow richer, this in itself is no objection if the rich are earning by just means. If it is said that the landowners will come to 'monopolize' all the land, then why should land continue to be the most profitable investment? As the economy grows, one can expect newer and more dynamic sources of wealth to arise. Landed wealth has to be given special status for such arguments to hold.

5. Folke Dovring (1972, 532), for example, found the case for land reform to be so cut and dried that he pointed out how generations of economists had been misled by the propaganda of large farmers in England.

6. For Latin America in particular, de Janvry and Sadoulet (1989b) have found new hope for agriculture in these difficult circumstances. The unexpected feature of agriculture was that its growth rate, relatively speaking, accelerated in hard times. It is notable, however, that while the authors state their desired policies to be a supplement to land reform and not a substitute for it, very little stress is laid upon land reform in the article. This would suggest that de Janvry, who has provided some of the most penetrating assessments of the political economy of land reform, no longer considers the redistribution of land to be a politically viable measure.

7. The information cited in this section is taken from Otsuka (1993).

8. Data reveal that there is always much greater inequality in ownership distribution than in operational distribution of land.

9. This portrayal of Shaw remains accurate in the main despite the growth of a middle class in agriculture (Thiesenhusen and Melmed-Sanjak 1990).

10. There is a large and burgeoning literature on the theory of sharecropping. For recent surveys of the literature see Bliss and Stern 1982; Binswanger and Rosenzweig 1984; Quibria and Rashid 1984; Otsuka and Hayami 1988; Singh 1989.

11. It can even be shown that the comparative statics results generated by a model incorporating dual labor market accords with most of the known facts for agrarian economies such as those of Bangladesh (Quibria and Rashid 1986).

12. Srinivasan (1972) provides yet another explanation of the size productivity relationship in terms of uncertainty and risk aversion. Under some plausible assumptions regarding risk attitude, he shows that the small farms will apply more inputs per unit of land as compared to large farms.

13. Much of the deprivation of women can also be traced to disparity in intrahousehold allocation between sexes. There is limited scope for government policies to influence intrahousehold allocation (Quibria 1994).

14. We do have empirical studies on the conservation measures induced by cash crops versus food crops. The difference between the systems lies not so much in the type of crop as between the explicit integration of natural resource management into the agricultural plans (Barbier 1989).

15. Nor should we forget that much of the earlier Western hope was based on the example of some Chinese communes such as Tachai (Perelman 1977). Who could guess that most of the purported facts about Tachai were fabricated?

16. Problems of land reform have been discussed elaborately in the framework of the traditional political economy. For some recent discussion of land reform in the context of the so-called neoclassical political economy, see Hayami (1991) and the comments on the paper.

17. Some scholars have even put almost the entire onus of real change on land reform. For example, Braverman and Srinivasan (1984, 64) argue that policies other than land reform will leave the welfare of each potential tenant unaltered while affecting the level of output, the extent of tenancy, and the welfare of the landlord.

References

Banerji, S., and S. Rashid, 1994. "Tournaments and Sharecropping." Working Paper. University of Illinois.

Barbier, E. B., 1989. "Cash Crops, Food Crops, and Sustainability: The Case of Indonesia." *World Development* 17(6):879-95.

Bell, C., 1977. "Alternative Theories of Sharecropping: Some Tests Using Evidence from Northeast India." *Journal of Development Studies* 13:317-46.

Berry, R. A., and W. R. Cline, 1979. *Agrarian Structure and Productivity in Developing Countries*. Geneva: International Labour Organisation.

Bhaduri, A., 1973. "A Study in Agricultural Backwardness Under Semi-Feudalism." *Economic Journal* 83:120-37.

Binswanger, H. P., K. Deininger, and G. Feder, 1993. "Power Distributions and Reform in Agricultural Land Markets." In J. Behrman and T. N. Srinivasan, eds., *Handbook of Development Economics*. Vol. III. New York: North-Holland Publishers.

Binswanger, H. P., and M. R. Rosenzweig, 1984. "Contractual Arrangements, Employment, and Wages in Rural Labor Markets: A Critical Review." In H. P. Binswanger and M. R. Rosenzweig, eds., *Contractual Arrangements, Employment, and Wages in Rural Labor Markets in Asia*. New Haven: Yale University Press.

Bliss, C. J., and N. H. Stern, 1982. *Palanpur: The Economy of an Indian Village*. Delhi: Oxford University Press.

Boyce, J., 1987. *Agrarian Impasse in Bengal*. Cambridge: Cambridge University Press.

Braverman, A., and T. N. Srinivasan, 1984. "Agrarian Reforms in Developing Rural Economics Characterized by Interlinked Credit and Tenancy Markets." In H. P. Binswanger and M. R. Rosenzweig, *Contractual Arrangements, Employment, and Wages in Rural Labor Markets in Asia*. New Haven: Yale University Press.

Chao, K., 1983. "Tenure Systems in Traditional China." *Economic Development and Cultural Change* 31(2):295-314.

Cheung, N. S., 1979. *The Theory of Share Tenancy*. Chicago: University of Chicago Press.

Dasgupta, P., and D. Ray, 1986. "Inequality as a Determinant of Malnutrition and Employment Theory." *Economic Journal* 96:1011-34.

———, 1987. "Inequality as a Determinant of Malnutrition and Unemployment Policy." *Economic Journal* 97:177-88.

de Janvry, A., 1981. The Role of Land Reform in Economic Development: Policies and Politics." *American Journal of Agricultural Economics* 63(2):389-92.

de Janvry, A., and E. Sadoulet, 1989a. "Alternative Approaches to the Political Economy of Agricultural Policies: Convergence of Analysis, Divergence of Implications." In A. Maunder and V. Valdés, eds., *Agriculture and Government in an Interdependent World*. Aldershot, Hants: Dartmouth.

———, 1989b. "A Study in Resistance to Institutional Change: The Lost Game of Latin American Land Reform." *World Development* 17(9):1397-407.

Dovring, F., 1965. *Land and Labour in Europe in the Twentieth Century*. The Hague: Nijhoff.

———, 1972. "Land Reform: A Key to Change in Agriculture." In N. Islam, ed., *Agricultural Policy in Developing Countries*. New York: John Wiley & Sons.

Dumont, R., 1957. *Types of Rural Economy*. London: Methuen.

El-Ghonemy, M. R., 1990. *The Political Economy of Rural Poverty. The Case for Land Reform*. London: Routledge.

Ellis, G., 1980. "Land Tenancy Reform in Ethiopia: A Retrospective Analysis." *Economic Development and Cultural Change* 28(3):523-45.

Feder, G., 1985. "The Relation Between Farm Size and Farm Productivity. The Role of Family Labor, Supervision and Credit Constraints." *Journal of Development Economics* 18:297-313.

Feder, G., R. E. Just, and D. Zilberman, 1985. "Adoption of Agricultural Innovations in Developing Countries: A Survey." *Economic Development and Cultural Change* 33:254-98.

Georgescu-Roegen, M., 1969. "The Institutional Aspects of Peasant Communities: An Analytical View." In C. Wharton, ed., *Subsistence Agriculture and Economic Development*. Chicago: Aldine Publishing Company.

Glover, D., and K. Kusterer, 1990. *Small Farmers, Big Business: Contract Farming and Rural Development*. New York: St. Martins.

Hansen, S., 1993. "Environment and Rural Poverty." In M. G. Quibria, ed., *Rural Poverty in Asia: Priority Issues and Policy Options*. Hong Kong: Oxford University Press.

Hayami, Y., 1991. "Land Reform." In G. Meier, ed., *Politics and Policy Making in Developing Countries Perspectives on the New Political Economy*. With comments by R. Junguito, 171-73 and by T. P. Tonrich, 173-77. San Francisco: ICS Press.

Heston, A., and D. Kumar, 1983. "The Persistence of Land Fragmentation in Peasant Agriculture: South Asia." *Explorations in Economic History* 20:199-220.

Hossain, M., 1977. "Farm Size, Tenancy, and Land Productivity: An Analysis of Farm Level Data in Bangladesh Agriculture." *Bangladesh Development Studies* 5:285-345.

Johnson, D. G., 1950. "Resource Allocation under Share Contracts." *Journal of Political Economy* 58(April):111-23.

Marshall, A., 1956. *Principles of Economics.* 8th ed. London: Macmillan [1890].

Meyer, C. A., 1991. "A Hierarchy Model of Associative Farming." *Journal of Development Economics* 34:371-83.

Moore, M., 1989. "The Fruits and Fallacies of Neoliberalism: The Case of Irrigation Policy." *World Development* 17:1733-50.

Newbery, D. M. G., 1977. "Risk Sharing, Sharecropping and Uncertain Labor Markets." *Review of Economic Studies* 44:585-94.

Nove, A., 1969. *An Economic History of the USSR.* London: Penguin Books.

Otsuka, K., 1991. "Determinants and Consequences of Land Reform Implementation in the Philippines." *Journal of Development Economics* 35(2):339-55.

———, 1993. "Land Tenure and Rural Poverty." In M. G. Quibria, ed., *Rural Poverty in Asia: Priority Issues and Policy Options.* Hong Kong: Oxford University Press.

Otsuka, K., H. Chuma, and Y. Hayami, 1992. "Towards a General Theory of Land and Labor Contracts in Agrarian Economies." *Journal of Economic Literature* 30:1965-2018.

Otsuka, K., and Y. Hayami, 1988. "Theories of Share Tenancy: A Critical Survey." *Economic Development and Cultural Change* 37:31-68.

Perelman, M., 1977. *Farming for Profit in a Hungry World: Capital and the Crisis in Agriculture.* New Jersey: Allanheld, Osmun & Co. Publishers, Inc.

Powelson, J. P., and R. Stock, 1987. *The Peasant Betrayed, Agriculture and Land Reform in the Third World.* Washington: Lincoln Institute of Land Policy.

Quibria, M. G., 1994. "The Gender and Poverty Nexus: Issues and Policies." *Economics Staff Paper Series* 51 (November).

Quibria, M. G., and S. Rashid, 1984. "The Puzzle of Sharecropping: A Survey of Theories." *World Development* 12:103-114.

———, 1986. "Sharecropping in Dual Agrarian Economies: A Synthesis." *Oxford Economics Papers* 38:94-111.

Ravallion, M., 1989. "Land-Contingent Poverty Alleviation Schemes." *World Development* 17(8):1223-33.

Ruttan, V. W., 1977. "The Green Revolution: Seven Generalizations." *International Development Review* (December):16-22.

Sen, A. K., 1964. "Size of Holdings and Productivity." *Economic and Political Weekly* Annual Number(February).

Shaban, R. A., 1987. "Testing Between Competing Models of Sharecropping." *Journal of Political Economy* 96:893-920.

Shaw, R. P., 1974. "Land Tenure and the Rural Exodus in Latin America." *Economic Development and Cultural Change* 23(1):123-32.

Singh, N., 1989. "Theories of Sharecropping." In P. K. Bardhan, ed., *The Economic Theory of Agrarian Institutions.* Oxford: Oxford University Press.

Srinivasan, T. N., 1972. "Farm Size and Productivity: Implications of Choice Under Uncertainty." *Sankhya* 34:409-20.

Stiglitz, J. E., 1987. "Pareto Efficient and Optimal Taxation and the New Welfare Economics." In A. Auerbach, and M. Feldstein, ed., *Handbook of Public Economics*. Vol. 2. Amsterdam: North-Holland Publishers.

Thiesenhusen, W. C., 1991. "Implications of the Rural Land Tenure System for the Environmental Debate: Three Scenarios." *Journal of Developing Areas* 26:1-24.

Thiesenhusen, W. C., and J. Melmed-Sanjak, 1990. "Brazil's Agrarian Structure. Changes from 1970 through 1980." *World Development* 18(3):393-415.

Tjondronegoro, S. M. P., I. Soejono, and J. Hardjono, 1994. "Indonesia." In M. G. Quibria, ed., *Rural Poverty in Developing Asia*. Vol. 2. Manila: Asian Development Bank.

United Nations, 1951. *Land Reform: Defects in Agrarian Structure as Obstacles to Economic Development*. New York: United Nations Publications.

Verma, B. N., and D. W. Bromley, 1987. "The Political Economy of Farm Size in India: The Elusive Quest." *Economic Development and Cultural Change* 35(4):791-807.

Warriner, D., 1969. *Land Reform in Principle and Practice*. Oxford: Clarendon Press.

World Bank, 1990. *World Development Report 1990*. Oxford: Oxford University Press.

Zaman, M. R., 1973. "Sharecropping and Economic Efficiency in Bangladesh." *Bangladesh Economic Review* 1(April):149-72.

Chapter Seven

Economic Development and the Environment: Issues, Policies, and the Political Economy

Partha Dasgupta

Introduction

The Resource Basis of Rural Production

People in poor countries are in the main agrarian and pastoral folk. In 1988, rural people accounted for about 65 per cent of the population of what the World Bank classifies as low income countries. The proportion of the total labor force in agriculture was a bit in excess of this. In addition, the share of agriculture in the gross domestic product of these countries was 30 per cent. These figures should be contrasted with those from industrial market economies, which are 6 per cent and 2 per cent, respectively.

Poor countries are for the most part *biomass-based subsistence economies*, in that their rural folk eke out a living from products obtained directly from plants and animals. For example, in their informative study of life in a microwatershed of the Alaknanda River in the central Himalayas in India, the (Indian) Centre for Science and Environment (1990) reports that of the total number of hours worked by the villagers sampled, 30 per cent was devoted to cultivation, 20 per cent to fodder collection, and about 25 per cent was spread evenly between fuel collection, animal care, and grazing. Some 20 per cent of time was spent on household chores, of which cooking took up the greatest portion, and the remaining 5 per cent of the hours worked was involved in other activities, such as marketing. In their work on Central and West Africa, Falconer and Arnold (1989), and Falconer (1990) have shown how vital forest products are to the lives of rural folk in those regions. Come what may, poor countries can be expected to remain largely rural economies for a long while yet.

What are Environmental Resources?

The environment comprises a gigantic capital asset. It is also a very heterogenous asset. In what follows we will refer to the environment in its most extensive reach, including not only the atmosphere and the stratospheric layers, but also such assets as soil and soil cover, forests, rivers, aquifers and other water bodies, fisheries, vegetation, animal life, and the rich genetic pool we all depend upon.

Environmental problems are almost always associated with resources that are regenerative (we could call them *renewable natural resources*), but that are in danger of exhaustion from excessive use.[1] The earth's atmosphere is a paradigm of such resources. In the normal course of events, the atmosphere's composition regenerates itself. But the speed of regeneration depends upon, among other things, the current state of the atmosphere and the rate at which pollutants are deposited. It also depends upon the nature of the pollutants. (Smoke discharge is clearly different from the release of chemicals or radioactive material.) Before all else, we need a way of measuring such resources. In the foregoing example, we have to think of an atmospheric quality index. The net rate of regeneration of the stock is the rate at which this quality index changes over time. Regeneration rates of atmospheric quality are complex, and often ill-understood. There is a great deal of synergism associated with the interaction of different types of pollutants in the atmospheric sink, so that, for example, the underlying relationships are almost certainly nonlinear, and, for certain compositions, perhaps greatly so. What are called 'nonlinear dose-response relationships' in the ecological literature, are instances of this.[2] But these are merely qualifications; and so, the analytical point we are making, that pollution problems involve the degradation of renewable natural resources, is both true and useful (see Ehrlich, Ehrlich, and Holdren 1977).

Animal, bird, plant, and fish populations are other examples of renewable natural resources, and there are now a number of studies that have addressed the reproductive behavior of different species under a variety of 'environmental' conditions, including the presence of parasitic and symbiotic neighbors.[3] Land is also such a commodity, for the quality of arable and grazing land can be maintained only by careful use. Population pressures can result in an extended period of overuse. By overuse we mean not only an unsustainable shortening of fallow periods, but also deforestation, and the cultivation and grazing of marginal lands. This causes the quality of the land to deteriorate, until it eventually becomes a wasteland.

The symbiotic relationship between soil quality and vegetation cover is central to the innumerable problems facing sub-Saharan Africa, most especially the Sahel.[4] The management of the drylands in general has to be sensitive to such relationships. It is, for example, useful to distinguish between, on the one hand, a reduction in soil nutrients and humus, and, on the other, the loss of soil due to wind and water runoff. The depletion of soil nutrients can be countered by fertilizers (which, however, can have adverse effects elsewhere in the ecological system), but in the drylands, a loss in topsoil cannot be made good. (In river valleys the alluvial top soil is augmented annually by silt brought by the rivers from mountain slopes. This is the obverse of water runoff caused by a lack of vegetation cover.) Under natural conditions of vegetation cover, it can take from 100 to 500 years for the formation of one centimeter of topsoil. Admittedly, what we are calling 'erosion' is a redistribution of soil. But even when the relocation is from one agricultural field to another, there are adjustment costs. Moreover, the relocation is often into the oceans and nonagricultural land. This amounts to erosion.[5]

Soil degradation can occur if the wrong crops are cultivated. Contrary to general belief, in subtropical conditions most export crops tend to be less damaging to soils than are cereals and root crops. (Groundnuts and cotton are exceptions.) Many export crops, such as coffee, cocoa, oil palm, and tea, grow on trees and bushes that enjoy a continuous root structure and provide continuous canopy cover. With grasses planted underneath, the rate of soil erosion associated with such crops is known to be substantially less than the rate of erosion associated with basic food crops (see Repetto 1988, table 2). But in poor countries, problems are compounded upon problems. In many cultures, the men control cash income while the women control food. Studies in Nigeria, Kenya, India, and Nepal suggest that, to the extent that women's incomes decline as the proportion of cash cropping increases, the family's nutritional status (most especially the nutritional status of children) deteriorates (Gross and Underwood 1971; Kennedy and Oniang'o 1990). The indirect effects of public policy assume a bewildering variety in poor countries, where ecological and technological factors intermingle with norms of behavior that respond only very slowly to changing circumstances.[6]

The link between irrigation and the process by which land becomes increasingly saline has also been much noted in the ecological literature (see Ehrlich, Ehrlich, and Holdren 1977). In the absence of adequate drainage, continued irrigation slowly but remorselessly destroys agricultural land through the salts left behind by evaporating water. The surface area of agricultural land removed from cultivation worldwide through salinization is thought by some to equal the amount added by irrigation (see United Nations 1990). Desalinization of agricultural land is even today an enormously expensive operation.

The environment is affected by the fact that the rural poor are particularly constrained in their access to credit, insurance, and capital markets. Because of such constraints, domestic animals assume a singularly important role as an asset (see, for example, Binswanger and Rosenzweig 1986; Rosenzweig and Wolpin 1989; Hoff and Stiglitz 1990). But they are prone to dying when rainfall is scarce. In sub-Saharan Africa, farmers and nomads therefore carry extra cattle as an insurance against droughts. Herds are larger than they would be were capital and insurance markets open to the rural poor. This imposes an additional strain on grazing lands, most especially during periods of drought. That this link between capital and credit markets (or rather, their absence) and the degradation of the environmental resource base is quantitatively significant (World Bank 1992) should come as no surprise. The environment is itself a gigantic capital asset. The portfolio of assets that a household holds, depends on what is available to it. In fact, one can go beyond these rather obvious links and argue that even the fertility rate is related to the extent of the local environmental resource base, such as fuelwood and water sources. Later in this chapter we will see not only why we should expect this to be so, but we will also study its implications for public policy.

Underground basins of water have the characteristic of a renewable natural resource if they are recharged over the annual cycle. The required analysis is a bit more problematic though, in that we are interested in both its quality and its quantity. Under normal circumstances, an aquifer undergoes a self-cleansing process as pollutants are deposited into it. (Here, the symbiotic role of microbes, as in the case of soil, is important.) But the effectiveness of the process depends on the nature of pollutants and the rate at which they are discharged. Moreover, the recharge rate depends not only on annual precipitation and the extent of underground flows, but also on the rate of evaporation. This in turn is a function of the extent of soil cover. In the drylands, reduced soil cover beyond a point lowers both soil moisture and the rate of recharge of underground basins, which in turn reduces the soil cover still more, which in turn implies a reduced rate of recharge, and so on.[7] With a lowered underground water table, the cost of water extraction rises.

In fact, aquifers display another characteristic. On occasion the issue is not one of depositing pollutants into them. If, as a consequence of excessive extraction, the groundwater level is allowed to drop to too low a level, there can be saltwater intrusion in coastal aquifers, and this can result in the destruction of the basin.

Environmental resources, such as forests, the atmosphere, and the seas, have multiple competing uses. This accentuates management problems. Thus, forests are a source of timber, bark, saps, and, more particularly, pharmaceuticals. Tropical forests also provide a habitat for a rich genetic pool. In addition, forests influence local and regional climate, preserve soil cover on site, and, in the case of watersheds, protect soil downstream from floods. Increased runoff of rainwater arising from deforestation helps strip soil away, depriving agriculture of nutrients, and clogging water reservoirs and irrigation systems. The social value of a forest typically exceeds the value of its direct products, and, on occasion, exceeds it greatly (see Ehrlich, Ehrlich, and Holdren 1977; Hamilton and King 1983; Anderson 1987).

It is as well to remember that the kinds of resources we are thinking of here are on occasion of direct use in consumption (as with fisheries), on occasion in production (as with plankton, which serves as food for fish species), and sometimes in both (as with drinking and irrigation water). Their stock are measured in different ways, depending on the resource: in mass units (for example, biomass units for forests, cowdung, and crop residues), in quality indices (such as water and air quality indices), in volume units (as acre-feet for aquifers), and so on. When we express concern about environmental matters, we in effect point to a decline in their stock. But a decline in their stock, on its own, is not a reason for concern. This is seen most clearly in the context of exhaustible resources, such as fossil fuels. To not reduce their stocks is to not use them at all, and this is unlikely to be the right thing to do. Thus even a casual reading of the foregoing examples suggests that a number of issues in environmental economics are 'capital-theoretic'. A few such issues will be discussed in this article.[8]

Institutional Failure and Poverty as Causes of Environmental Degradation

If these were all, life would have been relatively simple. But these are not all. Admitting environmental resources into economic modeling ushers in a number of additional, potent complications for development policy. They occur for two reasons: institutional failure and poverty.

The early literature on the subject identified failure of market institutions as the underlying cause of environmental problems (see, for example, Pigou 1920; Meade 1973; Mäler 1974; Baumol and Oates 1975; Dasgupta and Heal 1979). Indeed, more often than not, environmental economics is even today regarded as a branch of the economics of externalities. Recently, however, certain patterns of environmental deterioration have been traced to inappropriate government policies, not market failures (Feder 1977; Dasgupta 1982; Mahar 1988; Repetto 1988; Binswanger 1989; Dasgupta and Mäler 1991). Taken together, they reflect institutional failures. Later in this paper, we will place these matters within the context of the thesis that environmental degradation is a cause of accentuated poverty among the rural poor in poor countries. (See Dasgupta and Mäler 1993, for an extended discussion.)

At the same time, poverty itself can be a cause of environmental degradation. This reverse causality stems from the fact that, for poor people in poor countries, a number of environmental resources are complementary in production and consumption to other goods and services, while a number of environmental resources supplement income, most especially in times of acute economic stress (see, for example, Falconer and Arnold 1989; Falconer 1990). This can be a source of cumulative causation, where poverty, high fertility rates, and environmental degradation feed upon one another. In fact, an erosion of the environmental resource base can make certain categories of people destitute even while the economy on average grows (see Dasgupta 1993, chapter 16).

These two causes of environmental degradation (namely, institutional failure and poverty) pull in different directions, and are together not unrelated to an intellectual tension between concerns about externalities (such as, for example, the increased greenhouse effect, acid rains, and the fear that the mix of resources and manufactured capital in aggregate production is inappropriate in advanced industrial countries) that sweep across regions, nations, and continents; and about those matters (such as the decline in firewood or water availability) that are specific to the needs and concerns of poor people in as small a group as a village community. This tension should be borne in mind, and we will elaborate upon an aspect of it in the following section, when we come to evaluate an empirically-based suggestion by the World Bank (1992) concerning the nature of a possible tradeoff faced by poor countries between national income per head and environmental quality.

Environmental problems present themselves differently to different people. In part it is a reflection of the tension we are speaking of here. Some people identify environmental problems with the wrong sorts of economic growth, while others view them through the spectacles of poverty. It seems that both visions are correct. There is no single environmental problem; rather, there is a large collection of them. Thus, for example, growth in industrial wastes has been allied to increased economic activity, and in industrialized countries (especially those in the former Socialist block), neither preventive nor curative measures have kept pace with their production. These observations loom large not only in environmental economics, but also in the more general writings of environmentalists in the West.

On the other hand, economic growth itself has brought with it improvements in the quality of a number of environmental resources. For example, the large scale availability of potable water, and the increased protection of human populations against both water- and air-borne diseases in industrial countries, have in large measure come in the wake of the growth in national income that these countries have enjoyed over the past 200 years or so. Moreover, the physical environment inside the home has improved beyond measure with economic growth. (Cooking in South Asia continues to be a central route to respiratory illnesses among women.) Such positive links between wealth and environmental quality have not been much noted by environmental economists, nor by environmentalists in general. This lacuna may be yet another reflection of the fact that it is all too easy to overlook the enormous heterogeneity of the earth's natural consumption and capital base, ranging as it does from landscapes of scenic beauty to watering holes and sources of fuelwood. This heterogeneity should constantly be kept in mind.

Kuznets' Curves: Economic Growth and the Environment

In its admirable document on development and the environment, the World Bank (1992, chapter 1) suggests on empirical grounds that there is a relationship between gross domestic product (GDP) per head and concentration levels of industrial pollutants. Summarizing the historical experience of member countries of the Organisation for Economic Co-operation and Development (OECD), the document argues that concentrations of a number of atmospheric pollutants (such as sulfur dioxide) are increasing functions of GDP per head when GDP per head is low, and are decreasing functions when GDP per head is high. In short, the typical curve has the inverted-U shape (see the accompanying figure). It will be recalled that the so-called Kuznets' curve relates indices of income inequality to real national income per head in much the same way. So we will call this putative empirical relationship between national income per head and concentration levels of industrial pollutants the *environmental Kuznets' curve*.

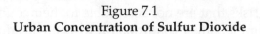

Figure 7.1
Urban Concentration of Sulfur Dioxide

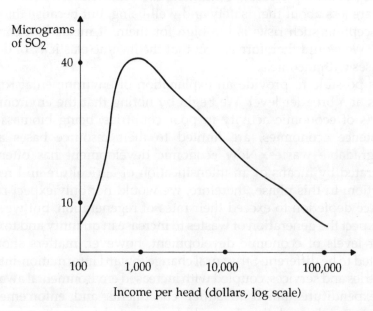

Income per head (dollars, log scale)

Source: World Bank, 1992. *World Development Report*. New York: Oxford University Press.

Panayotou (1992) has observed the inverted-U shape in cross-country data on deforestation, and emissions of SO_2, NO_x, and SPM (particulate matters). Sweden, for example, was found to lie on the downward part of the curve. Indeed, time series on timber stocks and sulfur and nitrogen emissions in Sweden, covering the decade of the 1980s, are consistent with this: timber stocks have increased, and the emission rates of sulfur and nitrogen have declined (see also Grossman forthcoming).

Like all broad generalizations in the social sciences, the environmental Kuznets' curve is almost certainly something of a mirage. Nevertheless, the idea behind it has an intuitive appeal, since environmental commodities are often thought to be luxury goods. We suggested earlier that a number of them are in fact necessities; most especially for the poor. In fact, such evidence as has been accumulated (in Sweden and the United States; see Kanninen and Kristrom 1993) suggests that income elasticities of demand are less than one, even for such goods as virgin forests and places of scenic beauty (even these goods are not luxuries). However, this finding is consistent with the thought that poor countries cannot afford clean technologies because they are expensive. The latter is in part reflected in the incontrovertible fact that citizens in poor countries absorb environmental risks that are not acceptable to their counterparts in rich nations (for example, safety conditions at work). They do so not because they care less about their safety and well-being, but because the cost of not accepting such risks is too high for them: it means not earning a living. We would therefore expect that the income elasticity of demand increases with income.

It is possible to provide an explanation of environmental Kuznets' curves at a broader level. We begin by noting that the environmental impacts of economic activity in poor countries, being biomass-based subsistence economies, are limited to their resource bases and to biodegradable wastes. Now economic development has often been accelerated by means of an intensification of agriculture and resource extraction. In this phase, therefore, we would not only expect rates of resource depletion to exceed their rates of regeneration, but we would also expect the generation of wastes to increase in quantity and toxity. At higher levels of economic development, however, matters should be expected to be different. Structural change toward information-intensive industries and services, coupled with increased environmental awareness and expenditure (allied to stiffer enactments and enforcements of environmental regulations), would be expected to result in a gradual decline in deterioration of the environment.

This is an intuitively plausible scenario. But we should be circumspect before using it to conclude that there are environmental Kuznets' curves associated with all environmental resources. First of all, the observations are based on the assumption that environmental damages are reversible. This is true only for some resources, and is not a good approximation for many others (for example, when investment is directed at hydroelectric power, or when the activity extinguishes an entire species). More generally, environmental 'threshold effects' provide instances where the reversibility of the impact of economic decisions is not a good or realistic assumption.

Second, if there really are quantifiable relationships between income per head and environmental quality to be discovered, they must surely depend on other factors as well; in particular, the characteristics of growth strategies pursued by countries. If economic growth were to be encouraged by means of an improved institutional structure (for example, by a removal of large scale distortions), rather than by the decimation of forests and extractive ores, then it is not clear if poor countries would face a tradeoff between increased national income and environmental quality. Zylics (1990) has attributed the high levels of pollution in the former socialist countries of Europe to the adoption of inappropiate industrial technologies. He has argued, for example, that by setting artificially low prices for energy, these countries consumed (and continue to consume) much more energy than the rest of Europe.[9] Further in this paper, we will see analytically why an improvement in production efficiency could be expected to be beneficial to the environment, broadly defined, so that even while some resources deteriorate in quality (or reduce in quantity), others would show an improvement, at least in the long run. However, partial improvements in prevailing resource allocation mechanisms cannot be guaranteed to enhance environmental quality: if important distortions persist elsewhere in the economy, the elimination of market or policy failure in a given sector would not necessarily lead to an improvement in human well-being. This is the central message of the theory of the second-best in welfare economics.

All this has a bearing on structural and sectoral adjustment programs. If they are carefully designed, such programs should not be unfriendly toward the environment.[10] Furthermore, the elimination of price distortions would make economic analyses of environmental problems that much more transparent. In the presence of government-induced distortions, it is often very difficult to locate the ultimate causes of any particular environmental problem. In such situations, the temptation of governments is to enact ad hoc policies aimed at countering the problem in question. Over time this can result in a patchwork of taxes and subsidies, quotas, and regulations, so intricate, that it proves virtually impossible to devise ways of sustaining anything like an optimal pattern of resource use.

Implicit in the environmental Kuznets' curve depicted in the accompanying figure are two key assumptions: (1) the variable measured along the horizontal axis is GNP per head, conventionally measured, and (2) the vertical axis measures industrial pollution. The nature of the tradeoff between poverty and environmental quality is conditional on both assumptions. In the next sections of this paper, we will focus on (1) and study why and how conventionally measured GNP ought to be replaced by an index of real net national product (NNP) that takes into account depreciation (or appreciation) of the natural resource base. If living standards were to be assessed by a correct measure of NNP, then the nature of tradeoffs between human well-being and environmental quality, even for poor countries, should be expected to be different from that implied by the environmental Kuznets' curve. Later, we will focus on (2) and develop a point stressed earlier, that with regard to local environmental resources (such as local forest products, grazing lands, and water sources), the link between poverty and the environment is different from that suggested in the environmental Kuznets' curve.

Project Evaluation and the Measurement of Net National Product

There are two ways of assessing changes in aggregate well-being. One would be to measure the value of changes in the constituents of well-being (utility and freedoms), and the other would be to measure the value of the alterations in the commodity determinants of well-being (goods and services that are inputs in the production of well-being). The former procedure measures the value of alterations in various 'outputs' (such as indices of health, education, and other social indicators), and the latter evaluates the aggregate value of changes in the 'inputs' of the production of well-being (namely, real national income). A key theorem in modern resource allocation theory is that, provided certain technical restrictions are met, for any conception of aggregate well-being, and for any set of technological, transaction, information, and ecological constraints, there exists a set of shadow (or accounting) prices of goods and services that can be used in the estimation of real national product. The index in question has the following property: small investment projects that improve the index are at once those that increase aggregate well-being.[11] We may state the matter more generally: provided the set of accounting prices is unaffected, an improvement in the index owing to an alteration in economic activities reflects an increase in aggregate well-being. This is the sense in which real national income measures aggregate well-being. Moreover, the sense persists no matter what is the basis upon which aggregate well-being is founded. In particular, the use of national income in measuring changes in aggregate well-being is not restricted to utilitarian ethics.

The theorem should be well-known, but it often goes unrecognized in development economics, and today the use of real national income as an indicator of economic development is held in disrepute. For example, Anand and Ravallion (1993) criticize the use of national income in assessing relative well-being in poor countries, on grounds that income is a measure of opulence, and not of well-being (nor, as they say, of 'capability'; see Sen 1992). They assert that using the former for the purposes of measuring the latter constitutes a philosophical error, and imply that development planners would have been better placed to make recommendations in poor countries if they had only read their Aristotle, a thinker who had earlier stressed the importance of 'capabilities' as constituents of well-being. The authors divide national income into two categories, personal income and public services, and show that there are a number of countries with a better-than-average personal income per head that display worse-than-average social indicators, such as health and basic education.

But it has long been a tenet of resource allocation theory that public health and basic education ought not to be a matter of private consumption alone. One reason for this view is that they both display strong externalities, and are at once merit goods (Musgrave 1959). Another reason is that the credit and savings markets work especially badly for the poor in poor countries. In short, the theory has always informed us that a community's personal consumption would not tell us much about its health and education statistics. As this is standard fare in public economics, one can but conclude that if the majority of poor countries have a bad record in the provision of public services, it is not due to a philosophical error on the part of their leadership, nor a lack of knowledge of resource allocation theory: it is something else. In any event, reliance on national income as an indicator of aggregate well-being does not reflect any particular brand of ethics. Its justification rests on a technical result in economics, and is independent of the ethical stance that is adopted.

To be sure, if real national income is to reflect aggregate well-being, accounting prices should be used. Recall that the accounting price of a resource is the increase in the maximum value of aggregate well-being if a unit more of the resource were made available without cost. (It is a Lagrange multiplier.) Accounting prices are, therefore, the differences between market prices and optimum taxes and subsidies. This provides us with the sense in which it is important for poor countries to 'get their prices right'. Moreover, by real national product for an intertemporal economy, we mean real *net* national product. The accounting value of the depreciation of fixed capital (and by this we mean both manufactured and natural capital) needs to be deducted if the index of national product is to play the role we are assigning to it here (see Dasgupta and Heal 1979; Solow 1986; Hartwick 1990; Dasgupta and Mäler 1991; Mäler 1991; Lutz 1993). Thus, NNP, when correctly measured in a closed economy, reads as follows:

NNP = Consumption + net investment in physical capital + the value of the net change in human capital + the value of the net change in the stock of natural capital - the value of current environmental damages.

Consumption is regarded as the numeraire in this measure of NNP. So the 'values' referred to in the equation are consumption values, and are evaluated with the help of shadow prices. Dasgupta and Mäler (1991, 1993), while studying an optimizing economy, present an account of how net national product ought ideally to be computed in an intertemporal economy. The optimization exercise enables one to estimate accounting prices. These prices can then in principle be used for the purposes of project and policy evaluation even in an economy that is currently far off the optimum (see, for example, Little and Mirrlees 1974; Squire and Van der Taak 1975).

There is a close link between real NNP and what is known as the current-value Hamiltonian associated with intertemporal optimization exercises. It takes us into somewhat technical matters, but it is well worth noting the central features. The theory of intertemporal planning tells us to choose current controls (for example, current consumptions and the mix of current investments) in such a way as to maximize the current-value Hamiltonian of the underlying planning problem.[12] As is well known, the current-value Hamiltonian is the sum of the flow of current well-being and the shadow value of all the net investments currently being undertaken. (The planning exercise generates the entire set of intertemporal shadow prices.[13]) It can be shown that the current-value Hamiltonian measures the social return on the value of all capital assets (see Solow 1986; Mäler 1991; Dasgupta 1993, chapter 10). In short, it is a measure of wealth. This provides us with the necessary connection between the current-value Hamiltonian and real net national product. NNP is merely a linearized version of the current-value Hamiltonian, the linearization amounting to a representation of the current flow of well-being by the shadow value of all the determinants of current well-being. In the simplest of cases, where current well-being depends solely on current consumption, NNP reduces to the sum of the shadow value of an economy's consumptions and the shadow value of the changes in its stocks of real capital assets.

The Hamiltonian calculus in fact implies something more. It implies that the present discounted sum of today's current value Hamiltonian is equal to the maximum present discounted value of the flow of social well-being (see Solow 1986; Mäler 1991; Dasgupta 1993, chapter 10). Thus the current-value Hamiltonian is the maximum sustainable flow of social well-being. Therefore if all commodities are priced appropriately, so that poverty itself is based on the notion of ill-being, the alleged tradeoff between poverty and the environment becomes blunt.

An alternative way of interpreting the aforementioned NNP equation is to think of public policy as a sequence of reforms. Accounting prices in this framework would be estimated from the prevailing structure of production and consumption (and not from the optimum). If the economy has a convex structure, then a sequence of such reforms would in principle take the economy ultimately to the optimum (see, for example, Dasgupta, Marglin, and Sen 1972; Ahmad and Stern 1990). The aforementioned equation reflects the correct notion of NNP in both the optimizing and reformist frameworks.[14]

It is useful to note here that the convention of regarding expenditures on public health and education as part of final demand implicitly equates the cost of their provision with the contribution they make to aggregate well-being. This in all probability results in an underestimate in poor countries.[15] We should note as well that current defensive expenditure against damages to the flow of environmental amenities ought to be included in the estimation of final demand. Similarly, investment in the stock of environmental defensive capital should be included in NNP.

By 'investment' we mean the value of net changes in capital assets, and not changes in the value of these assets. This means that anticipated capital gains (or losses) should not be included in NNP (see Dasgupta and Heal 1979; Dasgupta and Mäler 1991). As an example, the value of the net decrease in the stock of oil and natural gas (net of new discoveries, that is) ought to be deducted from GNP when NNP is estimated. The answer to the question of how we should estimate NNP should not be a matter of opinion today: it is a matter of fact.

Current estimates of NNP are biased because the depreciation of environmental resources is not deducted from GNP. Stated another way, NNP estimates are biased because a biased set of prices is in use. Prices imputed to environmental resources on site are usually zero. This amounts to regarding the depreciation of environmental capital as zero. But these resources are scarce goods, so we know that their shadow prices are positive. Profits attributed to projects that degrade the environment are therefore higher than the social profits they generate. This means in turn that the wrong sets of projects get chosen—in both the private and public sectors.

The extent of the bias will obviously vary from project to project, and from country to country. But it can be substantial. In their work on the depreciation of natural resources in Costa Rica, Solorzano et al. (1991) have estimated that, in 1989 the depreciation of three resources—forests, soil, and fisheries—amounted to about 10 per cent of gross domestic product and over a third of gross capital accumulation. Resource-intensive projects look better than they actually are. Installed technologies are usually unfriendly toward the environment.

Biases in Technological Adaptation

One can go further: the bias extends to the prior stage of research and development. When environmental resources are underpriced, there is little incentive on anyone's part to develop technologies that economize on their use. The extent of the distortion created by this underpricing will vary from country to country. Poor countries inevitably have to rely on the flow of new knowledge produced in advanced industrial economies. Nevertheless, poor countries need to have the capability for basic research. The structure of shadow prices there is likely to be different from those in advanced industrial countries, most especially for non-traded goods and services. Even when it is publicly available, basic knowledge is not necessarily usable by scientists and technologists, unless they themselves have a feel for basic research. Often enough, ideas developed in foreign lands are merely transplanted to the local economy; whereas, they ought instead to be modified to suit local ecological conditions before being adopted. This is where the use of shadow prices is of help. It creates the right set of incentives both among developers and users of technologies. Adaptation is itself a creative exercise. Unhappily, as matters stand, it is often bypassed. There is loss in this.

There is further loss associated with a different kind of bias: that arising from biased demand. For example, wherever household demands for goods and services in the market reflect, in the main, male (or, for that matter, female) concerns, the direction of technological change would be expected to follow suit. Among poor countries, we would expect technological inventions in farm equipment and techniques of production to be forthcoming in regions where cultivation is a male activity (there would be a demand for them); we would not observe much in the way of process innovations in threshing, winnowing, the grinding of grain in the home, and in the preparation of food. Thus, cooking in South Asia is a central route to respiratory illnesses among women: women sit hunched over ovens fueled by cowdung, wood, or leaves. It is inconceivable that improvements in design are not possible to realize. But entrepreneurs have little incentive to bring about such technological innovations. Household demand for them would be expected to be low.

The argument extends to collective activity in general, and State activity in particular. In poor communities, men typically have the bulk of the political voice. We should then expect public decisions over rural investment and environmental preservation also to be guided by male preferences, not female needs. Over afforestation in the drylands, for example, we should expect women to favor planting for fuelwood and men for fruit trees, because it is the women and children who collect fuelwood, while men control cash income. And fruit can be sold in the market. Such evidence on this is only anecdotal. But as it is confirmed by theory, it is reasonable to imagine that this must quite generally be true.

Such biases in NNP as identified here occur in advanced industrial countries as well. So then why is their importance in the context of poor countries stressed here? The reason is that poor people in poor countries cannot cope with the same margin of error as people living in rich countries: a 10 per cent drop in the standard of living imposes greater hardship on a poor household than a rich one. Recall too that the rural poor are especially dependent upon their local environmental resource base. Losses in well-being due to an underpricing of this base are absorbed by them disproportionately. The estimation of accounting prices of environmental resources should now be high on the agenda of research in the economics of poor countries.

The Valuation of Environmental Resources

The question, How should we estimate shadow prices for environmental resources? is a complex one. But it is not uniformly complex. There are now standard techniques of evaluation for commodities like irrigation water, fisheries, and agricultural soil. These techniques rely on the fact that such resources are inputs in the production of tradable goods. For others, such as firewood, and drinking and cooking water, the matter is more complex. But even they are inputs in production, namely, in household production. This implies that we need to have an estimate of household production functions. As an example, transportation costs (in particular, calorie costs) for women and children would be less were the sources of fuelwood and water not far away and receding. The value of water or fuelwood resources for household production can then be estimated from these caloric needs (see Dasgupta and Mäler 1993). In some situations (as on occasion with fuelwood) the resource is a substitute for a tradable input (for example, kerosine); in others (as with cooking water) it is a complement (sometimes a weak complement) to tradable inputs (for example, food grain). Such facts allow one to estimate shadow prices of nonmarketed goods in terms of the shadow prices of marketed goods.

The approach outlined above allows us to capture only the known use value of a resource. As it happens, its shadow price may well exceed this. Why? The reason is that there may be additional values embodied in a resource stock. One additional value, applicable to living resources, is their intrinsic worth as living resources. (It is absurd to suppose that the value of a blue whale is embodied entirely in its flesh and oil, or that the value of the game in Kenyan safari parks is simply the present discounted value of tourists' willingness to pay.) The idea of 'intrinsic worth' of living things is inherent not only within traditional religious systems of ethics, but also in the modern 'utilitarian' tradition. Therefore, the question is not so much whether living things possess intrinsic worth, but rather, about ways of assessing this worth. It is almost impossible to get a quantitative handle on intrinsic worth. So the right thing to do is to take note of it, keep an eye on it, and call attention to it in public debate if the resource is threatened with extinction.

What is the point of basing shadow prices solely on use value when we know that resources often possess intrinsic value as well? It is that such estimates provide us with biased shadow prices, and this can be useful information. For example, in his classic paper on the optimal rate of harvest of blue whales, Spence (1974) took the shadow price of these creatures to be the market value of their flesh, a seemingly absurd and repugnant move. But he showed that under a wide range of plausible parametric conditions, it would be most profitable commercially for the international whaling industry to agree on a moratorium until the desired long run population size was reached, and for the industry to subsequently harvest the creatures at a rate equal to the population's sustainable yield.[16] In other words, preservation is recommended solely on commercial grounds. But if preservation is justified when the shadow values of blue whales are estimated from their market prices, the recommendation would, obviously, be reinforced if their intrinsic worth were to be added. This was the point of Spence's exercise.

There is another source of value of environmental resources, which is more amenable to quantification. It arises from a combination of two things common to them: uncertainty in their future use values, and irreversibility in their use. (Genetic material in tropical forests provides a prime example.) The twin presence of uncertainty and irreversibility implies that, even if the aggregate well-being function were neutral to risk, it would not do to estimate the accounting price of an environmental resource solely on the basis of the expected benefit from its future use. Irreversibility in its use implies that preservation of its stock has an additional value—the value of extending society's set of future options. Future options have an additional worth because, with the passage of time, more information is expected to be forthcoming about the resource's use value. This additional worth of a resource is often called an *option value*. Thus, the accounting price of a resource is the sum of its use value and its option value.[17]

Environmental Degradation and Children as Income Earners

As mentioned earlier, the alleged curve between GDP and environmental pollution ignores the environmental resource base upon which rural people in poor countries depend for their livelihood. Poor countries for the most part are biomass-based subsistence economies. Rural folk there eke out a living from products obtained directly from plants and animals. Production throughput is low. Households there do not have access to the sources of domestic energy available to households in advanced industrial countries. Nor do they have water on tap. (In the semi-arid and arid regions, water supply is not even close at hand.) This means that the relative prices of alternative sources of energy and water faced by rural households in poor countries are quite different from those faced by households elsewhere. Indirect sources (such as tap water nearby) are often prohibitively expensive for the household. As we will see presently, this provides a possible link between high fertility, degradation of the environmental resource base of a rural community, and an accentuation of hardship among its members.

From about the age of six years, children in poor households in poor countries mind their siblings and domestic animals, fetch water, and collect fuelwood, dung, and fodder. These are complementary to other household activities. They are needed on a daily basis if the household is to survive. As many as five hours a day may be required for obtaining the bare essential firewood, dung, and fodder. (One should contrast this with the direct time spent by households in acquiring water and fuel in advanced industrial economies, which is nil.)

All this may be expected to relate to the high fertility and low literacy rates in rural areas of most poor countries. Poverty, the thinness of markets, and an absence of basic amenities make it essential for house-holds to engage in a number of complementary production activities: cultivation, cattle grazing, fetching water, collecting fodder and fuel-wood, cooking food, and producing simple marketable products. Each is time consuming. Labor productivity is low not only because capital is scarce, but also because environmental resources are scarce too.[18] Children are then continually needed as workers by their parents, even when parents are in their prime. They are not only consumer goods and a security for old age; but they are also producer goods. A small household simply will not do. Each household needs many hands, and it can be that the overall usefulness of each additional hand increases with declining resource availability.[19] In their study of work allocation among rural households in the foothills of the Himalayas, the Centre for Science and Environment (1990) recorded that children in the age range of 10 to 15 years work one-and-a-half times the number of hours adult males do, their tasks consisting of fuelwood, dung, and fodder collection, grazing domestic animals, household chores, and marketing. Now, a high rate of fertility and population growth further damages the environmental resource base (to the extent they are unprotected common property), which, in a wide range of circumstances, provides further (private) incentives for large families, which in turn further damages the resource base . . . and so on; until some countervailing set of factors (whether public policy, or some other form of check) stops the spiraling process. But, by the time this happens, millions of lives have usually suffered.[20] Such an explosive process can be set off by any number of factors. Government or private usurpation of resources to which rural communi-ties have had historical access is a potential source of the problem. As well, the breakdown of collective agreements among users of common property resources is a triggering mechanism. Indeed, even a marginal decline in compliance can trigger the process of cumulative causation. The static efficiency loss associated with minor violations is, to be sure, small; but over time the effect can be large.

The motivation for fertility emphasized here springs from a general absence of certain basic needs in rural parts of poor countries: public health services, old age security, water, and sources of fuel. Children are born in poverty, and they are raised in poverty. A large proportion suffer from undernourishment. They remain illiterate, and are often both stunted and wasted. Undernourishment retards their cognitive (and often motor) development (see, for example, Dasgupta 1993, chapter 14). Labor productivity is dismally low also because of a lack of infrastructure, such as roads. Given this background it is hard to make sense of the oft-expressed suggestion (see Simon 1977) that there are increasing returns to scale in population size even in poor countries; that human beings are a valuable resource. They are potentially valuable as doers of things and originators of ideas, but for this they require inputs of the means for development. Historical evidence on how the pressure of population led to changes in the organization of production, property rights, and in ways of doing things, which is what Boserup (1965, 1981) studied in her far reaching work, also does not seem to speak to the population problem as it exists in sub-Saharan Africa and the Indian subcontinent today. Admittedly, the central message one reads in these writings is that the spectre of the Malthusian trap is not to be taken seriously. But we should be permitted to ask of these modern writers what policy flows from their visions. The Boserup-Simon thesis implies that households confer an external benefit to the community when they reproduce. This means fertility ought to be subsidized. This implication has not, however, been advocated by its proponents.

Conclusions

In the present article, we have first argued that much resource allocation failure can be traced to the underpricing of various environmental resources, and that the time has come for the systematic use of accounting prices in the estimation of real net national product. When this is appropriately done, household income will itself come to be revalued. Our idea of poverty is not independent of this exercise. The tradeoff between poverty and the environment is likely to be more tenuous when poverty is measured properly.

We have also argued that there are conceptual dangers in aggregating environmental resources into an all purpose notion of the environment. At the very least, a distinction should be made between that portion of the environment (for example, the atmosphere and water bodies) that is used as a sink for industrial effluents, and the portion that provides a source of the biomass that is necessary for rural production. Admittedly, discharges of industrial and automobile effluents have reached staggering levels in the large metropolises of poor countries. But over 70 per cent of the populations of South Asia and sub-Saharan Africa are rural folk, and the environmental degradation they face is of a different kind. We have argued that the stress on the local environmental resource base of these communities is related directly to their poverty and this relationship may well be synergistic via people's fertility behavior. This suggests that policies that may be effective for growth in income may have salutary effects on the local environmental resource base and fertility behavior. In short, what are multiple social objectives may not be in conflict with one another.[21] This is, no doubt, a pleasing conclusion in what is a most depressing subject of research.

Acknowledgments

The author would like to thank Tariq Banur, Marian de los Angeles, and Gene Owens for their comments. Over the years he has gained much from discussions with Karl-Göran Mäler on the subject matter of this article. Some of the material here has been taken from Dasgupta and Mäler (1993).

Notes

1. Minerals and fossil fuels are not renewable (they are a prisitine example of exhaustible resources), but they raise a different set of issues. For an account of what resource allocation theory looks like when exhaustible resources are included in the production process, see Dasgupta and Heal (1979), Hartwick and Olewiler (1986), and Tietenberg (1988). For a nontechnical account of the theory and the historical role that has been played by the substitution of new energy resources for old, see Dasgupta (1989).

2. The economic issues arising from such nonlinearities are analyzed in Dasgupta (1982).

3. Ehrlich and Roughgarden (1987) is an excellent treatise on these matters.

4. Anderson (1987) contains an authoritative case study of this.

5. One notable, and controversial, estimate of worldwide productivity declines in livestock and agriculture in the drylands due to soil losses was offered in the United Nations Environmental Programme (1984). The figure was an annual loss of $26 billion. For a discussion of the United Nations Environmental Programme estimate, see Gigengack et al. (1990). The estimate by Mabbut (1984), that approximately 40 per cent of the productive drylands of the world are currently under threat from desertification, probably gives an idea of the magnitude of the problem. For accounts of the economics and ecology of drylands, see Falloux and Mukendi (1988), and Dixon, James, and Sherman (1989, 1990).

6. Such observed features of household allocations as just mentioned suggest that utility-maximizing models of the household are misleading. When peering inside the household, bargaining models would seem to be more illuminating (see Dasgupta 1993).

7. See, for example, Falkenmark (1986, 1989); Olsen (1987); Nelson (1988); Reij, Mulder, and Begemann (1988); Falkenmark and Chapman (1989).

8. There are added complications, among which is that the impact on the rate of regeneration of environmental resources of a wide variety of investment

decisions is not fully reversible, and in some cases is quite irreversible. The capital-theoretic approach guides the exposition in Clark (1976), who, however, concentrates on fisheries. The argument that environmental pollution presents the same analytical structure as renewable natural resources, such as fisheries and groundwater, was developed in Dasgupta (1982), which developed a unified capital-theoretic treatment of environmental management problems in the context of poor countries.

9. Poland's GNP represents about 3 per cent of European GNP (excluding the former Soviet Union); but its energy consumption is about 8 per cent of the corresponding European figure.

10. World Bank (1992) offers a similar viewpoint.

11. See Dasgupta (1993, chapters 7 and 10). The technical restrictions amount to the requirement that the Kuhn-Tucker Theorem is usable; that is, that both the set of feasible allocations and the ethical ordering reflected by the aggregate well-being function are convex. The assumption of convexity is dubious for pollution problems. Nevertheless, in a wide range of circumstances, it is possible to separate out the 'nonconvex' sector, estimate real national income (or product) for the 'convex' sector, and present an estimate of the desired index as a combination of the real product of the convex sector and estimates of stocks and their changes in the nonconvex sectors. This is a simple inference from Weitzman (1970), and Portes (1971). See also Starrett (1972).

12. The best economics treatment of all of this is still Arrow and Kurz (1970).

13. The current-value Hamiltonian will, in general, also contain terms reflecting the social cost of breaking any additional (second-best) constraint that happens to characterize the optimization problem. Such additional constraints are ignored here for expositional ease.

14. For a simplified exposition of the connection between these two modes of analysis (reforms and optimization), see Dasgupta (1982, chapter 5).

15. If education is regarded as a merit good, and not merely as instrumental in raising productivity, then its accounting price would be that much higher.

16. During the moratorium the whale population grows at the fastest possible rate. In his numerical computations, the commerically most profitable duration of the moratorium was found to be some 10 to 15 years.

17. The pioneering works are Arrow and Fisher (1974), and Henry (1974).

18. Cooking in a poor household is a vertically integrated activity: nothing is processed to begin with. It is time intensive.

19. This can happen especially if households discount the future at a high rate.

20. For an account of this kind of spiraling process, see Nerlove and Meyer (1991), and Dasgupta and Mäler (1991). In an important empirical document, the World Bank (1991) has provided some support for the thesis in the context of sub-Saharan Africa.

21. For more detail, see Dasgupta (1993).

References

Ahmad, E., and N. Stern, 1990. *The Theory and Practice of Tax Reform for Developing Countries*. Cambridge: Cambridge University Press.

Anand, S., and M. Ravallion, 1993. "Human Development in Poor Countries: On the Role of Private Incomes and Public Services." *Journal of Economic Perspectives* 7(1):133-50.

Anderson, D., 1987. *The Economics of Afforestation: A Case Study in Africa*. Baltimore: Johns Hopkins University Press.

Arrow, K. J., and A. Fisher, 1974. "Preservation, Uncertainty and Irreversibility." *Quarterly Journal of Economics* 88(2):312-9.

Arrow, K. J., and M. Kurz, 1970. *Public Investment, the Rate of Return, and Optimal Fiscal Policy*. Baltimore: Johns Hopkins University Press.

Baumol, W. M., and W. Oates, 1975. *The Theory of Environmental Policy*. Englewood Cliffs, NJ: Prentice-Hall.

Binswanger, H., 1989. "Brazilian Policies that Encourage Deforestation in the Amazon." Environment Department Paper No. 16. World Bank, Washington, D.C.

Binswanger, H., and M. Rosenzweig, 1986. "Credit Markets, Wealth and Endowments in Rural South India." Agriculture and Rural Development Department Report No. 59. World Bank, Washington, D.C.

Boserup, E., 1965. *The Conditions of Agricultural Growth*. London: Allen & Unwin.

———, 1981. *Population Growth and Technological Change: A Study of Long-Term Trends*. Chicago: Chicago University Press.

Clark, C. W., 1976. *Mathematical Bioeconomics: The Optimal Management of Renewable Resources*. New York: John Wiley & Sons.

Centre for Science and Environment (CSE), 1985. *The State of India's Environment: A Citizens' Report*. New Delhi: CSE.

———, 1990. *Human-Nature Interactions in a Central Himalayan Village: A Case Study of Village Bemru*. New Delhi: CSE.

Dasgupta, P., 1982. *The Control of Resources*. Oxford: Basil Blackwell.

———, 1989. "Exhaustible Resources." In L. Friday and R. Laskey, eds., *The Fragile Environment*. Cambridge: Cambridge University Press.

———, 1993. *An Inquiry into Well-Being and Destitution*. Oxford: Clarendon Press.

Dasgupta, P., and G. M. Heal, 1979. *Economic Theory and Exhaustible Resources*. Cambridge: Cambridge University Press.

Dasgupta, P., and K.-G. Mäler, 1991. "The Environment and Emerging Development Issues." *Proceedings of the World Bank Annual Conference on Development Economics, 1991*. Supplement to the *World Bank Economic Review* and the *World Bank Research Observer*.

———, 1993. "Poverty and the Environmental Resource Base." In J. Behrman and T. N. Srinivasan, eds., *Handbook of Development Economics*. Vol. III. Amsterdam: North-Holland.

Dasgupta, P., S. Marglin, and A. Sen, 1972. *Guidelines for Project Evaluation*. New

York: United Nations.

Dixon, J. A., D. E. James, and P. B. Sherman, 1989. *The Economics of Dryland Management*. London: Earthscan Publications.

———, eds., 1990. *Dryland Management: Economic Case Studies*. London: Earthscan Publications.

Ehrlich, P., A. Ehrlich, and J. Holdren, 1977. *Ecoscience: Population, Resources and the Environment*. San Francisco: W.H. Freeman.

Ehrlich, P., and J. Roughgarden, 1987. *The Science of Ecology*. New York: Macmillan.

Falconer, J., 1990. *The Major Significance of 'Minor' Forest Products*. Rome: Food and Agriculture Organization.

Falconer, J., and J. E. M. Arnold, 1989. *Household Food Security and Forestry: An Analysis of Socio-Economic Issues*. Rome: Food and Agriculture Organization.

Falkenmark, M., 1986. "Fresh Water: Time for a Modified Approach." *Ambio* 15(4):192-200.

———, 1989. "The Massive Water Scarcity Now Threatening Africa: Why Isn't It Being Addressed?" *Ambio* 18(2):112-8.

Falkenmark, M., and T. Chapman, eds., 1989. *Comparative Hydrology: An Ecological Approach to Land and Water Resources*. Paris: United Nations Educational, Scientific and Cultural Organization.

Falloux, F., and A. Mukendi, eds., 1988. *Desertification Control and Renewable Resource Management in the Sahelian and Sudanian Zones of West Africa*. Technical Paper No. 70. Washington: World Bank.

Feder, E., 1977. "Agribusiness and the Elimination of Latin America's Rural Proletariat." *World Development* 5(5-7):559-71.

Gigengack, A. R., et al., 1990. "Global Modelling of Dryland Degradation." In J. A. Dixon, D. E. James, and P. B. Sherman, eds., *Dryland Management: Economic Case Studies*. London: Earthscan Publications.

Gross, D. R., and B. Underwood, 1971. "Technological Change and Calorie Costs: Sisal Agriculture in North-Eastern Brazil." *American Anthropologist* 73.

Grossman, G., forthcoming. "Pollution and Growth: What Do We Know?" In I. Goldin and A. Winters, eds., *Sustainable Economic Development: Domestic and International Policy*. Cambridge: Cambridge University Press.

Hamilton, L. S., and P. N. King, 1983. *Tropical Forested Watersheds: Hydrologic and Soils Response to Major Uses or Conversions*. Boulder, Colorado: Westview Press.

Hartwick, J., 1990. "Natural Resource, National Accounting, and Economic Depreciation." *Journal of Public Economics* 43(3):291-304.

Hartwick, J., and N. Olewiler, 1986. *The Economics of Natural Resource Use*. New York: Harper & Row.

Henry, C., 1974. "Investment Decisions under Uncertainty: the Irreversibility Effect." *American Economic Review* 64(6):1006-12.

Hoff, K., and J. E. Stiglitz, 1990. "Introduction: Imperfect Information and Rural Credit Markets: Puzzles and Policy Perspectives." *World Bank Economic Review* 4(3):235-50.

Kanninen, B. J., and B. Kristrom, 1993. "Welfare Benefit Estimation and Income

Distribution." Revised version of Beijer Discussion Paper Series No. 20. Beijer International Institute of Ecological Economics, Stockholm.

Kennedy, E., and R. Oniang'o, 1990. "Health and Nutrition Effects of Sugarcane Production in South-Western Kenya." *Food and Nutrition Bulletin* 12.

Little, I. M. D., and J. A. Mirrlees, 1974. *Project Appraisal and Planning for Developing Countries*. London: Heinemann.

Lutz, E., ed., 1993. *Toward Improved Accounting for the Environment*. Washington: World Bank.

Mabbut, J., 1984. "A New Global Assessment of the Status and Trends of Desertification." *Environmental Conservation* 11(2):103-11.

Mahar, D., 1988. "Government Policies and Deforestation in Brazil's Amazon Region." Environment Department Working Paper No. 7. World Bank, Washington, D.C.

Mäler, K.-G., 1974. *Environmental Economics: A Theoretical Enquiry*. Baltimore: Johns Hopkins University Press.

————, 1991. "National Accounting and Environmental Resources." *Journal of Environmental Economics and Resources* 1.

Meade, J. E., 1973. *The Theory of Externalities*. Geneva: Institute Universitaire de Hautes Etudes Internationales.

Musgrave, R., 1959. *Theory of Public Finance*. New York: McGraw Hill.

Nelson, R., 1988. "Dryland Management: The 'Desertification' Problem." Environment Department Working Paper No. 8. World Bank, Washington, D.C.

Nerlove, M., and A. Meyer, 1991. "Endogenous Fertility and the Environment: A Parable of Firewood." In P. Dasgupta and K.-G, Mäler, eds., *The Environment and Emerging Development Issues*. Oxford: Clarendon Press.

Olsen, W. K., 1987. "Manmade 'Drought' in Rayalseema." *Economic and Political Weekly* 22.

Panayotou, T., 1992. "Environmental Kuznets Curve: Empirical Tests and Policy Implications." Harvard Institute for International Development. Mimeographed.

Pigou, A. C., 1920. *The Economics of Welfare*. London: Macmillan.

Portes, R., 1971. "Decentralised Planning Procedures and Centrally Planned Economies." *American Economic Review* (Papers & Proceedings) 61(2):422-9.

Reij, C., P. Mulder, and L. Begemann, 1988. "Water Harvesting for Plant Production." Technical Paper No. 91. World Bank, Washington, D.C.

Repetto, R., 1988. "Economic Policy Reform for Natural Resource Conservation." Environment Department Working Paper No. 4. World Bank, Washington, D.C.

Rosenzweig, M., and K. I. Wolpin, 1989. "Specific Experience, Household Structure and Intergenerational Transfers: Farm Family Land and Labour Arrangements in Developing Countries." *Quarterly Journal of Economics* 100:961-87.

Sen, A., 1992. *Inequality Reexamined*. Oxford: Clarendon Press.

Simon, J., 1977. *The Economics of Population Growth*. Princeton, NJ: Princeton University Press.

Solorzano, R., et al., 1991. *Accounts Overdue: Natural Resource Depreciation in Costa Rica*. Washington: World Resources Institute.

Solow, R. M., 1986. "On the Intergenerational Allocation of Natural Resources." *Scandinavian Journal of Economics*, 88(1):141-9.

Spence, A. M., 1974. "Blue Whales and Optimal Control Theory." In H. Gottinger, ed., *Systems Approaches and Environmental Problems*. Gottingen: Vandenhoek and Ruprecht.

Squire, L., and H. Van der Taak, 1975. *Economic Analysis of Projects*. Baltimore: Johns Hopkins University Press.

Starrett, D., 1972. "Fundamental Non-Convexities in the Theory of Externalities." *Journal of Economic Theory* 4(2):180-99.

Tietenberg, T., 1988. *Environmental and Natural Resource Economics*. 2nd ed. Glenview, Illinois: Scott, Forsman Publishers.

United Nations, 1990. *Overall Socioeconomic Perspectives of the World Economy to the Year 2000*. New York: United Nations Department of International Economic and Social Affairs.

United Nations Environmental Programme (UNEP), 1984. *General Assessment of Progress in the Implementation of the Plan of Action to Combat Desertification 1978-1984*. Report of the Executive Director. Nairobi.

Weitzman, M., 1970. "Optimal Growth with Scale Economies in the Creation of Overhead Capital." *Review of Economic Studies* 37(4):555-7.

World Bank, 1991. *The Population, Agriculture and Environmental Nexus in Sub-Saharan Africa*. Washington, D.C.

————, 1992. *World Development Report*. New York: Oxford University Press.

Zylics, T., 1990. "Miljopolitik for Fore Detta Centralplanerade Ekonomier." *Ekonomisk Debatt* 4.

Chapter Eight

Trade and Sustainable Development

Robert Repetto

Introduction

There is no doubt that international trade liberalization has been crucial to economic success in the Asian region. The so-called 'Asian tigers', which have sustained high rates of economic growth for decades, have provided the model for outward-looking development strategies. More recent converts to open trade regimes in Southeast and South Asia refute the often repeated contention that the experience of the 'tigers' is not replicable, or could not be generalized to all the developing world. As Table 8.1 shows, Indonesia, Thailand, and Malaysia have also achieved remarkable growth rates in exports, manufacturing output, and aggregate income (World Bank 1993a). Perhaps even more striking are the high growth rates achieved in the People's Republic of China (PRC), by far the largest East Asian developing country. Trade liberalization has been only a part of PRC's economic reforms, but liberalization, in addition to its direct benefits, has provided essential support for price rationalization, private sector development, openness to foreign capital and technology, and other policy reforms. The question now is whether trade liberalization also supports the goal of environmentally sound and sustainable economic development.

The Effects of Trade Policy on the Environment

Trade Liberalization

It is indisputable that outward-looking trade policies have had significant environmental effects. Trade expansion has led to rapid growth in export-oriented industries. The composition of exports has varied across countries and over time, depending on the resource endowment and stage of industrialization. At the early stages of export expansion, internationally competitive industries have been mostly labor-intensive

Table 8.1
Growth in East and Southeast Asia

	Average Annual Growth Rate (per cent)					
	Exports		*GDP*		*GNP/cap.*	
	1970-80	*1980-91*	*1970-80*	*1980-91*	*1960-80*	*1980-91*
Hong Kong	9.7	4.4	9.2	6.9	6.8	5.6
Singapore	4.2	8.9	8.3	6.6	7.5	5.3
Korea, Rep. of	23.5	12.2	9.6	9.6	7.0	8.7
Indonesia	7.2	4.5	7.2	5.6	4.0	3.9
Thailand	10.3	14.4	7.1	7.9	4.7	5.9
Malaysia	1.8	10.9	7.9	5.7	4.3	2.9
China, People's Rep. of	8.7	11.5	5.2	9.4	–	7.8

Source: World Bank, 1993. *The East Asian Miracle, Economic Growth and Public Policy*. New York: Oxford University Press.

processing and assembly operations, or downstream processing of local raw materials. Extractive and processing industries generate large quantities of wastes. At later stages of industrialization, exports have included a larger proportion of machinery, industrial materials, and products with higher technological content. Many such industries produce large quantities of hazardous wastes.

Export-led growth has also engendered rapid expansion of industries providing intermediate industrial materials and equipment, and of industries—energy industries, in particular—serving the domestic market. Energy industries have many serious environmental impacts. Industrial employment opportunities have drawn migrants to the cities, contributing to rapid urbanization. Rising incomes have brought construction booms and a virtual explosion in motor vehicle traffic. All these growth-related phenomena have, in the aggregate, generated new and increased environmental pressures (French 1993).

In Thailand, for example, rapid industrial growth has raised hazardous waste generation to 1.9 million tons per year in 1990, and industry's share has doubled to 58 per cent in a decade. A four-fold increase in the volume of hazardous waste is expected by 2001. Conventional biodegradable industrial wastes are also rising rapidly, severely polluting rivers and estuaries. Until recently, the government of Thailand did not insist that new investments include adequate emissions controls.

Energy consumption is growing at 8 per cent per year, faster than the gross domestic product (GDP), and Thailand is shifting toward domestic lignite, a very dirty fuel, for electricity generation. This will have unfortunate implications for air quality. Bangkok already exceeds World Health Organization health standards for several air pollutants. Lead, mainly from vehicle emissions, is found in blood samples at levels three times higher than in the United States and Europe, increasing the risk of strokes in adults and the incidence of mental retardation in children (Phantumvanit and Panayotou 1990).

Rapid industrialization in the People's Republic of China, much of it associated with increased openness to international trade, has generated similar problems. Industrial wastewater discharges more than doubled in the latter half of the 1980s, far outstripping treatment capacities and heavily polluting surface and groundwaters. Consequently, most of the urban Chinese population depends on unsafe drinking water, with severe health consequences. For example, a massive epidemic of hepatitis A in Shanghai afflicted 300,000 people.

Rapidly increasing energy generation from coal, three quarters of which is for industrial or electric power use, has led to some of the world's highest concentrations of fine particulates and sulphur oxides, some of the most acidic rainfall in the world, and chronic obstructive pulmonary disease five times more prevalent in urban populations than in the United States. Problems of untreated and improperly discharged toxic and hazardous wastes are also of great concern to drinking water supplies and fisheries (World Bank 1992).

In Indonesia, industrial output has increased eight-fold since 1970 and is expected to grow another 13-fold by 2020. Three quarters of all industry is located on the small island of Java, 60 per cent in urban areas. Industrial and household effluent loadings have grossly polluted most urban ground and surface water supplies. Consequently, even after treatment, most drinking water supplies are contaminated. Rapid growth of energy use, especially by vehicles, has degraded urban air quality beyond health limits: in Jakarta, for example, 28 per cent of women and children suffer from respiratory disease. Projections of future industrialization suggest that total emissions of conventional air and water pollutants will increase six-fold over the next 20 years (World Bank 1993b).

These growing environmental problems by no means imply that trade liberalization and its associated outward-looking development strategy have been a mistake or are inconsistent with sustainable development. Outward-looking strategies, especially in the Asian region, have dramatically reduced poverty and raised living standards for a large fraction of the world's population. They have provided the financial resources, technological capabilities, and institutions with which environmental problems can be managed. By raising living standards and strengthening communications, they have also created social and political conditions in which people demand environmental improvements.

The challenge is to ensure that newly created resources and capabilities are used to contain and diminish environmental pressures. Countries that are industrializing rapidly, with access to international technologies, are in a decidedly advantageous position, in that a large part of their capital stock is relatively new. New plants can readily incorporate up-to-date process technologies that use materials and energy more efficiently, minimize emissions, improve product quality, and reduce costs. The costs of building environmental controls into new plants are much less than the costs of retrofitting pollution abatement equipment onto old plants. Companies are more willing and able to meet strict emissions standards when building new facilities. For example, most first rank multinational companies' policies are to build overseas facilities to their own environmental standards or the host government's, whichever is higher. Countries that apply demanding environmental standards to new investments can thereby rapidly improve the environmental performance of an industry.

Rapidly industrializing countries can control environmental degradation if they apply effective environmental regulations, provided they are consistent, reasonable, and enforced effectively and evenhandedly. Most firms can reduce emissions substantially at modest cost. Even in member countries of the Organisation for Economic Co-operation and Development (OECD), where regulations are strict, pollution control costs rarely exceed 2 per cent of the value of sales. Problems are encountered in most industrializing countries because environmental standards are vague; monitoring is inadequate; and enforcement is lax, discriminatory, or sometimes nonexistent.

Land use regulations, which are weak in many developing countries, can also go far to minimize environmental degradation. With effective land use controls, ecologically vulnerable and vital areas can be protected, environmentally damaging activities can be restricted to locations where they do the least harm or where their effects can be mitigated more easily, and residential development can be kept apart from potential exposure to environmental hazards. However, even where elaborate urban and regional development plans and land use guidelines have been drawn up at substantial expense, implementation is often inadequate. Industrial locations—especially of small and medium enterprises—are typically haphazard, zoning regulations are weakly enforced, and supposedly protected areas often are not.

In many rapidly industrializing regions, infrastructure development is unbalanced. For example, many such regions have no safe and approved facilities for the collection, treatment, storage, and disposal of hazardous wastes. Although the chemicals, metal fabricating, fabric finishing, and other industries that generate significant volumes of hazardous wastes are growing rapidly, there are no environmentally sound facilities to receive those wastes. Consequently, they are stored or disposed of improperly on land or into water bodies. The resulting poisoning of aquifers and sediments is difficult or impossible to remedy and may produce long-lasting damage to human health or ecological systems.

Similarly, development of urban infrastructure to serve the rapidly growing urban population in such regions lags behind. Water and sanitation facilities remain inadequate for much of the expanding population. Urban transportation infrastructure is overwhelmed, leading to growing costs of congestion and air pollution.

In effect, countries suffer from underinvestment in institutional capacity and infrastructure for environmental management. The problem is one of underinvestment, in that the averted damages and costs would generously repay the needed expenditures. Although the costs of environmental degradation, in terms of increased sickness or reduced productivity, may not be adequately captured by market valuations, they are often implicitly overlooked as real costs to the economy.

Trade economists are fond of pointing out that trade restrictions are not the first-best measure with which to address environmental market failures (Low 1992). The best approach is to tackle the market failure at its source through appropriate environmental regulations, policies, or infrastructure investments. While this proposition is undoubtedly true in theory, few countries that have experienced a rapid growth spurt fueled by trade liberalization have adequately invested in environmental management or established effective regulations.

It is also true that the second-best policy, in the absence of effective domestic environmental policy, is not necessarily to go ahead with trade liberalization anyway (Anderson and Blackhurst 1992). The increased environmental damage generated by expanded exports might outweigh the increased gains from trade. This is not merely a hypothetical theoretical curiosity. Even partial economic accounting for resource degradation and depletion in developing countries suggests that the costs are large—in the order of 4 to 5 per cent of GDP per year (Tropical Science Center and World Resources Institute 1991; Repetto et al. 1989). Country case studies of previous trade liberalization programs suggest that the expansion of export sectors and the absence of effective domestic policies can exacerbate these environmental damages significantly (Cruz and Repetto 1992; Reed 1992).

The implications for development institutions, such as the Asian Development Bank, seem clear. To ensure that rapid export-led growth in the region is environmentally sound and the potential economic gains from trade expansion are realized, increased investments are required to strengthen institutional capacity and to provide necessary infrastructure. These investments should be made in anticipation of export-led growth because the costs of prevention are much less than the costs of remediation, or of the economic damages of environmental degradation. Unfortunately, decades of underinvestment in environmental protection and significant unmet needs for infrastructure and institutional strengthening have allowed damages to accumulate.

Trade Restriction

The argument that environmental protection has been neglected should not be interpreted as an attack on the outward-looking development model (Broad and Cavanagh 1993). Continued inward-looking, trade-restricting development policies might have produced equally serious environmental problems along with significantly lower living standards. Certainly, the People's Republic of China, in the years prior to economic reform, experienced severe environmental degradation (Smil 1984). Inefficient state-owned heavy industries generated enormous pollution. Misguided centrally planned management of agriculture, forests, and other sectors led to severe resource degradation.

Similarly, India, which has only begun to dismantle its inward-looking development regime, has experienced slow growth in incomes and substantial environmental degradation. Much of this degradation stems from the persistence of widespread rural and urban poverty. In the industrial sphere, obsolete technologies, overemphasis on highly polluting heavy industries, financial constraints, and lack of effective environmental controls have combined to produce pollution problems (Centre for Science and Environment 1985). By comparison to the Indian experience, outward-looking development has more rapidly increased the resources, and technological and institutional capabilities with which environmental problems can be addressed.

Trade restrictions in member countries of OECD also have adverse environmental and economic consequences for their own societies as well as for their Third World trading partners. Escalating tariffs according to the stage of processing inhibits the development of finishing industries that add value to raw materials produced in the South. The Multi-Fibre Agreement and other trade barriers impose serious quantitative restrictions on exports of labor intensive manufactures from developing countries. Such barriers affect not only textiles and apparel, but also footwear and other relatively labor-intensive products. By impeding the access of low cost producers with comparative advantage in these manufactures to industrial country markets, these restrictions substantially lower incomes in developing countries and raise consumer prices in industrial countries. For example, in the 1980s, American consumers paid about $18 billion per year in excess costs just for clothing and textiles (World Bank 1987). Protection reduces potential employment in developing countries but has done little to save jobs in industrialized countries where producers have rapidly automated production to raise productivity (World Bank 1987).

At the same time, these trade barriers exacerbate environmental pressures in developing countries by forcing them to intensify exports of natural-resource-based commodities. Most newly industrializing countries have a comparative advantage in the production and export of labor-intensive or resource-intensive commodities, but can't compete in high technology or capital-intensive industries. In the late 1980s, about half of all developing country exports still comprised fuels, minerals, and other primary commodities. By impeding exports of labor-intensive manufactures and downstream processing industries, especially when pressures on developing countries to meet high debt-servicing requirements are intense, these trade barriers virtually force developing countries to raise exports of natural-resource-based commodities. Eliminating these trade barriers would have significant economic and environmental benefits. Output would expand in labor-intensive processing industries, enabling developing countries to add more value to their exported primary materials. Growth of alternative sources of foreign exchange earnings would mitigate the overexploitation of natural resources for export.

Trade restrictions imposed by OECD countries also damage their own environments, while reducing incomes domestically and abroad. Agricultural protectionism in Europe, the United States, and Japan leads to much more intensive farming in these regions than is environmentally or economically justified. By inflating prices and per acre revenues, while (in some cases) limiting the acreage that can be planted, agricultural policies induce farmers to use more inputs on each acre planted than they otherwise would. Driven by these incentives, farmers adopt chemical-intensive monocultures that lead to more soil erosion, chemical runoff, loss of biological diversity, and conversion of once natural ecosystems to cropland than would otherwise take place (Faeth et al. 1991; Reichelderfer 1990; Runge 1991).

These domestic agricultural policies are supported by barriers to imports and subsidies to exports—trade distorting measures that impose heavy costs on domestic consumers and taxpayers, as well as on third-country producers. Within the OECD countries, agricultural protectionism costs consumers and taxpayers approximately $150 billion annually, more than double what farmers in these countries gain (Sanderson 1990). Current policies grossly distort world agricultural trade patterns, sacrificing static gains from trade of roughly $70 billion annually in the OECD countries alone (OECD 1989-1990). In addition, lower world prices depress returns to developing countries and other exporting country producers, inhibit badly needed investments in agriculture in those countries, and result in the spread of low yielding farming and ranching into ecologically vulnerable tropical forests.

Sugar Protectionism: A Case Study

Protectionism by the United States against sugar imports is an egregious example. Domestic price supports linked to a tariff-quota system keep US sugar prices two to three times higher than world levels and have reduced imports, predominantly from developing countries, by three quarters since the 1970s. The sugar industries in the Caribbean Basin and other low income countries have been crippled, with a loss of 400,000 jobs in Caribbean countries alone (Tucker and Chambers 1989).

These levels of protection are equivalent to a subsidy to US producers of 60 to 79 per cent, and a tax on US consumers of 43 to 59 per cent (Haley et al. 1993; Webb et al. 1990). The industry in the United States is highly concentrated. Thus, the largest 1 per cent of producers obtain 58 per cent of all producer benefits—more than a million dollars per producer per year—and the largest 10 per cent obtain more than 80 per cent (United States Government Accounting Office 1993). Large producers also benefit from subsidized irrigation and flood control works. The welfare cost to US consumers has been estimated in various studies to fall between $1 billion and $4 billion per year. The overall economic loss, net of benefits to US producers, probably lies between $100 million and $1 billion per year. The sugar protection program is a highly inefficient means of transferring income to large growers and processors in the United States from sugar producers in low income countries and average consumers in the United States.

The environmental consequences are most dramatic in South Florida where water and chemical uses by Florida sugarcane growers have imperiled the unique Everglades ecosystem. Two large companies are responsible for the entire crop in the Everglades Agricultural Area. The Everglades is a freshwater wetland of marshes, wet prairies, swamps, and tree islands. Described as a 'River of Grass', it once flowed in a 65 by 170 km basin from the southern shore of Lake Okeechobee to the mangroves on Florida's southwestern coast. Rainfall, formerly the main nutrient source, provided a slow, continuous sheetflow through the basin into Florida Bay, feeding North America's only living coral reef and a tremendous diversity of marine life (Rader and Richardson 1992; Everglades Coalition 1993). Since the turn of the century, 65 per cent of this wetland has been drained; the sheetflow has been channelized and diverted; water quantity and quality have drastically decreased; and severe ecological deterioration has occurred.

Only about one half of the original Everglades ecosystem remains, divided into three Water Conservation Areas and the Everglades National Park. The Park—a Biosphere Reserve, World Heritage Site, National Wilderness Area, and Wetland of International Significance—supports 16 endangered species, including wood storks, snail kites, Florida panthers, and American crocodiles. This remnant is threatened by sugar producers in the Everglades Agricultural Area to the north, formed by draining and irrigating nearly one third of the original Everglades. Without major changes in water management and agriculture, the remaining Everglades could become an oxygen-starved cattail marsh supporting none of the original diversity of plants and animals. The downstream mangroves and estuaries could continue disappearing until the well-spring of Florida Bay's reefs and fisheries are gone.[1]

Because water has been diverted for irrigation and urban use, the Everglades now receives less than half its historic flow, and instead of a long, continuous flow of rainwater, stagnant water is released from impoundments in massive pulses in the wet season and the marsh lacks water in the dry season. Drainage water from the agricultural area is massively enriched by fertilizers and nutrients released from exposed soils to a concentration hundreds of times higher than natural background levels. The sawgrass-dominated wetland ecosystem, adapted to a nutrient-poor environment, is taken over by phosphorus-tolerant cattails, which have already intruded far into the National Park. The cattails choke the aquatic ecosystem, disrupting the food chain and extinguishing species at all trophic levels, including the snails, shrimp, insects, crustaceans, and fish. Higher on the food chain, the population of wading birds has already declined by 93 per cent since the 1930s, because of a lack of food and nesting sites. With enough nutrient enrichment, a foul smelling, anaerobic mat of green filamentous algae eventually takes over, in which only cattails and few other species can survive (Nearhoof 1992; Davis 1993).

The likely extinction of the Florida panther, of which only 30 to 50 individuals now survive, is due partly to food chain disruption but mainly to bioaccumulation of mercury deposited in ash from burned sugarcane fields and bagasse and released from exposed peat as it oxidizes. Infant mortality from mercury poisoning in these top predators is high. In the bay, high salinity and temperatures caused by interruption of freshwater flows have produced massive seagrass die-offs and algal blooms, lowering dissolved oxygen levels and killing corals, sponges, and other marine animals. The shrimp harvest has fallen 80 per cent in the last decade, destroying an important commercial fishery.

Attempted solutions have focused on complex water and nutrient management systems, rather than the fundamental problem: highly uneconomic sugarcane production by large, heavily protected corporations. If sugar price supports and protectionist barriers to imports are dropped, and the industry faced is forced to pay the full costs of its water and drainage works, then sugar production in South Florida (and other high-cost producing areas) will fall dramatically. Consumers will benefit; efficient foreign producers will benefit; and the principal threat to the Everglades will be resolved. This is a prime example of complementarity between trade and environment objectives. Trade liberalization accompanied by strengthened environmental protection and better resource management can be a 'win-win' option for countries in the North and the South.

The Effects of Environmental Policies on Trade

The Competitiveness Issue

Firms in OECD countries fear that competitors in developing or transitional economies where environmental standards are less stringent or less strictly enforced derive an advantage in the marketplace from lower compliance costs. Meanwhile, labor unions fear relocation of factories in developing countries to take advantage of lax environmental standards. Simultaneously, firms in developing countries fear that if they are forced to meet environmental standards as strict as those in OECD countries, they will be unable to compete because of higher production costs.

To some extent, such professed fears are designed to bluff, intimidate, or otherwise influence government decisions regarding environmental standards. Companies have always used the threat of reduced employment or investment to deter governments from setting strict standards, oftentimes successfully. Governments must, therefore, examine carefully the basis for such implicit threats. Similarly, some environmental groups oppose trade liberalization because they fear that with lower trade barriers, the risk of competitive dislocations will force environmental standards in OECD countries down to some least common denominator. They, too, must examine the basis for such fears.

First, should potential competitive effects be judged at the level of the firm, the industry, or the total economy? Although the entrepreneurs making representations on environmental policy are interested primarily in the competitiveness of their own company, this is too narrow a base for public policy. An interesting case study of the Indian leather industry illustrates why this is so (Indira Gandhi Institute of Development Research 1993).

Exports of Indian leather and leather goods, mostly to the European Community, have increased rapidly and are expected to continue to do so. However, much of the tanning industry still consists of small establishments using backward technologies. Less than 25 per cent of such tanneries treat their effluents before discharging them into rivers or evaporation ponds. These practices impair the health of workers and neighboring residents, salinize adjoining farmlands, contaminate aquifers, and lead to the discharge of organic wastes and chromium, a toxic metal, into surface waters. Producers of Indian leathers are being forced to change their tanning processes to meet European product standards that forbid the contamination of leathers with pentachlorophenol, a toxic fungicide, and the use of dyes containing formaldehyde and benzidine. Indian leathers are also subject to packaging and labeling regulations. In addition, producers are concurrently being forced by Indian environmental regulations to install individual or common waste treatment plants.

The estimated cost impacts of these measures range from 1.5 to 3.0 per cent of finished product prices on average, but they affect specific segments of the industry quite differently. Small tanneries located around urban areas that use backward technologies, are the most seriously affected. Larger modern tanneries, which under a liberalized trade policy are able to import modern equipment and processing chemicals to produce a consistently higher quality product with fewer effluents, are able to capture a growing share of the market. Leather manufacturers, who can now import leather required for production of higher quality products at a labor cost advantage, are least affected.

Clearly, evaluating the competitive effects of Indian process standards and European product standards at the level of the individual tannery is inadequate. Both sets of standards are contributing to the modernization of the industry, accelerating the replacement of small, inefficient, unsafe, and highly polluting establishments. Such establishments and their workers may be losers from the change, but other, more efficient, Indian firms are gaining, and overall, output and employment in the industry are increasing. As modern technologies replace older ones, not only are productivity and product quality improving, but environmental damages can also be controlled.

However, evaluating competitiveness effects at the level of the industry is also too narrow. Other segments of the Indian economy have suffered substantial costs as a result of environmental spillovers from the leather industry. First of all, the 1.4 million people working in the industry, mostly low paid women and children, are exposed to unsafe levels of toxic, carcinogenic, and potentially lethal chemicals, including ammonia, formaldehyde, and hydrogen sulfide—and suffer numerous health impacts. It is hardly acceptable to say that for the industry to remain competitive, the lives of those who work in it must be put in jeopardy.

Furthermore, the land and groundwater supplies of the surrounding villages have been poisoned by salts and other effluents, so that they are fit only for use as dumping grounds for the tanneries. The livelihoods of the inhabitants have been destroyed. Finally, every year the establishments, located in Uttar Pradesh, discharge at least 10,000 tons of chromium, along with other wastes, into the Ganges River. This river is not only the source of drinking water for millions of people but is also sacred to hundreds of millions of Hindus.

It would be inconsistent for a government dedicated to poverty alleviation and development to ignore these significant costs to its own people. For this and other reasons, the question of competitiveness should be addressed not at the level of the individual firm, nor at the level of the individual industry, but at the level of the entire economy. The costs of pollution abatement forced on the industry are real costs to the Indian economy, but so are the costs of illness, loss of productive land, and pollution of ground and surface waters.

Even viewed from the perspective of a single industry, to what extent are environmental control costs likely to shift competitive advantage in world trade? It is conventional in this regard to make a distinction between *product standards*, which refer to the physical characteristics or composition of the traded item or its packaging, and *process standards*, which refer to the way in which it is manufactured, including the extent and composition of residual emissions. It has long been held under the rules of the General Agreement on Tariffs and Trade (GATT) that importing countries are free to regulate products entering their borders to protect health, safety, or natural resources, as long as such regulations treat domestically produced goods and imports alike, do not discriminate between foreign sources, are not covert protectionist measures, and are not arbitrary barriers to trade. It has generally been held under GATT rules that countries are not free to regulate the processes by which imported goods are made, since that would treat identical products made by different processes differently and violate the exporting country's sovereign right to set its own health and safety standards.

Of course, as the Indian tannery example illustrates, the distinction between product and process standards is becoming less and less distinct. Since sensitive tests of the product can recognize minute residual amounts of materials used in the processing, regulations banning those trace chemicals can force exporters to alter their production methods. Other product regulations, such as those governing recyclability, energy efficiency, or the tolerable amounts of pollutants a product can emit when used, can also force manufacturers to redesign industrial goods and the processes used to make them.

It is safe to predict that international differences in process standards will have small competitive impacts in world trade. Even in the United States, where regulatory standards are strict but not particularly cost effective, pollution control costs average only about 1.5 per cent of the value of the total sales of manufacturing industries. Only in a very few subsectors do they rise above 3 per cent of the value of sales (Pearson 1993). Thus, even if environmental controls brought no benefits whatever to the firm itself through reduced materials and energy use, or reduced liability or worker disability; and even if competing firms in other countries incurred no environmental control costs at all, the resulting cost disadvantage to American firms would be less than 2 per cent of the sales price for the large majority of industries. Compared to other competitive factors in international trade, such as differences in labor, transportation, or materials costs; differences in productivity and product quality; or differences in brand recognition and marketing ability; differential environmental control costs stemming from varying environmental process standards are unlikely to be noticeable, let alone decisive.

The parallel fear that companies will relocate their operations to 'pollution havens' is equally implausible. The idea that a company will move its production—a step that involves selling its plant, severing its workforce, persuading key personnel to relocate, acquiring a new site, building a new facility, recruiting and training new workers, and undergoing a shakedown period for a new plant—only to save pollution control costs, totaling less than 2 per cent of sales, absolutely strains credulity. When companies move their plants, other forces are at work.

These a priori predictions are borne out by many empirical studies, dating back two decades and extending up to the present (Dean 1992; Pearson 1993). Few of them find that differences in regulatory stringency or environmental control costs are at all useful in explaining patterns of international trade and investment, or changes in the location of production. The gross facts bear out these statistical findings: Japan and Germany, two countries with strict environmental standards, have never proven to be uncompetitive in international trade; India and the former Soviet Union, despite weak or ineffective environmental standards, have been strikingly uncompetitive in world markets. Obviously, other factors are determining the market outcomes. Although there are some reported cases of firms seeking out overseas production locations with weak environmental standards, by far the greatest amount of direct foreign investment is in countries that have high environmental standards.

Indeed, there is evidence that lax environmental standards can act as a deterrent to direct foreign investment. For example, Western firms have been unwilling to buy industrial plants in some heavily polluted regions of Eastern Europe at any price, because the potential liability for clean-up costs outweighs any reasonable expectation of profit. Regions interested in attracting industrial investment would do better by simplifying economic regulations, improving infrastructure and communications, and ensuring a stable economic, legal, and political climate than they would by abandoning environmental standards.

Although it would be irrational for developing countries to forego reasonable environmental controls, it would be equally irrational for northern environmentalists to demand that developing countries adopt the same process standards as OECD countries. For one thing, identical process standards in two settings will not achieve the same degree of environmental quality: other factors, such as the concentration of emissions sources and the assimilative capacity of the environment, also matter. In any case, rational developing countries will not have the same priorities for environmental quality as rich countries. For example, since cancer is a leading cause of death in an aging population, fear of carcinogens looms large in environmental regulations in the United States. However, in most developing countries, with a much younger age structure and high mortality rates from poverty-related diseases, cancer is a relatively minor cause of death. Furthermore, the effectiveness of environmental measures will vary between developed and developing countries. Would the ambitious and expensive goal of zero discharges for industrial plants, embodied in the US Clean Water Act, make sense in India, where less than 20 per cent of household sewage is even collected, let alone treated, and surface waters are highly contaminated with household wastes? Finally, imposing the same process standards on different plants would not 'level the playing field' in a competitive sense anyway, since the compliance costs will vary significantly across plants according to their age, layout, and technology. The principle of national sovereignty in the design and implementation of domestic environmental standards is sound and should be respected.

Process Standards, the Polluter Pays Principle, and Terms of Trade

Twenty years ago governments of OECD member countries agreed to the *polluter pays principle*. This was done to avoid trade displacements and distortions that might result if some governments subsidized industries' costs of compliance with environmental standards while others made the polluters pay. This principle has been useful, even though applied only spottily within the OECD. Non-OECD countries have not even universally adopted the principle, let alone the practice.

There are many reasons why they should. Governments of developing countries do not have the fiscal capability to subsidize pollution control expenditures to any great extent, and there are more worthy potential beneficiaries for limited government funds. The polluter pays principle will complement market liberalization programs underway in many developing countries by ensuring that prices include the full incremental costs of production, and environmental costs. There would be an additional economic benefit to developing countries. Trade experts in developing countries have long maintained that demand for their natural-resource-based exports is price inelastic—at least in the short or medium term. Table 8.2 provides estimated price elasticities of demand for some traded commodities. If the price elasticity of demand for a commodity is less than one in absolute value, an increase in its price will increase sale revenue. Table 8.3 shows that production of many internationally traded commodities is concentrated in developing countries. Thus, Third World countries have long attempted—with little success—to form commodity agreements or international associations to restrict supply and push up export prices and earnings, often in the name of price stabilization.

Table 8.2
World Elasticity of Demand for LDC[a] Export Commodities

Agricultural Commodities	
Coffee	-0.27[b]
Cocoa	-0.19[b]
Bananas	-0.40[b]
Tea	-0.20[c]
Rubber	-0.50[c]
Sugar	-0.04[c]
Cotton	-0.18[c]
Palm oil	-0.47[c]
Nonagricultural Commodities	
Phosphate rock	-0.70[c]
Tropical timber	
Nonconifer logs	-0.16[d]
Nonconifer sawnwood	-0.74[d]
Nonconifer plywood	-1.14[d]
Nonferrous metals	-0.55[e]
Ferrous metals	-0.65[e]
Aggregate energy	-0.50[e]

[a] Less developed country (LDC).

[b] Islam, N., and A. Subramanian, 1989. "Agricultural Exports of Developing Countries: Estimates of Income and Price Elasticities of Demand and Supply." *Journal of Agricultural Economics* 40(2):221-31.

[c] Demand from developed countries only. Karunasekera, M. J., 1984. "Export Taxes on Primary Products: A Policy Instrument in International Development." *Commonwealth Economic Papers* (19):53.

[d] Barbier, E., J. Burgess, J. Bishop, B. Aylward, and C. Bann, 1992. "The Economic Linkages between the International Trade in Tropical Timber and the Sustainable Management of Tropical Forests." [draft] Table 4.6: 31. International Institute for Environment and Development, London Environmental Economics Centre, London.

[e] Slade, M. E., 1992. "Environmental Costs of Natural Resource Commodities: Magnitude and Incidence." Working paper for *World Development Report*. Washington: World Bank.

If developing countries collectively adopt reasonable environmental process standards in commodity producing industries and adopt the polluter pays principle, the damage to their own natural resources would be curtailed, and the cost of environmental compliance would be internalized in the prices of their exports. Certificates and labeling systems indicating the use of sustainable and environmentally sound production methods, if organized by Third World producer groups, would support such collective standards (Kox 1992). Their terms of trade

Table 8.3
**The Share of Developing Countries in World Trade
of Major Primary Products during the Late 1980s**
(per cent)

Primary Commodity	Share in World Gross Exports	Six Largest LDC[a] Exporters' Share of World Exports
Coffee[b]	89.0	53.0
Cocoa[b]	90.2	78.4
Tea[b]	82.1	73.8
Sugar[b]	74.8	65.2
Beef[b]	14.8	8.1
Bananas[c]	93.1	75.9
Citrus fruits[c]	48.5	43.0
Rice[b]	58.7	50.1
Soybeans[b]	24.8	24.6
Copra[b]	90.8	79.7
Groundnuts[b]	52.1	44.7
Palm oil[b]	77.9	76.9
Cotton[c]	54.6	24.3
Jute[c]	95.1	75.5
Sisal & agaves[d]	96.6	95.2
Rubber[b]	97.4	93.3
Tobacco[c]	62.2	42.1
Veneer/sawlogs[c]	85.3	70.7
Sawnwood[c]	66.0	56.2
Bauxite[b]	90.1	80.0
Copper[b]	70.0	54.4
Iron ore[b]	59.8	41.0
Lead[b]	34.6	27.8
Manganese ore[b]	83.5	56.9
Nickel[b]	37.3	30.0
Tin[b]	77.8	73.4
Zinc[b]	29.5	22.6
Phosphate rock[b]	72.4	63.4

[a] Less developed country (LDC).

[b] 1985-87 average for 'low- and middle-income economies.' World Bank, 1993. *Commodity Trade and Price Trends*. 1989-91 edition. Washington: World Bank.

[c] 1988 figures. World Bank, 1990. *Price Prospects for Major Primary Commodities*. Washington: World Bank.

[d] 1989 figures. Food and Agriculture Organization, 1991. *Trade Yearbook*. Geneva: United Nations.

would improve, because northern consumers, whose demand is relatively insensitive to price, would be paying a larger share of the environmental costs associated with their consumption patterns. To illustrate, if environmental control costs averaged roughly 1.5 per cent of production costs, as they do in the United States, then the $500 billion in annual exports from developing countries would include payments of up to $7.5 billion by importers, mostly in the North, to help defray the costs of environmental controls. This sum is far greater than the annual flows of development assistance to the South for environmental programs. It should be a high priority for commodity associations, such as the International Tropical Timber Organization, and for international trade forums, such as the United Nations Conference on Trade and Development (UNCTAD), to promote agreements among Third World commodity exporters that they will adopt environmentally sound and sustainable production standards and apply the polluter pays principle.

Product Standards and Green Protectionism

Many developing countries fear that environmental product standards adopted by advanced countries will be serious barriers to trade, either because they are designed and applied as protectionist measures or simply because they are too strict for Third World producers with limited technology to attain. Although there is indeed a persistent tendency to use product standards and regulations—not just environmentally motivated ones—to protect domestic producers, fears of 'green protectionism' are exaggerated.

Safeguards against product standards becoming nontariff trade barriers are needed. These should include such disciplines as those in the GATT text barring standards that are arbitrary, discriminatory, or disguised protectionist measures. Trade dispute mechanisms are needed so that injured parties can appeal to impartial bodies for redress. These safeguards must draw the line between legitimate environmental regulation and protectionism.

However, recent GATT decisions have shifted this line to limit unduly the scope of environmental policy (Charnovitz 1992; Repetto 1993). Trade officials have interpreted the GATT text to be far more restrictive of environmental policy than that agreement was originally intended to be. They have, in effect, changed the GATT agreement through interpretation to circumscribe national discretion in setting environmental policy (Charnovitz 1992). Notably, GATT dispute resolution panels have placed the burden of proof in disputes over environmental standards on standard-setting countries to justify their environmental measures. This interpretation in itself weakens the presumption that countries are entitled to set their own national environmental standards and policies.

In a dispute over Thailand's restrictions on cigarette imports, a panel ruled that measures for the protection of human health must be 'the least GATT-inconsistent' of all available environmental measures. A variant, requiring such measures to be 'the least trade restrictive' has been used in other GATT trade disputes and in the Dunkel draft Standards Code. However, the GATT text does not require that measures necessary to protect life and health be the least GATT-inconsistent or the least trade restrictive of international trade of all measures available. This criterion might call into question many existing environmental regulations, on the grounds that they are not the least trade restrictive of available measures. Under most circumstances, for example, a pollution tax would be less trade restrictive than a command-and-control regulation or ban, but the former is rarely adopted by environmental policymakers.

The recently negotiated text of the North American Free Trade Agreement (NAFTA) and side agreements provide an improved model for safeguarding both trade and environmental protection. For example, NAFTA shifts the burden of proof to the party challenging a nation's environmental standards to demonstrate that they are arbitrary, discriminatory, or protectionist. It also allows for the use of panelists with environmental expertise in dispute resolution proceedings. GATT dispute resolution procedures are flawed in that they make panels composed overwhelmingly of trade experts, with no environmental expertise, pass on the legitimacy of environmental regulations.

More important than safeguards against 'green protectionism' written into trade agreements, there are broad and powerful economic forces at work to discourage the manipulation of product standards for protectionist purposes. They are summed up in the phrase 'globalization of the world economy'. A remarkably large and growing fraction of world trade consists of shipments between one branch of a company and another, or between a company and its foreign affiliate. As long ago as the mid-1980s, 52 per cent of imports in the United States and 57 per cent of Japan's were intracompany transactions of this kind (Julius 1990). Intracompany trade is buffered against the protectionist manipulation of product standards. The Ford Motor Company, for example, has no incentive to keep the components made in its Mexican plant out of the United States, since it built or acquired the Mexican facility precisely to supply those components to its factories in the United States and probably in other parts of the world as well. Instead, it would want to resist impediments to shipments among the nodes in its worldwide production network.

A large additional share of world trade in manufactures consists of 'outsourcing' by companies in advanced markets whose own capabilities lie in design and marketing. Benetton or Bloomingdale's, for example, have clothes sold under their labels manufactured all over the developing world by companies operating under contract. Contractors are held to strict specifications on design, materials, quality, and delivery time. They must also meet the environmental and other product standards in force in the import market. Clearly, Benetton and other importers have no incentive to manipulate such product standards to keep their contractors from selling into the importing market, since they have developed the 'outsourcing' relationship precisely to find a low cost and reliable supplier. In this way, globalization trends in the world economy provide a powerful countervailing force against the protectionist use of environmental product standards.

Some developing country producers may nonetheless find those standards hard to meet, and may thus be at a disadvantage to other firms, in the North or South, with more refined production processes or greater capital and technical resources. However, environmental standards are no different in this respect than product standards imposed by the importer with respect to quality or delivery time. Meeting such standards is the competitive prerequisite for supplying a demanding market. Not all companies can do so. However, the virtual explosion of intracompany trade, outsourcing, and South to North trade in industrial and manufactured products demonstrates that many Third World companies are able to manufacture to the high standards demanded by the importing market. For such firms, product standards are valuable guideposts, helping potential developing country exporters know how to break into advanced markets.

Green protectionism undoubtedly exists, but its extent is relatively small. In agriculture, which is probably more subject to covertly protectionist product standards than manufacturing, empirical studies have shown that less than 5 per cent of shipments of fruits, vegetables, fish, and shellfish to the United States are detained at the border for noncompliance with product standards. Of these, 15 per cent was detained for environmental reasons such as the presence of pesticides, heavy metals, or unsafe additives. A larger fraction was detained for ordinary quality defects, such as decomposition, presence of salmonella, or contamination by filth. Other more common reasons for rejection were improper labeling and defective canned foods (Pearson 1993). Less than one per cent of food shipments is rejected on environmental grounds; these are overwhelmingly for noncompliance with unchallenged US environmental standards.

Today, what threatens the world trading system and market access for developing countries is not green protectionism. It is ordinary, dirty brown, protectionism. The Uruguay Round may well fail, severely weakening the GATT, the multilateral trading system, and progress in dismantling barriers to trade in textiles, food, and other products of concern to developing countries. The Uruguay Round is endangered primarily but not exclusively by agricultural protectionism, especially in Europe and Japan. Agricultural protectionism is driven by concern not for the rural environment but for the rural vote. NAFTA may well not pass the US Congress. Although some environmental groups in the United States oppose it, most have endorsed it and support its passage. Should it fail, the reason will be the opposition of the labor union movement fearful of competition in labor-intensive manufacturing processes, and agricultural interests subject to Mexican competition.

Trade barriers are not maintained today as a second-best approach to environmental protection, a widely accepted policy goal. They are maintained, as in the past, to protect the incomes of politically well-organized minorities at disproportionately high cost to the majority. The economic costs of so-called green protectionism to the developing countries are trivial compared to the costs of barriers erected in the North against labor-intensive manufactures such as textiles and apparel, and against competing agricultural commodities such as sugar or bananas. They are also tiny compared to the cost of barriers erected by developing countries to the expansion of South-South trade, or to the costs of biases in developing countries' own trade regimes that reduce their ability to export. Concern over potential protectionist barriers created by environmental product standards is excessive, and deflects attention from much more critical trade issues.

Sustainable Development Principles for Trade and Environmental Policy

In many ways, liberal international trade and sustainable development are complementary, or could be reconciled through changes in policy. There are many trade policy changes that would benefit the environment, and environmental policy changes that would help secure the benefits of liberalized trade. Implementing such changes would produce significant economic and environmental benefits. This section identifies some important principles for integrating trade and sustainable development.

1. Reorient Agricultural Policy and Reduce Agricultural Protectionism in OECD Countries

As explained above, if the European Community, the United States, and Japan succeed in liberalizing agricultural trade and decoupling farm income support payments from production decisions, thus raising farm productivity and consumer welfare significantly, they can reduce fiscal burdens, expand international trade, and improve environmental quality. Developing countries will improve their market access and terms of trade. This is a prime example of complementarity between development and environment objectives.

2. Reduce Barriers in OECD Countries to Exports of Labor-Intensive Manufactures from Developing Countries

There would be substantial gains from increased trade in both exporting and importing countries if tariff escalation that inhibits processing of raw materials before export were scaled back, and if nontariff barriers against labor-intensive manufactures, such as the Multi-Fibre Agreement, were eliminated. These policy changes would reduce the pressure to over-exploit natural resources in developing countries.

Some of these complementarities are within reach. The Uruguay Round negotiators have made progress both in reducing agricultural protection-ism and in increasing market access in OECD countries for labor-intensive manufactures from developing countries. NAFTA offers similar benefits for Mexico in North American markets (Hufbauer and Schott 1992). Ensuring these gains by concluding and ratifying the Uruguay Round and NAFTA agreements, with adequate environmental safe-guards, would represent a step forward for environmental protection as well as for trade liberalization.

3. Use Trade and Investment Incentives to Induce Cooperation in International Environmental Protection

Using trade sanctions unilaterally or even multilaterally to discourage noncooperation in international environmental protection activities is controversial. For example, the unilateral US ban on Mexican tuna imports to protect dolphins in international waters led to a GATT dispute. The provisions in the Montreal Protocol that require signatories to ban imports of chlorofluorocarbons (CFCs) and products containing CFCs from nonsignatory countries is a multilateral example.

Because of the poor record of compliance with international environmental agreements and the long negotiations required to achieve even weak international agreements, a strong argument can be made that trade sanctions are needed to deter cheating or free riding on an agreement. The threat of possible trade sanctions can be an essential incentive to induce parties to negotiate an agreement.

Many environmentalists fear that, if challenged, such trade measures could be regarded as inconsistent with GATT obligations, as the Tuna-Dolphin dispute panel suggested. On the other hand, many developing or small industrial countries fear that such policies might be used coercively by powerful nations to impose their own environmental standards or preferences on other countries. Although they may sometimes be necessary, trade sanctions are not the ideal measure with which to achieve international environmental cooperation because they rely on one costly measure (trade restrictions) to discourage another (noncooperation in environmental protection). They hold out no guarantee that the result will be a net improvement in global welfare.

Sometimes, carrots may work better than sticks. Using trade concessions to elicit international environmental cooperation is much more likely to generate economic and environmental gains and an overall improvement in welfare. The proposed North American Free Trade Agreement may be an example. The prospect of substantially increased gains from trade and investment has induced the Mexican government to strengthen its enforcement of its own environmental regulations and to resolve the tuna-dolphin dispute. The potential gains have also induced the US and Mexican governments to agree to spend substantially more on badly needed environmental protection in the border area.

If successful, this approach could be applied to a wider round of negotiations over a Latin American Free Trade Agreement, and incorporated into subsequent negotiating rounds under the GATT. The Uruguay Round has demonstrated that agreements on trade liberalization can be linked to negotiations on other issues, such as intellectual property rights. Why can't agreements on trade liberalization also be linked to negotiations on transboundary environmental protection?

4. Enforce Reasonable Environmental Standards and the Polluter Pays Principle

If developing countries adopt reasonable environmental standards and adhere to the polluter pays principle, they can ensure that pollution control and environmental costs are internalized into enterprise costs and product prices. The severe damages they are now suffering from environmental degradation will be mitigated. Trade disputes over hidden environmental subsidies and *eco-dumping* will be reduced. In addition, concerns over the environmental consequences of trade liberalization will also be muted, because environmental control costs will be reflected in market prices.

5. Eliminate Natural Resource Subsidies

Natural resources, such as water and energy, are very often underpriced in both industrialized and developing countries. These policies distort international trade, whether the subsidized resource is directly exported or used as an input in the production of exported commodities. At the same time, such natural resource subsidies result in extensive environmental damage by encouraging the oversupply and overuse of the natural resource in question. For example, water subsidies in the western United States have led to severe environmental damages, including salinization of soils, contamination of wetlands, and reduction of fisheries and bird populations. Resource subsidies of this kind are often not considered to be environmental policies, but they significantly affect the use and management of natural resources. Eliminating them yields trade and environmental benefits.

In such Asian countries as Indonesia, Philippines, and Papua New Guinea, failure by governments to charge concession holders adequate royalties for timber harvested on public forests has led to wasteful overexploitation and ecological losses. At the same time, the public exchequer has been deprived of badly needed funds to finance development programs (Repetto and Gillis 1988). Austria and the Netherlands have proposed tariff or nontariff barriers to imports of tropical timber harvested unsustainably. These measures would surely be open to challenge under GATT rules. How much better it would be for tropical timber producing countries to reform their own timber royalty structures to reduce incentives for profiteering in tropical timber exports. The developing country government would receive the revenues directly, the incentives for improved timber management would apply to all production, for domestic use and for export to all destinations, and the measures would be completely consistent with GATT principles.

In Eastern Europe and Russia, underpricing of energy has fostered grossly inefficient domestic energy use, increased pollution, and deprived countries of badly needed potential export revenues. Eliminating such resource subsidies would constrain domestic consumption and release additional supplies for exports, as well as provide financial resources for investment in higher production and efficiency. Eliminating resource subsidies yields economic and environmental returns.

6. Harmonize Procedural Standards Governing Testing and Risk Assessment

While countries may understandably and legitimately adopt standards implying different levels of control over environmental risks, there are many economic and environmental gains to be obtained if the procedures for risk assessment are harmonized internationally. Such issues as, How should risks be assessed? What data are relevant, and how should they be collected? What tests and testing procedures are acceptable? can be agreed upon internationally without impinging on each country's authority to decide for itself the level of acceptable risk. Uncertainty regarding the actual quality of products entering the country from abroad would be reduced. The workload on environmental agencies would be reduced. Agreeing on these important procedural matters would decrease the regulatory costs of international investment and trade. It would also reduce the scope for trade disputes over the legitimacy and scientific basis for product standards.

In summary, fears over the impacts of environmental policies on trade have not been balanced by hopes for potential benefits. The two goals are potentially complementary. Good environmental policies can help secure the gains from trade and avert trade conflicts. Trade liberalization, if conducted with adequate safeguards, can lead to better environmental quality. What is needed is a consistent vision of sustainable development and a coherent set of domestic and international policies to promote both.

Acknowledgments

The paper has benefited from the helpful comments of Francis Harrigan, Narhari Rao, Mao Yushi, and other participants at the Second Asian Development Bank Conference on Development Economics.

Note

1. Personal communication with Garth Redfield, Director, South Florida Water Management District Research Program, 31 September 1993.

References

Anderson, K., and R. Blackhurst, eds., 1992. *The Greening of World Trade Issues*. London: Harrester Wheatsheaf.

Broad, R., and J. Cavanagh, 1993. *Plundering Paradise: The Struggle for Environment in the Philippines*. Berkeley: University of California Press.

Centre for Science and Environment, 1985. *The State of India's Environment, The*

Second Citizen's Report, 1984-85. New Delhi.

Charnovitz, S., 1992. "GATT and the Environment: Examining the Issues." *International Environmental Affairs* 4(3):203-33.

Cruz, W., and R. Repetto, 1992. *The Environmental Effects of Stabilization and Structural Adjustment Programs: The Philippines Case*. Washington: World Resources Institute.

Davis, S. M., 1993. "Phosphorous Inputs and Vegetation Sensitivity in the Everglades." South Florida Water Management. District Technical Publication (draft).

Dean, J. M., 1992. "Trade and the Environment: A Survey of the Literature." Background paper for *World Development Report 1992*, Washington: World Bank.

Everglades Coalition, 1993. The Greater Everglades Ecosystem Restoration Plan. Everglades Coalition, Florida.

Faeth, Paul, et al., 1991. *Paying the Farm Bill*. Washington: World Resources Institute.

French, H. F., 1993. *Costly Tradeoffs: Reconciling Trade & The Environment*. Washington: Worldwatch Institute.

Haley, S. L., et al., 1993. "Sugar Policy Reform in the United States and the European Community: Assessing the Economic Impact." Report No. 693. United States Department of Agricultural Economics & Agribusiness.

Hufbauer, G. C., and J. J. Schott, 1992. *North American Free Trade*. Washington: Institute for International Economics.

Indira Gandhi Institute of Development Research, 1993. "Trade and Environment Linkages: The Case of India." Draft report for the United Nations Conference on Trade and Development. Delhi, India.

Julius, D., 1990. *Global Companies and Public Policy: The Growing Challenge of Foreign Direct Investment*. New York: Council on Foreign Relations Press.

Kox, H. L. M., 1992. "Incorporating Environmental Considerations into Commodity Agreements." Paper presented at Organisation for Economic Co-operation and Development Workshop, Paris.

Low, P., 1992. *International Trade and the Environment*. Washington: World Bank.

Nearhoof, F. L., 1992. "Nutrient-induced Impacts and Water Quality Violations in the Florida Everglades." Water Quality Technical Series 3:24. Draft. Florida Department of Environmental Regulation, Tallahasse, Florida.

Organisation for Economic Co-operation and Development (OECD), 1989-90. "Modelling the Effects of Agricultural Policies." *OECD Economic Studies* 13(Winter).

Pearson, C., 1993. "Trade and Environment: The United States Experience." United Nations Conference on Trade and Development. United Nations, Geneva.

Phantumvanit, D., and T. Panayotou, 1990. *Industrialization and Environmental Quality: Paying the Price*. London: Tropical Development and Research Institute.

Rader, R. and C. Richardson, 1992. "The Effects of Nutrient Enrichment on Algae and Macroinvertebrates in the Everglades: A Review." *Wetlands* 12:121-35.

Reed, D., ed., 1992. *Structural Adjustment and The Environment*. Boulder: World Wide Fund for Nature.

Reichelderfer, K., 1990. "Environmental Protection and Agricultural Support: Are Trade-offs Necessary?" In K. Allen, ed., *Agricultural Policies in a New Decade*. Washington: Resources for the Future.

Repetto, R., 1993. "Trade and Environment Policies: Achieving Complementarities and Avoiding Conflicts." *Issues and Ideas*. Washington: World Resources Institute.

Repetto, R., and M. Gillis, eds., 1988. *Public Policies and the Misuse of Forest Resources*. London: Cambridge University Press.

Repetto, R., et al. 1989. *Wasting Assets: National Resources in the National Income Accounts*. Washington: World Resources Institute.

Runge, C. F., 1991. "Environmental Effects of Trade in the Agricultural Sector." Paper prepared for the Organisation for Economic Co-operation and Development, University of Minnesota.

Sanderson, F, H., ed., 1990. *Agricultural Protectionism in the Industrialized World*. Washington: Resources for the Future.

Smil, V., 1984. *The Bad Earth: Environmental Degradation in China*. New York: Sharpe Publishers.

Tropical Science Center and World Resources Institute, 1991. *Accounts Overdue: Natural Resource Depreciation in Costa Rica*. Washington, D.C.

Tucker, S. K. and M. Chambers, 1989. "U.S. Sugar Quotas and the Caribbean Basin." Overseas Development Council, Washington, D.C.

United States Government Accounting Office, 1993. "Sugar Program: Changing Domestic and International Conditions Require Program Changes." Washington, D.C.

United States Environmental Protection Agency, 1990. *Agriculture and the Environment: OECD Policy Experiences and US Opportunities*. Washington, D.C.

Webb, A. J., et al., 1990. *Estimates of Producer and Consumer Subsidy Equivalents: Government Intervention in Agriculture, 1982-1987*. United States Department of Agriculture, Economic Research Service, Statistics Bulletin 803, Washington, D.C.

World Bank, 1987. *World Development Report 1987*. Chapter 8. Washington: World Bank.

———, 1992. *China Environmental Strategy Paper*. Washington: World Bank.

———, 1993a. *The East Asian Miracle, Economic Growth and Public Policy*. New York: Oxford University Press.

———, 1993b. *Indonesia Environment and Development: Challenges for the Future*. Washington, D.C.

Chapter Nine

The Implications of New Growth Theory for Trade and Development: An Overview

Pranab Bardhan

Introduction

The theoretical literature on growth and trade flourished in the 1950s and 1960s, beginning with Hicks' famous Inaugural Lecture (1953). The literature first developed a framework for analyzing the comparative statics of the effects of capital accumulation and exogenous technical change on a country's terms of trade and balance of payments. Then in the second half of the 1960s, the dynamic analysis of neoclassical growth models was extended to the case of the open economy. For a review and extensions of this literature, see Bardhan (1970), and Findlay (1973). In the 1970s and almost up to the end of the 1980s, the theoretical literature on growth and trade was somewhat inactive, except for the development of several North-South models focusing on the impact on trade relationships of the various kinds of asymmetries between rich and poor countries (primarily in the structure of demand for importables and exportables, or in the labor markets). In the last few years, there has again been a spurt in the literature flowing from the application of the so-called new growth theory following upon the leading contributions of Romer (1986, 1990), and Lucas (1988). The Grossman-Helpman book (1991) is the major example of this application to an open economy.

Two misperceptions exist about this new literature. First, it has often been claimed that the new growth theory has endogenized technical progress in contrast to the old growth theory, the central case of the latter being the Solow (1956) growth model. This overlooks the tradition of endogenous growth in many of the growth models of the 1960s: apart from Arrow's (1962) learning-by-doing model where learning emanated from the dynamic externalities of cumulated gross investment, and Uzawa's (1965) model of investment in human capital generating technical change, there are the Kaldor-Mirrlees model (1962) where investment is the vehicle of technical progress, and Shell's (1967) model of inventive activity. Nor is the blurring of the distinction between capital accumulation and technical progress a new feature. It was the salient point of the Johansen-Solow type vintage-capital models as well as the many growth models of Kaldor. The idea of aggregate dynamic economies of scale in the form of the development of new inputs, expanding the productivity in the final goods sector using those inputs—which Romer borrows from Ethier (1982) and which actually goes back to Young (1928)—has in some sense been formalized already in vintage-capital models. In these models each new vintage of better machines expanded the range of higher productivity inputs used in final goods production. The major contributions of the new growth theory lie in combining all of these strands with a tractable imperfect-competition framework that provides some (Schumpeterian) private motivation for investment in research and development.

The major contribution of the open economy models in this literature is to give new insights on the effects of trade on growth. The East Asian success stories have given credence[1] to the belief of many neoclassical economists in a positive relationship between outward-orientation and economic development (although a rigorous empirical demonstration of the *causal* relationship between some satisfactory measure of outward-orientation and the rate of growth is rather scarce). Standard neoclassical growth theory did not provide any such general theorem. The second misperceived claim about the new literature is that it provides an unambiguous theoretical demonstration of the positive effects of trade expansion on the rate of development.

Trade Policy and the Traditional Growth Theory

Four strands in the earlier theoretical literature relate trade policy to the rate of growth in a developing country. One is a simple extension of the Solow model with an essential *imported* intermediate input, the growth in supply of which depends on the rate of growth of exports (see, for example, Khang 1968, and Bardhan 1970, chapter 4). In these models, the steady-state rate of growth of the economy is different from the rate of growth of population and labor-augmenting technical progress, depending on the rate of growth of the country's exports in the world market.

The second strand[2], following an older tradition, formalizes dynamic economies of scale associated with learning by doing (captured by the inter-firm spillover effects of cumulated gross output), thus rationalizing an old argument for support of 'infant' industry producing import-substitutes or new exports (see the models of Bardhan 1970, chapter 7; and Clemhout and Wan 1970).

Thirdly, in a small open dual-economy model with a tariff on capital-intensive capital goods and a fixed fraction of profits saved, Findlay (1982) demonstrated that protection can lower the steady-state rate of capital accumulation. In a more general three-good (including non-tradables), three-factor model of a small open economy with savings determined by intertemporal utility maximization, Buffie (1991) has recently shown, however, that the effect of protection on the rate of capital accumulation need not be negative.

The fourth strand in the earlier literature involves the effects of trade policy on the modernization of the capital stock, based on vintage-capital growth models. The first models to link comparative advantage to endogenous differences in the economic life of capital between countries (lower wages in poorer countries allowing for the use of older, less productive machines) were those of Bardhan (1966), and Bardhan (1970, chapter 5); Smith (1976) developed a more general model to include trade in secondhand equipment between rich and poor countries. Bardhan and Kletzer (1984) showed, in terms of a simple vintage-capital trade model with embodied technical progress, how the question of a policy of protection accelerating or delaying modernization of capital stock (thus helping or dampening growth of labor productivity) depends, among other things, on the technological characteristics of the protected sector. It does not have an unambiguous answer.

The new growth theory literature has not yet significantly followed up on this strand of the earlier literature. In fact, borrowing as it does the Dixit-Stiglitz-Ethier 'love of variety' models in terms of a production functional where endogenous growth takes the form of simply extending the range of new inputs, it overlooks the endogenous process of the economic obsolescence of some inputs: it is not necessarily the *width* of the range of inputs that enhances productivity. For example, in the new growth theory the production function for finished manufactured products is often something like

$$Q = F\left(L, \left[\int_0^n x^\beta(j)\,dj\right]^{\frac{1}{\beta}}\right), \qquad 1 > \beta > 0 \qquad (1)$$

where Q is output, L is labor, $x(j)$ is the produced input of type j—all symmetric but imperfect substitutes combined in a CES function—and n is the measure of continually augmented inputs (as well as of the stock of cumulative knowledge capital). There is no scope here for the scrapping of obsolete inputs; an old abacus keeps on being symmetrically used as does a new computer. In the old vintage-capital models, the production function may be written as

$$Q(v,t) = F(L(v,t), I(v))$$ (2)

where $I(v)$ is the number of machines of vintage v, $Q(v,t)dv$ and $L(v,t)dv$ are the rates of output produced and labor employed respectively, at time t on machines of vintage $v(v{\leq}t)$. Total output is therefore

$$Q(t) = \int_{t-T}^{t} Q(v,t)dv$$ (3)

where T is the vintage of the oldest machine in use. A machine is scrapped when the wage bill for operating it exhausts the value of its output:

$$W(t)L(t-T,t) = Q(t-T,t),$$ (4)

where $W(t)$ is the wage rate at time t.

Bardhan and Kletzer (1984) developed a vintage-capital model of endogenous growth with (linear) effects of learning by doing, where they trace the impact of trade policy on the time-path of productivity. Their fixed-coefficient production function is

$$Q(v,t) = min\{a(v)I(v), bq(v)L(v,t)\}$$ (5)

where $a(v)$ is the capital productivity coefficient on machines of vintage v, b is a positive constant and cumulated output, which is the index of experience and learning, is given by

$$q(v) = \int_{0}^{v} Q(t)dt$$ (6)

This is an endogenous growth model that allows for economic obsolescence of producer goods. This model needs to be extended to the case of imperfect competition.

Trade Policy and the New Growth Theory

A major result in the new literature is to show how economic integration in the world market, compared to isolation, helps long-run growth by avoiding unnecessary duplication of research in similar developed economies and thus increases aggregate productivity of resources employed in the research and development (R&D) sector (characterized by economies of scale). World market competition gives incentives to entrepreneurs in each of these countries to invent products that are unique in the world economy (see the models of Rivera-Batiz and Romer 1991; and Grossman and Helpman 1991, chapter 9). One has, of course, to keep in mind the fact that sometimes these unique products are unique in the sense of product differentiation but not in the sense of any technological advance. (It is well-known, for example, that in the pharmaceutical industry a majority of the so-called new products are really recombinations of existing ingredients with an eye to prolonging patent protection, and that they are new, not therapeutically, but from the marketability point of view). Besides, the presumption in these models of a common pool of knowledge capital created by international spillovers of technical information is not often relevant for a poor country.

When knowledge accumulation is localized largely in the rich country and the poor country is also smaller in (economic) size, particularly in the size of its already accumulated knowledge capital (which determines research effectiveness), the rich country captures a growing market share in the total number of differentiated varieties. The entrepreneurs in the poor country, foreseeing capital losses, may innovate less rapidly in long-run equilibrium with international trade than would happen under autarky, as shown by Feenstra (1990), and Grossman and Helpman (1991, chapter 9). Trade reduces the profitability of R&D in the poor country as it places local entrepreneurs in competition with a rapidly expanding set of imported, differentiated products. This may drive the poor country to specialize in production rather than research, and within production to move from high tech products to traditional, possibly stagnant, industries, which use the relatively plentiful supply of unskilled workers—thus slowing innovation and growth.[3] Of course, slower growth does not necessarily mean that the consumer loses from trade: apart from the usual static gains from trade, consumers may have access to more varieties innovated abroad. But trade may sometimes cause a net welfare loss, since in the poorer country it accelerates a market failure (underinvestment in research in the initial situation) by allocating resources further away from research.

One should note that the relevant R&D for a poor country is, of course, more in technological adaptation of products and processes invented abroad and in imitation. But even this kind of an R&D sector is usually so small that major changes in aggregate productivity and growth on the basis of the trade-induced general-equilibrium type reallocation of fully employed resources into or away from the R&D sector, as emphasized by Grossman and Helpman, will seem a little overdrawn if applied in the context of poor countries.[4] In any case, the ambiguity in the relationship between trade expansion and productivity growth in these general-equilibrium models only confirms similar conclusions in careful partial-equilibrium models, particularly when entry and exit from industries are not frictionless (see, for example, Rodrik 1992).

In the Grossman-Helpman model of the innovating North and the imitating South, with all firms in Bertrand competition with one another, labor costs form the only component of the cost of entry into the imitative-adaptive R&D activity in the South. So, armed with cheaper labor, the southern firms can relentlessly keep on targeting northern products for imitation, unhampered by many of the formidable real world, nonlabor constraints on entry (for example, those posed by the lack of a viable physical, social, and educational infrastructure or that of organizational know-how in a poor country). Also, the Grossman-Helpman models, by adopting the Dixit-Stiglitz-style consumer prefer-ences, assume a uniform price elasticity and a unitary expenditure elasticity for each of the differentiated products that enter symmetrically in the utility function. This, of course, immediately rules out what has been a major preoccupation of the trade and development literature: to explore the implications of sectoral demand asymmetries for trade relationships between rich and poor countries. The assumption of monopolistic competition and contestable markets in the models also precludes any serious examination of the impact of trade on growth through the lowering of entry barriers in oligopolistic industries, industry rationalization, and reduction of the gap between actual and best practice international technology that foreign competitive pressure may induce.

The slow diffusion of technology from rich to poor countries is often interpreted in the literature as reflecting the frequent laxity in the enforcement of patents in poor countries and innovators in rich countries thus compelled to protect their ideas through secrecy. This brings us to the controversial issue of intellectual property rights (IPR), which has sometimes divided the rich and poor countries, as was notable in the recent Uruguay Round discussions. Rich countries often claim that a tighter IPR regime encourages innovations (by expanding the duration of the innovator's monopoly) from which all countries benefit. Poor countries often counter this by pointing to their losses following increased monopoly power of the larger companies of rich countries. Since the poor countries provide a very small market for many industrial products, the disincentive effects of lax patent protection in those countries may be marginal on the rate of innovation in rich countries, and, as such, attempts at free riding by the poor countries may make sense, as Chin and Grossman (1990) suggest. To this, Diwan and Rodrik (1991) add the qualification that the disincentive effects may be very significant in the case of innovation in technologies or products that are particularly appropriate for poor countries (for example, drugs against tropical diseases). But both of these theoretical models use a static partial-equilibrium framework. Helpman (1993) recently constructed a dynamic general-equilibrium model of innovation and imitation to discuss the question of IPR. In the long-run equilibrium of his model, a tighter IPR (reducing the rate of imitation by the lower wage poor country) increases the fraction of the total number of products produced unchallenged by the rich country, but lowers the long-run rate of innovation of new products[5] (this works through the rise in the price-earning ratio of the R&D firm in the rich country, consequent upon the general equilibrium labor reallocation effect of a larger range of manufactured products produced in the rich country).[6] Even apart from this effect on the rate of innovation, a tighter IPR, by shifting production from the lower wage (and therefore lower price) country to the higher wage country, makes consumers in both countries worse off.

The discussion advocating a tighter IPR regime also ignores the cases of restrictive business practices of many multinational companies (like preemptive patenting and 'sleeping' patents where new patents are taken out in poor countries simply to ward off competitors but seldom are actually used in local production).[7] Furthermore, the flow of technology through direct investments by multinational enterprises to a poor country is often constrained not so much by restrictive government policy in the host country as by its lack of infrastructure (the development of which in turn is constrained by the difficulty of raising large loans in a severely imperfect international credit market).

The new models of trade and growth bring into sharp focus the features of monopolistic competition, particularly in the sector producing intermediate products and, in some models, the Schumpeterian process of costly R&D races with the prospect of temporary monopoly power for the winner. These aspects were missing in most of the earlier growth models. But there are other important aspects of imperfect competition as well. These aspects, such as the case of 'sleeping' patents above or how international credit market imperfections shape the pattern of comparative advantage[8], need formalizing in the literature on trade and development.

In another respect, the new literature marks a substantial advance over the old. This relates to what was identified previously as the second strand of the earlier literature on trade policy and growth, the one concerned with learning by doing. An important extension of the models of Bardhan (1970, chapter 7), and Clemhout and Wan (1970) has been carried out by Krugman (1987), and Boldrin and Scheinkman (1988), where, over time, the learning effects (emanating from production experience measured by cumulated industry output) enhance the existing sectoral patterns of comparative advantage. This may call for a deliberate trade policy, one that can orchestrate a breakout from such a historical 'lock-in'.[9]

But these models of learning share with the earlier ones the unrealistic feature of continued learning at a given rate on a fixed set of goods. As Lucas (1993) comments, evidence on learning on narrowly defined product lines often shows high initial learning rates, declining over time as production cumulates. For on-the-job learning to occur in an economy on a sustained basis it is necessary that workers and managers continue to take on tasks that are new to them, to continue to move up the quality ladder in goods. The major formulations that try to capture this in the context of an open economy are those of Alwyn Young (1991), and Stokey (1991). On the basis of learning by doing that spills over and across industries, although bounded in each industry, Young's model endogenizes the movement of goods out of the learning sector into a mature sector in which learning no longer occurs and thus gives a plausible account of an evolving trade structure. Stokey has a model of North-South trade, based on vertical product differentiation and international differences in labor quality; the South produces a low quality spectrum of goods and the North a high quality spectrum. If human capital is acquired through learning by doing and so is stimulated by the production of high quality goods, free trade (as opposed to autarky) will speed up human capital accumulation in the North and slow it down in the South. A similar result is obtained by Young. (It, of course, does not follow that the South would be better off under autarky.) It also indicates why a policy of protecting infant export industries is sometimes more growth-promoting in the long run than that of protecting infant import-substitute industries, since, in the former case, the opportunities for learning spillover into newer and more sophisticated goods are wider than when one is restricted to the home market. Through vertical linkage, export growth encourages accumulation of technological capability not only in the producer firms but also in the specialized supplier firms.

Finally, while the new literature has sharpened analytical tools and made our ways of thinking about the relationship between trade and growth more rigorous, it is high time that more attention is paid to the extremely difficult task of empirical verification of some of the propositions in the literature. (This remark, of course, does not count the largely vacuous cross-country regressions on the basis of very shaky, but easily available, international data, which some of the new growth theorists have been playing with). While some beginnings have been made—see, for example, the study by Feenstra, Markusen, and Zeile (1992) on the basis of a sample of industries in the Republic of Korea—to confirm the hypothesis of the new growth models that the creation of new inputs generates continuous growth in total factor productivity, the evidence on the link between trade and productivity growth is still scanty and rather mixed. On the basis of a sample of semi-industrial countries in the World Bank project on 'Industrial Competition, Productivity and their Relation to Trade Regimes', Tybout (1992, 207) observes: 'the lack of stable correlations (between trade and productivity) in sectoral and industry-level data is matched by a surprising diversity in the processes of entry, exit, and scale adjustment'. The theoretical models, for all their recent enrichment, have a long way to go before they can catch up with the complexity of the empirical reality.

Acknowledgments

The author would like to thank Basant Kapur, Jeffrey Liang, and Pak-Wai Liu for helpful comments.

Notes

1. It should, however, be noted that the export boom in manufactures for the Republic of Korea and Taipei,China in the 1960's came *before* any significant trade liberalization. As Rodrik (1992) suggests, a realistic exchange rate policy and a generous program of export subsidies, rather than trade liberalization per se, may be the key ingredients for successful export performance.

2. The first and the second strands have, in a sense, been combined and extended in the recent work of Quah and Rauch (1990).

3. This is at least consistent with the view in the historical studies of Japan's innovation system that restrictions on imports and foreign direct investment may have played a major positive role in regard to R&D effort until the early 1970s. See Odagiri and Goto (1993).

4. It may also be noted that in the Grossman-Helpman (1991, chapter 11) model of imitation, where the poor country grows faster with imitation and trade

than without them, it is the process of imitation rather than the integration of product markets per se that contributes to a more rapid pace of innovation in the poor country.

5. This result may not be robust for the case where direct foreign investment as well as imitation acts as a channel of technology transfer, as Lai (1993) shows.

6. In a different context, Mookherjee and Ray (1991) have shown that when a dominant firm decides on the adoption of a sequence of potential cost-reducing innovations with Bertrand competition in the product market, a faster rate of diffusion of the latest technology to a competitive fringe may, over some range, increase the competitive pressure on the leader, quickening the latter's pace of innovations.

7. Some estimates by the United Nations Conference on Trade and Development (1975) suggest that 90 to 95 per cent of foreign-owned patents in developing countries are not used in those countries.

8. Kletzer and Bardhan (1987) show how more costly credit under imperfect information may drive a poor country away from specializing in sophisticated manufactured products that require more selling and distribution costs than traditional primary products.

9. A similar model of hysteresis, based on self-reinforcing advantages, not of learning but of headstarts in R&D, is developed in Grossman and Helpman (1991, chapter 8).

References

Arrow, K. J., 1962. "The Economic Implications of Learning by Doing." *Review of Economic Studies* 29:155-73.

Bardhan, P., 1966. "International Trade Theory in a Vintage Capital Model." *Econometrica* 34:756-67.

———, 1970. *Economic Growth, Development and Foreign Trade: A Study in Pure Theory*. New York: Wiley-Interscience.

Bardhan, P., and K. Kletzer, 1984. "Dynamic Effects of Protection on Productivity." *Journal of International Economics* 16:45-57.

Boldrin, M., and J. A. Scheinkman, 1988. "Learning by Doing, International Trade and Growth: A Note." In P. W. Anderson, K. J. Arrow, and D. Pines, eds., *The Economy as an Evolving Complex System*. Reading: Addison-Wesley.

Buffie, E. F., 1991. "Commercial Policy, Growth and the Distribution of Income in a Dynamic Trade Model." *Journal of Development Economics* 37:1-30.

Chin, J. C., and G. M. Grossman, 1990. "Intellectual Property Rights and North-South Trade." In R. W. Jones and A. O. Krueger, eds., *The Political Economy of International Trade: Essays in Honor of Robert E. Baldwin*. Cambridge: Blackwell.

Clemhout, S., and H. Wan, 1970. "Learning by Doing and Infant Industry Protection." *Review of Economic Studies* 37:33-56.

Diwan, I., and D. Rodrik, 1991. "Patents, Appropriate Technology, and North-South Trade." *Journal of International Economics* 30:27-47.

Ethier, W. J., 1982. "National and International Increasing Returns to Scale in the Modern Theory of International Trade." *American Economic Review* 72:389-405.

Feenstra, R. C., 1990. "Trade and Uneven Growth." Working Paper No. 3276. National Bureau of Economic Research. Cambridge, Massachusetts.

Feenstra, R. C., J. R. Markusen, and W. Zeile, 1992. "Accounting for Growth with New Inputs: Theory and Evidence." *American Economic Review* 82:415-21.

Findlay, R., 1973. "International Trade and Development Theory." New York: Columbia University Press.

―――, 1982. "Protection and Growth in a Dual Economy." In M. Gersovitz et al., eds., *The Theory and Experience of Economic Development: Essays in Honor of Sir W. Arthur Lewis.* London: Allen and Unwin.

Grossman, G. M., and E. Helpman, 1991. "Innovation and Growth in the Global Economy." Cambridge: M.I.T. Press.

Helpman, E., 1993. "Innovation, Imitation, and Intellectual Property Rights." *Econometrica* 61:1247-80.

Hicks, J. R., 1953. "An Inaugural Lecture." *Oxford Economic Papers* 5:117-35.

Kaldor, N., and J. A. Mirrlees, 1962. "A New Model of Economic Growth." *Review of Economic Studies* 29:174-92.

Khang, C., 1968. "A Neoclassical Growth Model of a Resource-Poor Open Economy." *International Economic Review* 9:329-38.

Kletzer, K., and P. Bardhan, 1987. "Credit Markets and Patterns of International Trade." *Journal of Development Economics* 27:57-70.

Krugman, P., 1987. "The Narrow Moving Band, the Dutch Disease, and the Competitive Consequences of Mrs. Thatcher: Notes on Trade in the Presence of Dynamic Scale Economies." *Journal of Development Economics* 27:41-55.

Lai, E. L. C., 1993. "International Intellectual Property Rights Protection and the Rate of Product Innovation." Mimeographed.

Lucas, R. E., 1988. "On the Mechanics of Economic Development." *Journal of Monetary Economics* 22:3-42.

―――, 1993. "Making a Miracle." *Econometrica* 61:251-72.

Mookherjee, D., and D. Ray, 1991. "On the Competitive Pressure Created by the Diffusion of Innovations." *Journal of Economic Theory* 54:124-47.

Odagiri, H., and A. Goto, 1993. "The Japanese System of Innovation: Past, Present and Future." In R. R. Nelson, ed., *National Innovation Systems: A Comparative Analysis.* New York: Oxford University Press.

Quah, D., and J. E. Rauch, 1990. "Openness and the Rate of Economic Growth." University of California, San Diego. Mimeographed.

Rivera-Batiz, L. A., and P. M. Romer, 1991. "Economic Integration and Endogenous Growth." *Quarterly Journal of Economics* 106:531-55.

Rodrik, D., 1992. "Closing the Productivity Gap: Does Trade Liberalization Really Help?" In G. Helleiner, ed., *Trade Policy, Industrialization and Development: New Perspectives.* Oxford: Clarendon Press.

Romer, P. M., 1986. "Increasing Returns and Long-run Growth." *Journal of Political Economy* 94:1002-37.

————, 1990. "Endogenous Technological Change." *Journal of Political Economy* 98:S71-S102.

Shell, K., 1967. "A Model of Inventive Activity and Capital Accumulation." In K. Shell, ed., *Essays in the Theory of Optimal Economic Growth*. Cambridge: Massachusetts Institute of Technology Press.

Smith, M. A. M., 1976. "International Trade Theory in Vintage Models." *Review of Economic Studies* 43:99-113.

Solow, R. M., 1956. "A Contribution to the Theory of Economic Growth." *Quarterly Journal of Economics* 70:65-94.

Stokey, N., 1991. "The Volume and Composition of Trade between Rich and Poor Countries." *Review of Economic Studies* 58:63-80.

Tybout, J. R., 1992. "Linking Trade and Productivity: New Research Directions." *World Bank Economic Review* 6:189-211.

United Nations Conference on Trade and Development, 1975. *The Role of the Patent System in the Transfer of Technology to Developing Countries*. New York: United Nations.

Uzawa, H., 1965. "Optimal Technical Change in an Aggregative Model of Economic Growth." *International Economic Review* 6:18-31.

Young, A., 1928. "Increasing Returns and Economic Progress." *Economic Journal* 38:527-42.

Young, Alwyn, 1991. "Learning by Doing and the Dynamic Effects of International Trade." *Quarterly Journal of Economics* 106:369-405.

Chapter Ten

Recent Advances in Trade and Growth Theory

Ronald Findlay

Introduction

This paper, which focuses on recent advances in trade and growth theory, concentrates on developments since the mid-eighties. For a review of developments prior to that period, see Findlay (1984a). As it turns out, the mid-eighties is a very convenient point at which to break into the stream of this particular branch of intellectual history, since it was very shortly afterward that we had the sudden emergence of 'endogenous growth theory' in the work of Lucas (1988), and Romer (1986, 1990). From its very inception, at least in the case of Lucas, this approach has taken an international perspective. Romer himself and others have recently written several papers on endogenous growth in a trade context, and we have had a full blown treatise on *Innovation and Growth in the Global Economy* by Grossman and Helpman (1991). A large and growing literature on the subject exists, some of which is reviewed by Pranab Bardhan in a companion paper in this volume.

As argued in Findlay (1984a), the field of trade and growth goes back all the way to David Ricardo's *Essay on Profits,* which remains the most profound and original contribution to the subject. Recalling the classical origins of the concern about the links between trade and growth helps to remind us that the concept of the growth rate being an endogenous variable is, in itself, hardly new. It is, in fact, a feature of *all* the growth models from Marx to von Neumann, Arthur Lewis, and Harrod and Domar. In Ricardo, it is the relentless effect of diminishing returns on the land that drives down the rate of profit, and hence the rate of growth, even though trade with 'new' land-abundant countries could provide a long, but in the end only temporary, reprieve. This followed from his crucial assumption that the recipients of the rising land rents did not save but spent on luxury consumption. In our day, as the Dutch Disease literature has shown, resource windfalls do seem to induce both private and public profligacy. In Marx, von Neumann, Lewis, and Harrod and Domar, the economic system escapes from the law of diminishing returns by postulating linear technologies and removing land as a scarce factor.

It was Robert Solow (1956), in his celebrated paper, who brought diminishing returns back into the growth story by introducing capital-labor substitution and a fixed growth rate of the effective labor force, which meant that such factors as the rate of time preference and the propensity to save would have no *ultimate* effect on the rate of growth. As he said 'the long run is the domain of the neoclassical, the land of the margin'. Now, once again, we are attempting to escape from the tyranny of diminishing returns by the Promethean concept of the unlimited power of the human mind and the cumulative growth of knowledge, eloquently expounded by Paul Romer.

In making the rate of growth an endogenous variable the new theory has followed two separate tracks. One is the idea of 'learning by doing', associated of course with the famous model of Arrow (1962), but which can be traced back much earlier to the 'infant industry' argument of Hamilton and List. Formal restatements of the infant industry argument in the context of growth models along the lines of Arrow were made by Bardhan (1970), and Clemhout and Wan (1970). Lucas (1988), in one of the models that he presents based on Krugman (1987), candidly acknowledges that it is a restatement of the infant industry argument. Alwyn Young (1991), in a very ingenious model with a continuum of commodities, also shows that trade can set back the rate of technological progress of the 'latecomer' country, while it accelerates it in its more advanced partner.

The other idea, stressed by Romer, and by Grossman and Helpman, is that innovations creating new products or varieties are generated by the conscious expenditure of resources with a view to recouping the investment out of the future stream of profits created by the innovation. There is, however, a crucial externality, the contribution that the new idea makes to the pool of cumulative knowledge, thereby making it easier for subsequent new ideas to be generated. This is the 'dynamic' increasing returns to scale that characterizes the research and development (R&D) or 'knowledge' industry and which is the source of the endogeneity of the growth rate. As Joan Robinson would have put it, the thicker is the existing 'book of blueprints', the cheaper it is to add a new page.

These new 'varieties' can be considered as either final consumer goods that enter the Dixit-Stiglitz (1977) 'love of variety' utility function, or as in the clever adaptation by Ethier (1982), as intermediate inputs into a production function for a single final good with the same functional form as the Dixit-Stiglitz utility function. The market structure in either case is monopolistic competition *á la* Chamberlin. Just as trade between similar economies in the 'new' trade theory produces gains from greater variety to consumers, the alternative hypothesis has trade boosting final output through the provision of a wider mix of intermediate inputs.

In Clarida and Findlay (1991, 1992), we adopted the view that R&D is a *public* intermediate input, which is provided by the state to the private sector to augment its productivity over time. We could also imagine that this input is provided by a privately organized, industry-wide consortium, that internalizes the benefits of its R&D activities to its members, so that the full Lindahl price (the sum of the marginal value products to all firms) is charged and the optimal amount provided. In this model, the growth rate of a small open economy is shown to be endogenous and an increasing function of the provision of the public intermediate input.

The remainder of this paper is in four parts. The first discusses the concept of comparative advantage in a dynamic context, using the neoclassical growth model and the 'dual economy' approach of Arthur Lewis as the reference points. The impact of trade policy on the rate of growth is discussed in each of these settings, and it is shown how, in the Lewis setting, a constant tariff can *permanently* lower the rate of growth for as long as the surplus labor condition applies. The next section presents a simple model of learning by doing and endogenous growth, while the third develops a model of endogenous growth as a consequence of public R&D expenditures. The final section examines the record of the newly industrializing economies of East Asia in the light of trade and growth theory of both the 'old' and 'new' vintages.

Growth in a Small Open Economy: The Neoclassical and Dual Economy Models

All theories of economic growth have generally found it useful to drastically simplify the production structure under consideration, with output originating in one, or at most two, sectors. This 'heroic' aggregation can be made more palatable by adopting the trade theory device of a 'small open economy', one that faces fixed relative prices for all tradable goods on the world market. Given constant returns to scale production functions for all these goods, it is possible to show that these can be aggregated into a simple 'composite' or 'surrogate' production function for any individual good (see Findlay 1973, chapter 6; or Findlay 1984a).

With a continuum of tradable goods, each differing infinitesimally in capital-labor ratio from its 'nearest' partners, the production function is smooth and differentiable. With a finite number of tradable goods, it would have linear facets as segments joining adjacent goods but the essential properties of a neoclassical production function remain, even though they have to be suitably interpreted.

With the aid of this device a number of important points can be made quickly. First, let us consider the question of the difference between comparative advantage at given factor proportions, the traditional 'static' view, and what might be called 'dynamic' or 'long-run' comparative advantage. In Figure 10.1, the unit 'isoquant' FF' refers to the 'surrogate' production function for a unit of what may be termed 'international purchasing power' (IPP), that is to say combinations of capital and labor that can each produce tradable goods of constant *value* at *world prices*. Let the ray O_a from the origin indicate the initial capital-labor ratio k_0 for the small open economy. Making the standard neoclassical Solow-Swan assumptions of a fixed savings ratio s and rate of labor force growth in efficiency-units, denoted n, but using the technology defined by FF', it follows that we can define k^*, the long-run, steady state capital-labor ratio to which the small open economy will converge as

$$k^* = sf(k^*)/n \tag{1}$$

Let k^*, greater than k_0, be defined in Figure 10.1 by the slope of O_b. This enables us to identify 'momentary comparative advantage' with the good that is efficient to produce at k_0 and relative factor prices indicated by the slope of FF' at the point where it is intersected by k_0. The desired pattern of final demand and consumption is irrelevant, since whatever bundle is most desired can be purchased from the income that is maximized at world prices by specializing on the 'right' good, determined by the 'right' prices, which are the given vector of world prices, as well as the real wage w_0, return to capital r_0 corresponding to k_0, and the technology defined by FF'.

The 'long run' comparative advantage, on the other hand, is in the more capital-intensive good defined by k^*, with factor prices w^* and r^*, which maximize steady state income at the given world product prices. Any attempt to 'jump the gun' by producing the good corresponding to k^* before the steady state is reached will be inefficient, implying a loss of real income not only in the present but compounded into the future because it implies lower future capital stocks. As the economy develops from k_0 to k^*, comparative advantage steadily shifts up the 'ladder' of capital intensity.

Figure 10.1

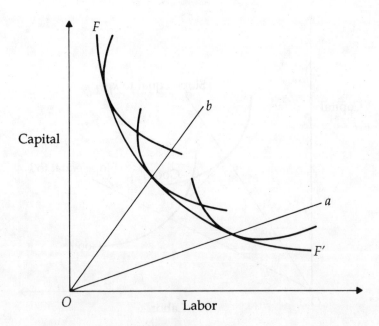

In Figure 10.2, we consider the more realistic case of a finite number of tradable goods, with goods j and $(j + 1)$ being adjacent in the ladder of capital intensity. When the aggregate capital-labor ratio of the economy $k(t)$ is equal to k_j the good j is the only product that the economy should produce to maximize its real income. As $k(t)$ increases, the economy will also engage in production of good $(j + 1)$, increasingly so $k(t)$ rises toward k_{j+1}, at which point it will abandon production of good j. If it took say three years for $k(t)$ to rise from k_j to k_{j+1}, and say five years to go from k_{j+1} to k_{j+2}, then the economy will produce good $(j + 1)$ for eight years in all, initially exporting it and then importing it. The economic history of the country would be a succession of overlapping histories of particular sectors, that are 'born' and 'die' as the capital-labor ratio $k(t)$ ascends remorselessly from k_0 to k^*.

Although we have been considering a highly abstract and simplified construct, it is nevertheless a very useful one. For one thing, it allows us to 'dynamize' the familiar Heckscher-Ohlin or factor proportions approach to comparative advantage in a very natural and useful way. Radical development economists are constantly denouncing classical notions of comparative advantage as hopelessly inadequate because they are allegedly inherently static. Our analysis demonstrates immediately the falseness of this widely prevalent and endlessly repeated view. In the

Figure 10.2

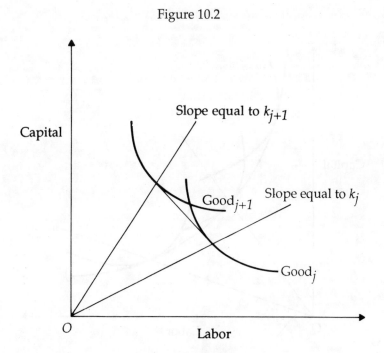

case of very rapidly growing economies, such as the Republic of Korea, the experience of the last 30 years or so is captured, in a stylized way, by the succession of increasingly capital-intensive and technologically sophisticated sectors into which its comparative advantage has evolved on the basis of its rising capital-labor ratio.

The model can also be used to analyze the recently fashionable topic of 'convergence'. All economies need not converge to the same capital-labor ratio, wiping out trade as a result. Even with the same constant returns to scale technology for all goods, countries could differ in their saving propensities. A possible scenario would be that countries could converge into *high savers*, with long-run, capital-labor ratios above a certain level k_1^*, *low savers* with capital-labor ratios below a certain level k_2^*, and *middle savers*, with capital-labor ratios between k_1^*, and k_2^*. Each of these groups would have price equalization factors between them, but with the real wage falling, and return to capital rising, as we move from high to middle to low savers.

Instead of assuming full employment of an exogenously growing labor force at rising real wages as capital grows faster than labor, we can follow Arthur Lewis and the classical economists by taking the real wage as exogenous in the early stages of development, where the bulk of the population is a rural peasantry with family farming as the dominant institutional mode. Not only the Republic of Korea and Taipei, China, but even the city states of Hong Kong and Singapore, with their hinterlands in China in the former case, and Malaysia and Indonesia in the latter, could be taken as representative of these conditions in the early phases of their remarkable expansions.

Using the same technology as represented by the IPP unit isoquant FF', we can derive the factor-price frontier RR' in Figure 10.3, which shows the maximum rate of profit ρ as a function $\rho(w)$ of the real wage w, with $\rho'(w)$ negative and the capital-labor ratio k defined by the absolute value of $\rho'(w)$ at each point on RR'. With the real wage $\bar{w}$ taken as determined by institutional conditions in the peasant hinterland, we have ρ determined as $\rho(\bar{w})$ and hence the growth rate g as well by the so-called Anglo-Italian equation where σ is the propensity to save out of profits.

$$g = \sigma \rho (\bar{w}) \tag{2}$$

Note that this rate of growth is truly 'endogenous' since it varies with the parameters $\bar{w}$ and σ.

Figure 10.3

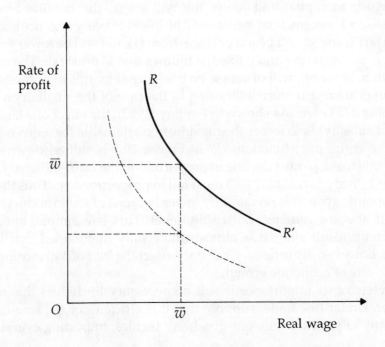

Rate of profit

$\bar{w}$

R

R'

O

$\bar{w}$

Real wage

Again, we may note that even though this Lewis model, extended to a small open economy (instead of a closed system as in his original work), is an extremely simplified and abstract framework, it nevertheless can account for the remarkably rapid growth of output, employment, capital, profits, and exports that were observed in the earlier stages of the 'outward-looking' development strategies pursued by the successful East Asian economies. Finding profitable 'niches' in the labor-intensive end of the spectrum of tradable goods, their low initial real wages combined with access to world technology and markets gave them high rates of profit, which their thrifty entrepreneurs and capitalists, reinforced by such measures as the Central Provident Fund in Singapore, ploughed back into investment and hence further profits in a virtuous circle of cumulative expansion. Eventually, the 'surplus labor' phase ended and wages started to rise and growth slowed down, but the fruits of progress are now being better distributed while growth, though slower than in the earlier phase, is still very rapid by the standards of the rest of the world.

We now turn to the vital question of trade policy, and of its effects on levels of real income and rates of economic growth. In the full employ-ment, neoclassical version of our small open economy model with a finite number of tradable goods, it is clear that under free trade the economy will produce only two goods, exporting at least one and importing all the rest. If the export good is the more labor intensive then a tariff will raise the return to capital and lower the real wage, the familiar Stolper-Samuelson Theorem. Real income will be lower at every instance because of the tariff, and k^* will be lower since, from (1), $f(k)$ will be lower for any given k, and so with s and n fixed, it follows that k^* must fall. The rate of growth n, however, will of course be unchanged by this hypothesis.

Things are much more interesting in the case of the small open dual economy à la Lewis. As shown in Findlay (1982), the effect of a tariff (or output subsidy) is to lower the maximum ρ attainable for a given w, so that the entire $\rho(w)$ function RR' in Figure 10.3 is shifted downward. Since $\bar{w}$ is fixed, ρ must decline in proportion to the tariff-induced fall in RR' and since ρ is constant $g(\bar{w})$ must fall in proportion to ρ. Thus the *rate* of economic growth is *permanently* lower because of the introduction of a tariff at some *constant*, not rising, level. This is a simple, but very important, result since it is almost universally maintained that trade policy, however, distortionary, can only affect the *level* of real income and *not* the rate of economic growth.

In view of its importance it will be necessary to discuss this result further. Under free trade, suppose that it is efficient for the small open economy to produce only one good, say textiles, importing everything else. Given the production function for textiles and the real wage, we can obtain the capital-labor ratio k_T^* in textiles and the return on capital ρ^* from the profit-maximizing condition that equates the real wage to the marginal product of labor that is

$$f_T(k_T^*) - f_T'(k_T^*)k_T^* = \bar{w} \qquad (3)$$

while

$$f_T'(k_T^*) = \rho^* \qquad (4)$$

gives us the return on capital. For an initial level of the aggregate capital stock K_0, we obtain the initial employment level L by dividing K_0 by k_T^*. The economy then expands capital, employment, and output exponentially at the rate of g^* equal to $\sigma\rho^*$.

Suppose now that another good, say steel, which it was not profitable to produce under free trade, is now given sufficient protection to make it viable in the small open economy. In Figure 10.4 we plot the unit isoquant for textiles and the capital-labor ratio k_T^*, which determines the factor cost line WW' tangent to the unit isoquant at that ratio. Let us say that the value for one unit of textiles at world prices is $100, and of one unit of steel is $20. The isoquant for five units of steel is WW', indicating that its production is not viable under free trade. If a tariff of 25 per cent is introduced, however, its domestic price will rise to $25, and four units of steel will be worth one unit of textiles at domestic prices, instead of five units as under free trade. The isoquant for four units of steel, which is more capital-intensive than textiles, is now tangent to WW' at the capital-labor ratio k_S^*, indicating that the tariff enables it to compete with textiles.

Production of steel in the economy is indeterminate between zero and self-sufficiency, however, so that there has to be a further decision, say by administrative means, on either production or trade to allocate the fixed initial capital between steel and textiles. Since k_S^* is greater than k_T^*, the more steel is produced the lower will be the total initial employment L_0.

The relation between the employment level and the rate of profit, both endogenous variables, can be derived from the following equations. Letting Y denote real national income at world prices, we have under free trade that

$$Y = \bar{w} L + \rho K_0 \qquad (5)$$

where $\bar{w}$ is the fixed real wage, K_0 the fixed initial capital stock, and ρ the rate of return on capital. After the tariff is introduced and the further decision on the level of steel output is made, L_0 and hence Y and ρ must fall since

$$dY/dL = \bar{w} + K_0 \, d\rho/dL \qquad (6)$$

Figure 10.4

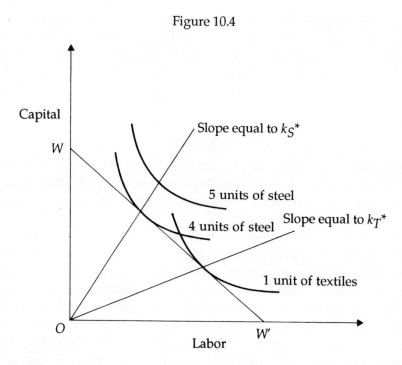

from which it follows that

$$(\eta - \lambda)\hat{L}/(1 - \lambda) = \hat{\rho} \qquad (7)$$

where $\eta = (L/Y)\, dY/dL$ is the elasticity of output with respect to labor, $\lambda = wL/Y$ is the share of labor in national income and $\hat{L}$ and $\hat{\rho}$ are the proportionate declines in employment and the return on capital at world prices respectively. It must be the case that η is greater than λ since dY/dL in (6) must be greater than $\tilde{w}$ because $d\rho/dL$ is negative. We therefore see from (7) that the profit rate and hence the growth rate fall in the same proportion as employment, which in turn depends upon the extent of import substitution that the tariff permits.

The analysis therefore shows why import substitution reduces not only real income but also employment in the 'modern' sector of the dual economy and the rate of growth itself.

Learning by Doing and Endogenous Growth

We now turn to introducing the basic ideas of endogenous growth into the model of a small open economy that we have used in the previous section to study neoclassical growth and the development of a dual economy. Starting again with a continuum of tradable goods varying in capital-intensity, we introduce a key hypothesis: the higher the capital-intensity of a good the greater is the degree of learning by doing acquired by the labor force. Under this hypothesis, letting n indicate the rate of labor-augmenting technical progress we postulate that

$$n = n(k) \qquad n'(k) > 0 \tag{8}$$

which is plotted as the upward sloping curve LL in Figure 10.5. Once again taking the 'surrogate' production function for a unit of IPP as an ordinary production function, the marginal product of 'capital' is the rate of profit ρ so that we have

$$\rho = f'(k) > 0 \qquad f''(k) < 0 \tag{9}$$

The Anglo-Italian equation is now

$$g = \sigma \rho = \sigma f'(k) \tag{10}$$

which is plotted as the downward sloping curve KK in Figure 10.5. The intersection of these two curves determines the steady state value k^* of the capital-labor ratio and the endogenous growth rate n^* by the condition

$$n^* = n(k^*) = \sigma f'(k^*) \tag{11}$$

The equilibrium is stable since to the left of k^* we have the growth rate of capital exceeding the growth rate of the effective labor force, so that k^* rises, while to the right of k^* we have the opposite, so that k^* falls.

Figure 10.5

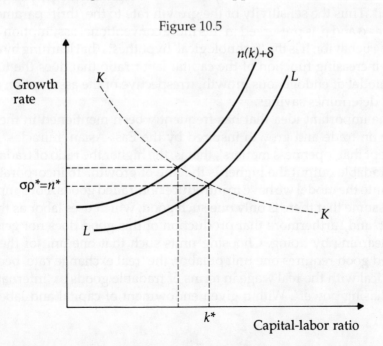

The fundamental difference with the Solow model of course is that LL is positively sloped, whereas it is horizontal in the Solow model, n being simply given and not a function of k as we have here. The immediate implication is that an increase in the propensity to save, shifting KK to the right, not only raises k^*, but n^* as well, since n is an increasing function of k. Thus not only is the steady state level of per capita output raised, but also the rate of growth itself—this is the main result of endogenous growth theory.

Our exposition is easily extended to the more conventional hypothesis about savings behavior: that it is determined by maximizing the integral of utility from the present to infinity discounted at a given rate of time preference δ. The equilibrium values of k^* and n^* can then be found from the well-known 'modified golden rule' condition that

$$f'(k^*) = n(k^*) + \delta \tag{12}$$

Figure 10.5 can easily be altered to accommodate this change in underlying assumptions. The negatively sloped curve KK is now simply $f'(k)$ as a function of k, instead of $\sigma f'(k)$ as before, and the positively sloped LL curve is $n(k) + \delta$ instead of just $n(k)$ as before. Once again, the intersection of the two curves determines k^* as well as the endogenous growth rate n^*.

A shift in time preference such as a reduction in the degree of 'impatience', which reduces δ, will shift the LL curve downward for each value of k and so result in a higher k^* and a higher endogenous growth rate n^*. Thus the sensitivity of the growth rate to the 'thrift parameters', such as σ and δ, is preserved in this more conventional assumption about saving behavior. It is the 'technological' hypothesis that learning by doing is an increasing function of the capital-labor ratio that does the trick in our model of endogenous growth, irrespective of the assumption about what determines savings.

One important idea that has frequently been mentioned in the literature on trade and growth inspired by the East Asian 'miracles' is the concept that 'openness matters', that is, the higher the ratio of tradable to nontradable output the higher is the rate of growth. To incorporate this idea into the model we have to introduce nontraded goods. For simplicity we assume that there is only one such good, which uses labor as the *sole* input, and furthermore that production of this good does not generate any learning by doing. Choosing units such that one unit of the non-traded good requires one unit of labor, the 'real exchange rate' becomes identical with the real wage in terms of tradable goods or 'international purchasing power'. With a given endowment of capital and labor, the higher the real wage the lower the employment in the tradable sector, and the greater, therefore, the output of the nontraded good, that is, the supply of the nontraded good is an increasing function of its price, the real exchange rate. With the demand for the nontraded good given by identical and homothetic utility functions for all consumers as a decreasing function of its price, it is clear that there is a unique real exchange rate and real wage that simultaneously clear the markets for the nontraded good and labor. Thus to any value k of the capital-labor ratio for the whole economy, we can associate a unique capital-labor ratio k_T for the tradable sector and a corresponding rate of profit ρ, since the profit rate and real wage are inversely related by the international purchasing power 'surrogate' production function.

For each value of k and hence of per capita income, we also know the proportion λ of the labor force that will be allocated to the tradable sector by the demand pattern implied by the homothetic utility function. Learning by doing will take place at the rate of n_T associated with k_T in the tradable sector while it will be zero by hypothesis in the nontraded sector. We therefore define learning by doing in the economy as a whole as

$$n(k) = \lambda n_T [k_T(k)] \tag{13}$$

that is, a weighted average of the two rates, one of which is assumed to be zero. We have also demonstrated above that

$$\rho(k) = f' [k_T(k)] \tag{14}$$

We now can investigate the effect of an increase in k on n and ρ in the presence of nontraded goods. An increase in k, at a constant real wage, would leave k_T unchanged, and hence imply a reduction in the supply of the nontraded good by the Rybczynski Theorem because more of the given labor force would have to be used in the tradable sector to maintain k_T constant at a higher k. With homothetic preferences, a higher k at a constant real exchange rate would lead to an increase in the demand for the nontraded good. Thus the higher k at a constant real wage and real exchange rate leads to an excess demand for the nontraded good that must result in a rise in its price, that is, in the real wage and real exchange rate. This in turn must imply a rise in k_T, and therefore a rise in n and a fall in ρ.

We have therefore demonstrated that the curves LL and KK in Figure 10.5 can continue to be drawn in the presence of nontraded goods and the steady state equilibrium values of k^* and n^* determined in essentially the same way.

In the case of a continuum of tradable goods with an IPP isoquant that is convex to the origin, only a single tradable good will be produced, though any number can be consumed in exchange for export of the sole tradable good produced. In other words, there is no import-competing production. To analyze the consequences of trade intervention on domestic production, we therefore assume a finite number of tradable goods with an IPP isoquant that has linear facets that are the common tangents to two successive isoquants for individual tradable goods. Leaving aside nontraded goods it is apparent that under free trade there will be some equilibrium value k^* of the capital-labor ratio that in general will lie in the 'cone of diversification' defined by the capital-labor ratios k_j^* and k_{j+1}^* of the two adjacent isoquants for goods j and $(j + 1)$. The equilibrium rate of growth n^* will be a weighted average of the growth rates n_j and n_{j+1}, with the weights λ^* and $(1 - \lambda^*)$ determined by

$$k^* = \lambda^* k_j^* + (1 - \lambda^*)k_{j+1}^* \tag{15}$$

Goods are numbered in increasing order of capital-intensity so n_{j+1} will be greater than n_j. Suppose that good j is the export and good $(j + 1)$ is the import-competing good. The profit rate ρ^* is determined by the marginal productivity of capital in terms of either of the two goods produced, and $\sigma \rho^*$ is of course equal to n^* by the steady state equilibrium condition.

Suppose now that production of good $(j + 1)$ is stimulated either by a tariff or output subsidy. This leaves world relative prices unchanged but raises the domestic relative price of the capital-intensive good n_{j+1}. By the familiar Stolper-Samuelson theorem, the profit rate ρ^* will be raised and the real wage w^* lowered as a result. Thus, on impact, the growth rate of capital $\sigma\rho$ will rise above $\sigma \rho^*$. The tariff or subsidy will shift resources into good $(j + 1)$ so that λ will rise, thus raising the growth rate of effective labor above n^*. So long as $\sigma \rho$ exceeds n, the capital-labor ratio will rise until a new steady state value k^{**} is attained, with a higher λ associated with it. The endogenous growth of productivity will therefore now be $n^{**} > n^*$. Trade will be restricted since the weight of the import-competing sector in production has been increased, but since this is the sector that is assumed to be more conducive to learning by doing, the endogenous growth rate of the effective labor force and the economy as a whole has gone up to n^{**} equal to $\sigma \rho^{**}$.

The echo of the infant industry argument, which we find in the models of Lucas, and Alwyn Young, is thus reproduced here.

R&D Expenditures and Endogenous Growth in a Small Open Economy

This section pursues the other major strand in the endogenous growth literature, that it arises from the deliberate allocation of resources to R&D rather than merely through the accumulation of experience in the form of learning by doing. We shall use the familiar three-sector version of the Heckscher-Ohlin model with a nontradable good, which in this case will be identified with the provision of R&D services to the tradable production sectors to enhance their efficiency. As before, capital and labor will be the primary inputs, and we will assume that the endowments of these factors remain unchanged, with technological progress the only source of growth. Production functions have constant returns to scale and the three sectors have a unique ranking of factor intensities. Consumer preferences will be identical and homothetic as before.

The production functions for the tradable goods X and Y can be written as

$$X(t) = A(t)L_x f_x(k_x)$$ (16)

$$Y(t) = A(t)L_y f_y(k_y)$$ (17)

where $A(t)$ is an index of technological efficiency that is uniform for both sectors and will change endogenously over time. Labor allocations to X and Y are denoted L_x and L_y, while $f_x(k_x)$ and $f_y(k_y)$ denote the production functions for each sector in intensive form, with k_x and k_y as the capital-labor ratios.

The crucial hypothesis of this section is that $A(t)$ changes endogenously over time at a rate determined by the per capita output of R&D services for the economy as a whole. These services are provided by a third nontraded sector of the economy denoted Z. We assume that

$$Z = L_z f_z(k_z)$$ (18)

$$L_x + L_y + L_z = L$$ (19)

$$\lambda_x k_x + \lambda_y k_y + \lambda_z k_z = k$$ (20)

where λ_x, λ_y and λ_z denote fractions of L allocated to the respective sectors, and

$$\dot{A} = A(t)\,\phi[\lambda_z f_z(k_z)]$$ (21)

where the function ϕ has the properties

$$\phi' > 0, \quad \phi'' < 0, \quad \phi(0) = 0$$ (22)

For most of this section we will make the 'small open economy' assumption that relative prices X and Y are given from outside, with Y as the *numeraire* and p_x denoting the relative price of X. At some initial time t_0, we can make $A(0)$ equal to unity and with all three goods produced that the real wage w, the capital rental r, the capital-labor ratios k_x, k_y, and k_z and the relative price p_z of the nontraded good will all be determined by p_x and the three production functions, independent of demand conditions.

As long as production of Z is not zero, we see from (21) that technological change will be taking place in the tradable sector at a uniform rate $A(t)$, with the pace depending upon the per capita level of R&D provision. The greater the production of Z, the greater the rate of technological progress, but not proportionately so because of the 'concavity' of the function assumed in (22). Thus we will have 'Hicks-neutral' technological change at a uniform rate in X and Y, with their relative price constant at the given value of p_x. It is apparent, however, that the real wage w, rental r, and nontradable goods price p_z will all have to *rise* relative to the *numeraire* at the same rate $A(t)$ that technological progress takes place in the tradable sector as a whole.

If L_z is held constant, the remaining labor $(L - L_z)$ will be allocated optimally between X and Y so that λ_x and λ_y will be determined. We define the per capital output of the tradable sector as a whole as

$$v(t) = A(t) \, [p_x \lambda_x f_x(k_x) + \lambda_y f_y(k_y)] \qquad (23)$$

in which $v(t)$ is a function of time only because of $A(t)$, the expressions inside the bracket being constant so long as L_z is held constant.

The key problem for the economy is how to determine L_z, the level at which R&D services are provided and hence the rate of endogenous technological change. The nontraded good Z, which we are identifying with R&D, is a public intermediate input to the tradable sector. It is 'public' because it is 'nonrival' and 'nonexcludable', the two essential characteristics of public goods. Firms in the X and Y sectors all benefit jointly from the knowledge generated by the R&D sector, and none can prevent access by others to the same knowledge if they refuse to contribute. The R&D sector must thus either be operated directly by the government and financed by taxes, or as a 'consortium' by firms in the X and Y sectors themselves and supported by some system of voluntary contributions in return for the benefits received and anticipated. Either alternative could be taken for our model. What matters is how the scale of the R&D effort of the economy is determined, and thus the allocation of resources between X, Y, and Z.

To determine the benefit of R&D expenditures on the future value of tradable output we first differentiate (23) with respect to time and using (21) we obtain

$$\dot{v} = A(t)\phi(z)v(z) \qquad (24)$$

where z refers to $\lambda_z f_z(k_z)$, the per capita output of Z. Raising z raises $\dot{v}$ by raising $\phi(z)$, since $\phi'(z)$ is positive, but raising z also implies less capital and labor for tradable output, so that $v'(z)$ is negative. Equation (24) therefore indicates the basic tradeoff involved in deciding the level of R&D expenditure, which is to balance the enhancement of technology $\phi(z)$ against the reduction of current output $v(z)$. Setting $A(t)$ equal to unity at time zero, we obtain the marginal benefit from R&D as

$$\frac{\partial \dot{v}}{\partial z} = \frac{\phi(z)v(z)}{z} \{ \frac{z}{v}\frac{dv}{dz} + \frac{z}{\phi}\frac{d\phi}{dz} \} \qquad (25)$$

where the two expressions in brackets are the elasticities of $v(z)$ and $\phi(z)$ with respect to z respectively.

This marginal benefit will be available from now to infinity and so the full benefit of the incremental expenditure of R&D will be the capitalized value at the given rate of interest ρ, which will be the right hand side of (25) divided by ρ.

The cost of a unit of R&D services, so long as all these goods X, Y, and Z are produced, is simple p_z as determined above, independently of the quantity demanded. Marginal benefit is therefore equated to marginal cost when

$$\frac{\phi(z)v(z)}{z} \{ \frac{z}{v}\frac{dv}{dz} + \frac{z}{\phi}\frac{d\phi}{dz} \} = \rho p_z \qquad (26)$$

Denoting the level of z that satisfies (27) as z^*, and the rate of technological progress $\dot{A}/A$ as g, we determine the growth rate g^* of the small open economy as

$$g^* = \phi(z^*) \qquad \phi'(z'') > 0 \qquad (27)$$

The determination of g^* can be clarified further by considering figure 10.6. The concave function OF plots $\dot{v}$, or $\phi(z)v(z)$, as a function of z. This function is concave because $v(z)$ is a negative linear function of z, since p_x and k_x, k_y and k_z are all fixed, and $\phi(z)$ is concave. As z increases, the proportionate increase in $\phi(z)$ exceeds the proportionate decline in $v(z)$ until a maximum is reached when both are equal, after which $\dot{v}$ declines.

The ray from the origin, OH, shows the interest cost of R&D expenditure $\rho p_z z$ as a function of z. Marginal benefit is equal to marginal cost, that is (27) is satisfied, when the slope of OF equals the constant slope ρp_z of the ray OH, which determines z^*.

Figure 10.6

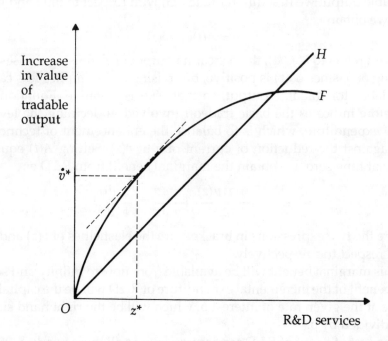

It is easy to show that z^* will remain optimal over time, even though the technological level of the economy is undergoing continuous improvement at the rate g^*. This is because the index of technological efficiency $A(t)$ and $p_z(t)$ increase over time at the rate g^*, along with real wages and the rental on capital goods.

The endogeneity of g^* is also easy to ascertain. An increase in ρ, for example, will rotate the OH ray upward, thus shifting z^* and hence g^* downward as a result, since the slope of OF will have to increase correspondingly to the rise in ρ.

There are many other ways in which the rate of technological change can be made to endogenously depend upon the pattern of resource allocation in the economy between 'invention', or the creation of new knowledge, on the one hand, and 'production', by the use of existing knowledge, on the other. Romer, and Grossman and Helpman, rely extensively on the Ethier modification of the Dixit-Stiglitz utility function mentioned earlier, and which Pranab Bardhan examines closely in his paper in this volume. What we have presented here is in some ways the polar alternative to this approach, but the results are not essentially altered in any way.

Trade and Growth Theory and the East Asian NIEs

In Findlay (1984b), we argued that the adoption of outward-looking liberal trade regimes by the fast growing newly industrializing economies (NIEs) of East Asia could not alone be regarded as responsible for this rapid growth. The traditional case for free trade only argued that real income would be maximized for *given* resources and was silent on the question of the growth rate and changes over time, which would depend on such factors as savings behavior and the rate of technological progress, neither of which had any direct connection to trade policy in the received doctrine of the time. In Findlay (1981) it was observed that there seemed to be a mysterious 'Omega Factor' at work, raising the rate of technological progress the more a country engaged in exports, a dynamic externality of some kind perhaps coming from the necessity to compete harder in world markets than in domestic ones. It is tempting to claim that the 'Omega Factor', like some sort of benign virus, has now been identified in the shape of the 'new' theories of growth and trade that we have been considering in the previous sections of this paper. There are several reasons, however, to be cautious about advancing any such claims.

First, consider the models that associate growth with R&D, of either the 'private' or 'public' types. It seems that R&D efforts in all of the East Asian NIEs are relatively modest, and for the most part confined to absorbing *existing* technology rather than extending the frontier. Thus we would have to fall back on learning by doing, but in this case on the *export* rather than the import-competing sectors, as in the ideas associated with the traditional infant-industry argument. On reflection, it seems that empirical research might support a view along these lines. These export lines have indeed been 'infants' in many, if not most cases, springing up almost overnight in response to opportunities opened up by the outward-looking policies. Youthful labor forces have entered them, acquired experience and on-the-job training in initially low skill activities, and then moved up the ladder of capital and skill intensity and technological sophistication. In this respect it makes a huge difference that the export sectors have been in *manufacturing*, rather than the traditional primary export sectors where this kind of productivity change is much more difficult to accomplish.

It seems that the success of the East Asian NIEs has much more to do with 'catching up' rather than the development of new technology. In Findlay (1978), the Veblen-Gerschenkron idea of the advantage of 'relative backwardness' was combined with the Nelson-Phelps model of technological diffusion and the Arrow (1969) concept of transmission of knowledge through 'contagion'. It was further assumed that the rate of productivity growth in a less developed country (LDC) would be an increasing function of the 'technology gap' between itself and the 'leader', whose growth rate was exogenous, as well as a variable representing 'contact' between the leader and the follower—in this case, the share of foreign direct investment to total investment in the host economy. More generally, this 'contact' variable can be extended to cover trade as well as some index of exposure of the local labor force to the ideas and practices of the leader. It is in *all* of these dimensions that the East Asian NIEs have excelled. Empirical support for the hypothesis of technology transfer through foreign direct investment is provided by Blomstrom (1989), and an elegant theoretical extension by Wang (1990). All of the ideas mentioned here are foreshadowed in the great chapter on 'Trade as a Highway of Learning' in the treatise on the economic development of Japan by Lockwood (1954), cited in Findlay (1984b).

One very important factor in the success of the East Asian NIEs has been the combination of liberal trade policy with highly elastic labor supplies, at least in the earlier stages of their development. As argued in the section on dualistic growth in the small open economy, this combination makes for a high rate of profit that permits, in turn, a high rate of physical capital accumulation. The elastic labor supplies do not need to come from the economy's own agricultural sector, as in the standard Lewis model. For Hong Kong and Singapore in the fifties and sixties, the 'peasant hinterland' could be China, or Indonesia and Malaysia. Another major source of labor force growth has been the remarkable increase in female labor force participation, as in Singapore and Taipei,China. As noted earlier, the fixed real wage assumption leads to a permanently higher rate of growth under free trade than under trade restriction, that is, for as long as the 'surplus' labor condition holds. Eventually, of course, real wages start to rise sharply, as they have in recent years for the NIEs, and the growth rates slow down, but only relative to the earlier phenomenal expansions.

The generous provision of infrastructure, particularly in the case of Singapore, has been another feature of the success of the NIEs. The role of this factor in trade and growth has been modeled in Findlay and Kapur (1991), and Clarida and Findlay (1991, 1992). The provision of infrastructure raises the return on both domestic and foreign direct private investment and so provides another explanation for the extraordinarily high rates of capital accumulation observed in the East Asian NIEs.

That factor, accumulation and *not* productivity growth, has been the main explanation of the remarkable rise in per capita incomes of the East

Asian NIEs and is the finding of recent careful exercises in growth accounting by Kim and Lau (1992), and Alwyn Young (1993a, 1993b). The first shows no technical progress at all in all four of the East Asian NIEs, with physical capital accumulation alone accounting for more than 80 per cent of the growth in each of them. Young finds total factor productivity growth slightly negative for Singapore, and only modest for the other three. Since technical progress was steadily positive for the major member countries of the Organisation for Economic Cooperation and Development (OECD), Kim and Lau find that despite their fantastic overall growth performance, the East Asian NIEs were falling even further behind the huge initial technology gap, which they had relative to the United States in 1970, of the order of about five to one.

In this connection it is interesting to note that in a characteristically insightful and stimulating paper entitled 'Making a Miracle', Robert Lucas (1993), the inspirer of endogenous growth theory, strives to capture, with 'pen and paper', the miracles that he assumed to have occurred in East Asia. In this venture, he relies on the learning models by Young, Stokey, Romer, Krugman, Grossman and Helpman, and others that we have referred to here. What appears to have happened in East Asia instead seems to have been the more humdrum, but nevertheless remarkable, feats of physical and human capital accumulation that these economies have accomplished. The main difference with the former Soviet bloc, which *also* had high rates of accumulation, lies in the openness of the East Asian economies. 'Getting prices right', meaning world prices, although much derided by radical critics of the World Bank and others, was essential in all these cases. For growth to continue and the remaining income gaps with the OECD to be closed, productivity itself must eventually start to rise and then perhaps the new models will come into their own. But for now the old masters, Solow and Lewis, appear to be doing just fine.

Acknowledgments

The author would like to thank Rodney Falvey, Junichi Goto, M. G. Quibria, and Min Tang for their helpful comments.

References

Arrow, K. J., 1962. "Economic Implications of Learning by Doing." *Review of Economic Studies* 29:155-73.

———, 1969. "Classificatory Notes on the Productivity and Transmission of Technological Knowledge." *American Economic Review* 59:29-35.

Bardhan, P. K., 1970. *Economic Growth, Development and Foreign Trade.* New York: John Wiley & Sons.

Blomstrom, M., 1989. *Foreign Investment and Spillovers.* London: Routledge.

Clarida, R., and R. Findlay, 1991. "Optimal Endogenous Growth, Public Capital and the Dynamic Gains from Trade." Discussion Paper No. 600. Economics Department, Columbia University, New York.

————, 1992. "Government, Trade and Comparative Advantage." *American Economic Review* 82(2):122-7.

Clemhout, S., and H. Y. Wan, 1970. "Learning by Doing and Infant Industry Protection." *Review of Economic Studies* 37(1):33-56.

Dixit, A. K., and S. Stiglitz, 1977. "Monopolistic Competition and Optimum Product Diversity." *American Economic Review* 67(3):297-308.

Ethier, W., 1982. "National and International Returns to Scale in the Modern Theory of International Trade." *American Economic Review* 72(3):389-405.

Findlay, R., 1973. *International Trade and Development Theory.* New York: Columbia University Press.

————, 1978. "Relative Backwardness, Direct Foreign Investment and the Transfer of Technology: A Simple Dynamic Model." *Quarterly Journal of Economics* 92 (February):1-16.

————, 1981. Comment on "Export-led Industrial Growth Reconsidered" by A. O. Krueger. In W. Hong and L. B. Krause, eds., *Trade and Growth of the Advanced Developing Countries in the Pacific Basin.* Seoul: Korea Development Institute.

————, 1982. "Protection and Growth in a Dual Economy." In M. Gersovitz et. al., eds., *The Theory and Experience of Economic Development.* London: George Allen and Unwin.

————, 1984a. "Growth and Development in Trade Models." In R. W. Jones and P. B. Kenen, eds., *Handbook of International Economics.* Vol. 1, Amsterdam: North-Holland Publishers.

————, 1984b. "Trade and Development: Theory and Asian Experience." *Asian Development Review* 2:23-42.

Findlay, R., and B. Kapur, 1991. "An Analytical Growth Model of the Singapore Economy." *Asian Economic Journal* VI(1).

Grossman, G., and E. Helpman, 1991. *Innovation and Growth in the Global Economy.* Cambridge: MIT Press.

Kim, J., and L. J. Lau, 1992. "The Sources of Economic Growth of the Newly Industrialized Countries of the Pacific Rim." Mimeographed.

Krugman, P. R., 1987. "The Narrow Moving Band, the Dutch Disease and the Competitor Consequences of Mrs. Thatcher." *Journal of Development Economics* 27 (October):41-55.

Lockwood, W. W., 1954. *The Economic Development of Japan.* Princeton: Princeton University Press.

Lucas, R. E., 1988. "On the Mechanics of Economic Development." *Journal of Monetary Economics* 22 (July):3-42.

———, 1993. "Making a Miracle." *Econometrica* 61(2):251-72.

Romer, P. M., 1986. "Increasing Returns and Long Run Growth." *Journal of Political Economy* 94:1002-37.

———, 1990. "Endogenous Technological Change." *Journal of Political Economy* 98(2):S71-102.

Solow, R. M., 1956. "A Contribution to the Theory of Economic Growth." *Quarterly Journal of Economics* 70:65-94.

Wang, J., 1990. "Growth, Technology Transfer and the Long-Run Theory of International Capital Movements." *Journal of International Economics* (November):255-71.

Young, A., 1991. "Learning by Doing and the Dynamic Effects of International Trade." *Quarterly Journal of Economics* 106(May):369-406.

———, 1993a. "The Tyranny of Numbers: Confronting the Statistical Realities of the East Asian Growth Experience." Mimeographed.

———, 1993b. "Lessons from the East Asian Newly Industrialized Countries: A Contrarian View." Mimeographed.

Author Index

Subject Index